Everyday Matters

EVERYDAY MATTERS

a love story

Nardi Reeder Campion

UNIVERSITY PRESS OF NEW ENGLAND

HANOVER AND LONDON

Published by University Press of New England,
One Court Street, Lebanon, NH 03766
www.upne.com
Text © 2004 by Nardi Reeder Campion
Foreword © 2004 by Hillary Rodham Clinton
First University Press of New England paperback edition 2006
Printed in the United States of America

5 4 3 2 1

ISBNs for the paperback edition:
ISBN–13: 978–1–58465–538–1
ISBN–10: 1–58465–538–0

Library of Congress Cataloging-in-Publication Data
Campion, Nardi Reeder.
Everyday matters : a love story / Nardi Reeder Campion.
p.   cm.
Includes index.
ISBN 1–58465–407–4 (alk. paper)
1. Campion, Nardi Reeder.   2. Campion, Thomas.
3. Journalists—United States—Biography.   4. Married people—
United States—Biography.   I. Title.
PN4874.C228A3   2004
070.92—dc22   2004010717

Many of these pieces originally appeared, in different forms, in the
Valley News and other publications.

This collection is a labor of love, a gift to my family, and, mostly, a valentine to my husband, Tom Campion. We met in 1938 and married in 1941, abiding together until death did us part in 2000.

Natural History
by E. B. White

The spider, dropping down from twig,
Unwinds a thread of his devising:
A thin, premeditated rig
To use in rising.

And all the journey down through space,
In cool descent, and loyal-hearted,
She builds a ladder to the place
From which she started.

Thus I, gone forth, as spiders do,
In spider's web a truth discerning,
Attach one silken strand to you
For my returning.

Contents

✤

Foreword

❦

I met Nardi when she interviewed me at Dartmouth during the 1992 Presidential campaign. What I remember from that first encounter is that we shared a devotion to our alma mater, Wellesley, and spent most of our time laughing. That convinced me right off that Nardi was no ordinary journalist; in fact, there is nothing at all ordinary about her. Others—and they are legion—will pay tribute to her remarkable marriage and family and her commitment to the community she serves in both word and deed.

I want to highlight her profligate generosity with her gifts of friendship. She was my faithful friend during the White House years, providing a steady stream of delightful letters and pithy aphorisms about life and politics. She unfailingly recommended good books to read and great places to visit. She brought her enthusiasm to every encounter we had and often boosted my own spirits. She became a friend I cherish and gladly share with all who know the joy of her company and caring.

Hillary Rodham Clinton,
United States Senator

From the Women's Fund of New Hampshire book *In Celebration of Women and Girls,* 2001.

The Gratitude Attitude

I am overflowing with gratitude to the people who made this book happen. They are legion.

First and foremost, I thank my family (see book). My husband, Tom, skillfully edited everything I wrote, and graciously (most of the time) accepted my writing obsession. Our children—Tommy, Tad, Toby, Cissa, and Russell—were pressed into early editorhood, sharpening pencils, changing typewriter ribbons (this book goes way back), doing research—not joyous about every task, but always supportive.

Seven strong, bright women have helped me at every step of the way: our dear in-laws, Suzanne Carrier, Ellen Feinman, Peggy McCarthy, Anita Montero (all now Campion); and our dear "outlaws," Lynn Campion Waddell, Anne Campion Hartman, Missy Jacobus Campion.

Our grandchildren—Ashley and husband Matt Semler, Peter and wife Amy Thomas, Berit, Manolo, Iris, Ned, Grady, and Maddy—helped, too: editing, filing, listening (every writer needs listeners), the younger ones teaching grandma the computer, the youngest sorting paper clips and applying stamps (licking is obsolete). Our first great-granddaughter, Anna Caitlin Semler, born November 13, 2003, inspired Gee-Gee to write for posterity.

My list is so long and my space is so short, only Biggies allowed. Biggest of all is my mentor, Dartmouth Professor of English Noel Perrin, who began pushing me to do a book in 1989. He and his wife, Sara Coburn, are brilliant editors and never-failing friends, writingwise and otherwise.

Nothing would have happened without my gifted, devoted young writing assistants (they know everything): Reverend Mary Kate Schroeder

(Dartmouth '93), Leyla Kamilick (Dartmouth '02), and Beth Zuttermeister, who manages me along with her twin daughters.

Henry Homeyer, *Valley News* "Gardening Guy," refused to listen when I wanted to give up. Without Henry, this book would never have been published.

Thomas Summerall is what every writer needs: a Blood Relative Techie. Thomas can and has solved 1,002 computer crises.

Alexandra Marshall and Jim Carroll are literary moguls who have encouraged me to keep writing since our friendship began thirty years ago.

And the list goes on: Tina White, adopted daughter, bookkeeper, editor; Heather McCutchen Kannam, original thinker, great (both senses) niece, and author of *Lightland;* Bin Lewis, former publisher of the *Valley News,* who made me a columnist; Anne Adams, brilliant features editor at the *Valley News* and promoter of clear thinking; Roz Wilfley Neilson, perceptive editor, friend forever; Betty Smith, perceptive editor, friend forever; Katharine Beal, gifted writer who contributed some of "my" best sentences; Sheba and Jim Freedman—as first lady and president of Dartmouth, they lent support at every turn, Sheba with psychological insights, Jim with erudition, both with humor; Sheila Harvey Tanzer, wordsmith, poet, spiritual director; Madalyn Gilligan, secretary extraordinaire; Mollie Brooks and Bob Simon, my therapists who miraculously dispelled deepest doubts.

To my omitted Biggies, who are legion: Gratitude unlimited (if unexpressed).

Everyday Matters

Introduction

We Were Before Pantyhose, Penicillin, and the Pill . . .

"There are Three Ages of Mankind," Tom used to say. "Youth, middle age, and 'you haven't changed.'" We both graduated from college in 1938 B.C. (Before Computers). For our generation, change is the name of the game. We were before the pill and the population explosion, which, inexplicably, went hand in hand.

We were before television. Before penicillin, nylon, Xerox, and Frisbees. We were before frozen orange juice, radar, credit cards, and ballpoint pens. Our Broadway was the "Great White Way"—we were before fluorescent lights. For us, a chip meant a piece of wood, hardware meant hardware, and software wasn't a word.

In our day closets were for clothes, not coming out of, and a bestseller about two young women traveling together could be called *Our Hearts Were Young and Gay*. At Harvard, "Playboy" referred to J. M. Synge's prevaricator of Ireland's Western World, bunnies were small rabbits, and rabbits were not Volkswagens. We were before Grandma Moses and Frank Sinatra and cup-sizing for bras. At Wellesley we wore Peter Pan collars and thought deep cleavage was something butchers did.

Tom and I were before *Grapes of Wrath, Stuart Little,* even Snoopy. Before vitamin pills, vodka (in the United States), disposable diapers, Jeeps, the white wine craze, and *Q.E. One.*

Before college students could take a term off or, heaven forbid, get married. Before the National Gallery of Art, scotch tape, Grand Coulee Dam, the automatic shift, and Lincoln Continentals. When we were in college, no one had ever heard of pizzas, Cheerios, instant coffee, or McDonald's. We thought fast food was what you ate during Lent.

This Wellesley reunion talk, published in the *Boston Sunday Globe* on July 17, 1993, has been published, republished, re-republished, and pirated. It has been reproduced endlessly on e-mail (uncredited, of course). People are still asking for copies.

We were before women could vote in France or use the Lamont Library at Harvard. (I said to Tom: "A *library* for men only?" No answer.) Before FM radio, tape recorders, electronic music, disco dancing—and that's not all bad. In 1938 the tallest building in Boston was the Custom House; "made in Japan" meant junk; and "making out" referred to how you did on an exam.

We were before air travel went commercial—no one flew across the country and transatlantic flight belonged to Charles Lindbergh and Amelia Earhart. Before LaGuardia and Logan Airports, most tunnels—Queens, Midtown, Sumner, Callahan, Chesapeake, and the Chunnel, of course. We had hilarious train trips cross country to college and giddy ocean voyages abroad.

We were before Israel and the United Nations. Before India, Pakistan, Indonesia, the Philippines, and Iceland became independent countries. Since our graduation, ninety-two countries—forty-eight of them African—have become nations. And, God help us all, we were before the cataclysm of nuclear fission.

We were before they discovered that the brain's preoptic hypothalamus stimulates sexual activity. We thought perfume, padded bras, and dancing cheek-to-cheek did that.

In our day Wellesley "girls" were forbidden to wear pants and Harvard "boys" thought only hillbillies wore blue jeans. We were before icemakers, dishwashers, clothes dryers, hair dryers, freezers, and electric blankets. Before pantyhose and drip dry clothes. Before students had cocktail parties on campus. Before the opposite sex was allowed above the first floor. Before Hawaii and Alaska became states. Before men wore long hair and earrings and women wore tuxedos.

We were before vending machines, jets, helicopters, interstate highways, even the Mass. Pike. How could anybody be before the Mass. Pike? Before Leonard Bernstein, yogurt, Ann Landers, plastics, the forty-hour week, the minimum wage, and premarital sex. We got married first, and then lived together. How quaint can you be?

In our day cigarette smoking was fashionable, grass was mowed, coke was something you drank, and pot was something you cooked in. We were before daycare centers, house-husbands, babysitters, computer dating, and commuter marriages. When we had a baby, it was a seven-day rest in the hospital for mama, not something she did on the way to work.

Some things we had are worth forgetting. In 1938 public schools were segregated; blacks were not allowed to eat in "white restaurants" nor to play major league baseball; and the D.A.R. refused to allow Marian Anderson to sing in Constitution Hall. (Eleanor Roosevelt to the rescue.)

There used to be five-and-ten-cent stores where you could buy things for five and ten cents. For a nickel you could ride a subway, or a ferry, or make a phone call, or buy a Coke, or buy two copies of *The New York Times* and get change, or buy enough stamps to mail one letter and two postcards. You could buy a new Chevy Coupe for $659, but who could afford that in 1938? Nobody. A pity, too, because gas was eleven cents a gallon.

If anyone had asked us to explain C.I.A., Ms., N.A.T.O., U.F.O, N.F.L, J.F.K., B.M.W., E.R.A., or I.U.D., we would have said alphabet soup. We were not before the difference between the sexes, but we were before sex changes. We just made do with what we had. And we were the last generation that was so dumb as to think you needed a husband to have a baby.

Consider what delights we *did* have. We had seated meals in our dorms with white tablecloths, candles, maids. We had housemothers and rooms that were never locked. We mailed our laundry home in cardboard containers and it came back with brownies.

We had real fountain pens with real bottles of ink. We danced to the big bands—Benny Goodman, Tommy Dorsey, Glenn Gray, Guy Lombardo. Unlike the remote control dancers of today, our partners held us close and double dipped.

In those days we had humorists who were funny—Thurber, Benchley, E. B. White, Charlie Chaplin, Bea Lillie, W. C. Fields, the Marx Brothers. Who can forget Groucho, as Dr. Quackinbush, taking a patient's pulse? "Either this man is dead or my watch has stopped."

We played our music on thick 78 RPM records with cactus needles that always needed sharpening. We had Toscanini and Koussevitsky and Flagstad and Edward VIII and saddle shoes and convertibles with rumble seats. And when Ray Noble sat at his piano and slowly sang "The Very Thought of You," we melted.

Like Kurt Vonnegut's Billy Pilgrim, Tom and I became "unstuck in time." In the springtime of our senility, we were misfits. We weren't into veggies or Yoga or Zen or Punk. We did not want to rock around the clock. We spent year after year after year married to the same spouse.

How embarrassing.

Who Am I? (As if I Knew)

Like Gaul, my life is divided into three parts: Before Tom, With Tom, and After Tom. I have nearly spanned the twentieth century, from coal stoves to microwaves, from windowless cars to air conditioning. My journey reflects, among other things, the forward march of American women from the vote (1920) to Secretary of State (2000).

I grew up an army brat—the old army, dependent on horses and bugles. Born in Hawaii, I was the petted baby of three much older siblings. I went to grade school in Virginia and Kansas, high school in Panama, and college in New England. I started out giddy, took some hard knocks, and ended up in love with education, monogamy, and Tom Campion.

Senior year at Wellesley I met my one and only husband, a senior at Harvard. Tom Campion taught me, among other things, that laughter is life's best solvent. In fifty-nine years, we moved from Cincinnati (Procter & Gamble) to Bronxville (*The New York Times*) to Amherst (UMass) to Hanover (Dartmouth) to Lebanon (retirement community).

In houses filled with laughter—and tears—we raised four boys and one girl, managing to educate them almost as much as they educated us. Our life has been enriched by those five engrossing, enabling children, eight evolving, enlightening grandchildren, one adorable, adored great grandchild, and, of course, the sexual revolution. Our marriage survived four jobs (Tom's); seven books (mine); nine homes; nineteen pets (gerbils don't count); and umpteen crises, some serious, some funny, all instructive.

How to account for our good luck? No way. I am awash with gratitude. In sharing our story, from the cradle to the grave (one of us), I want to pass one powerful lesson, which we learned the hard way. Anne Morrow Lindbergh said it best: "The most exciting thing in life is communication."

I. Before Tom

Army Brat

❧ 1. Votes for Women!

When I was two, my mother taught me to stand up in my playpen, shake my fist, and shout, "Votes for women!" After the Nineteenth Amendment passed (finally!), on August 26, 1920, there was wild rejoicing in our family.

"Women are on the move!" my mother cried.

"And high time, too," Father said.

At our dinner table, in addition to talking politics, we played games: "What is your first memory?" "Who was your best teacher?" "What's your favorite book?" "What's your pet peeve?" and my mother's favorite, "What famous woman would you like to be?"

My answer to "What is your scariest memory?": learning to swim in Honolulu. My father, an officer in the U.S. Army, was stationed there twice before I was ten.

I was born on the old army post, Fort Kamehameha, Territory of Hawaii, on June 27, 1917. My mother had me at home, of course; no maternity wards or birthing centers in those days. Later we lived at Fort Shafter, when my father was promoted to General Summerall's staff.

I loved Hawaii: the fragrant pink and white oleanders, the scarlet hibiscus, the liquid sunshine (rain to visitors), the succulent pineapples (unrelated to pineapples in the States), the juicy papayas and rich avocados growing in our yard, the blue ocean rollers thumping on deserted beaches.

There was a royal poinciana tree in our backyard at Fort Shafter, with lacy leaves, long pods, and scarlet blossoms. I would climb to the platform my brother Fred had built for me and think "green thoughts in a green shade." One day I decided to climb higher, lost my balance, and fell. I landed on my head and was knocked out cold. (I've never been the same since.)

Mother said finding me unconscious was her second most frightening memory. (Her first was little Nat's sudden death, before I was born.) She rushed me to the post dispensary. The doctor revived me and promised her my head would still function. She was a wreck. My mother's feelings were close to the surface; my father kept his submerged.

Daddy had no small talk, which put some people off. I adored him. He was a tall, heavyset man with a strong chin, blue eyes, rimless eyeglasses, and receding white hair. I thought he was handsome. He had style. His boots were highly polished, as was the Sam Browne belt strapped across his chest. When I was little, I thought the gold-framed miniature of Napoleon in uniform was a picture of Daddy as a young officer.

My tutors were my three siblings. They taught me everything from swimming to handling the parents. In 1922, when I was five, my brother Red was a cadet at West Point, playing first base, playing end, flunking thermodynamics. My sister Julia, eighteen, was a freshman at the University of Hawaii, prospecting for eligible men. My brother Fred, handsome as a prince but not as tall as he would like (he never would be), was at Punahoe High School.

Mother was forty when I was born—ancient, she thought. A supporter of Margaret Sanger's wildly controversial crusade for birth control, my mother often told me what an unwelcome surprise I was. Unwelcome, she always added, until she saw me. Then she lavished on me her lost love for little Nat.

In those days children carried on family names, not names of movie stars and football players. Red was named for Daddy, Fred for Grandfather Martin, Julia for Grandma Reeder, Nat for Daddy's brother. I was the fourth Narcissa.

One afternoon, we were all sitting on our fern-filled *lanai* when our guest, Colonel Hase, remarked, "Narcissa isn't a name, it's a complex." Those in the know used to work Freud into the conversation.

"We're not narcissists," my mother laughed, "we're the third and fourth.

The first one was my grandmother, Narcissa Pillow Martin of Columbia, Tennessee. The Old South cultivated things classical—Doric columns, Parthenon buildings, names like Lucius and Cassius. Narcissus is the masculine."

My father sprang to our defense. "Narcissus became the complex. He fell in love with his own face reflected in a pond, leaned down to kiss himself—and drowned."

"A white flower sprang up where he'd been lying," Mother added. "It's called the narcissus."

"Why have I never heard of Narcissa II?" I demanded.

Mother spoke softly. "Because Narcissa II—my mother's sister—is a terrible story. She'd been told over and over: never play with matches—matches were everywhere then—but she did it. She lit a match, sparks flew, and her organdy dress burst into flames. Before anyone could get to her, little Narcissa burned to death. My grandparents never got over it." My mother's eyes were swimming. "When your child dies, the pain is forever."

Nobody on the *lanai* spoke. Colonel Hase broke the silence. "I think Narcissa IV needs a nickname. What shall we call her?" He stopped to think. "Nardi. How about Nardi?"

My siblings adopted it; my parents ignored it.

My two most frightening memories have to do with Fred. Eleven years older than I, Fred was my hero. He knew everything. We used to sit on the back steps and grade the glorious Hawaiian sunsets. I'd say, "I give this one a C, not enough gold." He'd answer, definitively, "It's a B-plus. See how separate the red and blue streaks are." When the sky glowed red and gold through a purple haze, Fred would tell me, "No human spread those colors out. You know that, don't you?"

I was three years old and quivering with excitement because it was the Fourth of July. After dark, we'd have fireworks on the parade ground. Just before dinner I picked up a sparkler, held it to a burning candle, and started making circles in the air. Beautiful. A spark landed on my party dress. It caught fire and I shrieked.

Fred ran down the walk. He grabbed me as I tried to run, threw me on the ground, and rolled with me until the fire was out. I tried to scream, but I couldn't even breathe. I felt my heart throbbing. Mother, ghastly white, almost fainted. Daddy revived her with smelling salts. It wasn't just the fire. I had eerily invoked the death of Narcissa II.

Fred was the hero. Mother held him tight, kissing him and awarding her highest accolade. "You functioned in disaster, Fred."

After he saved my life, Fred felt responsible for me.

On my fifth birthday he said it was high time I learned to swim. Fred was a powerful ocean swimmer who had won the huge silver cup in the Australian crawl (new) race from Diamond Head to Waikiki Beach. He marched me across the parade ground to the post swimming pool. "Put your suit on. I'm going to throw you in and you'll do what comes natu-rally: swim. You'll paddle like a puppy dog," he chuckled. As always, I believed him. He had read about this teaching method in the *Honolulu Examiner*.

We stood on the edge of the pool in our one-piece black wool bath-ing suits. I tried to hide my fear. Suddenly, Fred picked me up and tossed me into the deep end. Down, down, down, terrified, unable to breathe, unable to open my eyes, I knew I was drowning.

After a long, long time, my head popped out of the water. Fred was right beside me. Frozen with fear, gasping and sputtering, I couldn't even dog-paddle. He threw a strong arm across my chest and towed me to safety. I lay on the hot cement, vomiting chlorine water and sobbing. I learned to swim in the shallow end.

At Fort Shafter I learned a lot of things. A nine-year-old boy named Boswell Osborne took me and another little girl up to his room. We were about seven. He unbuttoned his pants and showed us his little pink penis. He demonstrated how the foreskin worked. He was proud and seemed to think we were missing something. I didn't—he was welcome to his gadget. I never mentioned this to my mother, but I couldn't for-get it. The experience cured me of Boswell Osborne.

My parents were retrogressive *re* sex education but progressive *re* school. They sent me to one of the first progressive schools, Hanahou'oli in Honolulu. The young headmistress, Miss Louisa Palmer, was a pio-neer in "whole child education." Most classes were held outside and she let us go barefoot (no snakes in Hawaii).

Miss Palmer believed in hands-on education. We learned the multi-plication tables by sorting colored beans. We learned persistence by watch-ing a wasp trapped in a bottle, trying to get out. We acted out stories—and then read them. I was Cinderella in a white gauze, tinsel-trimmed gown and a silver crown. No wonder I couldn't wait to read the story.

I was struggling to write cursive when my mother came up with the carrot. "As soon as you can sign your name, you can get your own library card." She made it sound like the Holy Grail, which in a way it was.

Hanahou'oli School used the Palmer Method. "No relation," Miss Palmer told us. I mastered the connecting circles and slanting lines and moved on to the alphabet. "Narcissa Pillow Reeder" did not come trip-pingly off my pencil. One day my mother studied my best effort and ex-claimed, "Excellent! Now you can go to the library, get a card, and pick out your own book."

In the twenties children could go places by themselves. What caused the change? Maybe it was loss of community. On an army post, every-one looked out for everyone else. We had what Hawaiians call *kokua,* the spirit of helping.

I trotted over a long wooden footbridge to the part of the post known as "over the gulch," where non-commissioned officers lived. The Fort Shafter Library was in a converted barracks. No quiet carpeting or easy chairs, just long rows of dusty books on wooden shelves. The room was lit by bare light bulbs and smelled musty. An aging sergeant, too "stove up" to drill, was post librarian.

Sergeant O'Toole looked at me over his glasses. "What can I do for you, little lady?"

"I want to get a library card."

"Aren't you a little young for that?" His chuckle burned me up.

"I may look young to you," I said, "but I'm old to me. And I want a library card. Now." I didn't mean to sound rude. I was just naturally im-patient, a condition that hasn't improved with age.

"Can you write your name?"

"Of course."

"Temper, temper," he laughed, pulling out a pink card and handing it to me. "Let's see you do it."

I sat down opposite him, ready for the challenge. I dipped the steel penpoint into his well and slowly wrote my name on the dotted line. No ink blots. I put a flourish at the end.

I passed it to Sergeant O'Toole. He held the card at arm's length and read slowly: "Narcissa Pillow Reeder." He paused. "Jesus Christ!"

I took out *Little Black Sambo.* My mother was glad I picked a book she grew up on. In those politically incorrect times one could enjoy, without a twinge of guilt, the smart little black boy who outwitted all the tigers, turned them into butter, and ate them on his pancakes.

I loved school, but just as we got to the seven and eight tables, my education ground to a halt. My big sister got engaged to "the best dancer in Hawaii," a man my parents did not care for. I liked Steiny because he brought me beautiful picture books. To them, this recent Naval Academy graduate was unacceptable. Ensign Steinbar was a fine fellow. It was simply a matter of religion.

He was Jewish.

❦ 2. At Sea with General MacArthur

Julia told me that when she broke the news of her engagement to Steiny, Mother said not a word but two tears rolled down her cheeks. It hurts me to record my parents' anti-Semitism, but that's the way things were. Prejudice was the norm in America and rampant in the military.

It was really xenophobia. Fear of strangers led people to shun those who weren't L.U. (like us). Irish and Italians and Germans were considered worse than Jews. After my father returned from France at the end of World War I, he canceled Fred's nickname. "Fritz" was too German. Before President Kennedy, Irish Catholics were fish eaters, and Italians were gardeners.

With blacks it was different. My mother, having grown up in the South, had an abiding affection for Negroes, as they were called. She smoldered with indignation over the injustices they endured. But in her heart she believed that blacks and whites were happier living separately.

My mother wanted everybody to be happy, especially her children. But she didn't think anything of rearranging our lives to make us happy—whether we agreed or not.

I overheard her tell my father, "We have to handle this engagement with kid gloves. Julia is so hard headed, if we say no, she will marry him at once."

Julia was hard headed, all right. When she was little, Daddy handed her a quarter allowance (a fortune in those days) and told her she could not spend it. She had to learn to save her money. Julia ran upstairs and slammed the door. Later Mother found her facedown on the bed. It was January in Fort McKinley, Maine, where we lived, but the window was wide open. "What did you do with your quarter, Julia?"

"I threw the damned thing out the window. What good is a quarter if you can't spend it?"

My sister came by her stubbornness naturally. Our father was diffident, disciplined, intellectual, determined. Our mother was warm, intuitive, impulsive, determined. Mother was an optimist. Daddy said, "A pessimist is someone who lives with an optimist." They often disagreed, but they agreed wholeheartedly on one thing: Ensign Steinbar did not belong in our family, and we did not belong in his family. The motto on both sides was "Stick to your own kind."

"Russell," my mother said to my father, "can't you arrange for us to go to the Philippines on an Army transport? I want Julia to meet other men. There'll be bachelors on board. Propinquity works magic—and there's a lot of propinquity in an ocean voyage." My mother may have been educated at a finishing school in Little Rock, Arkansas, but she was a wordsmith.

In those days the army was full of bachelors, and with reason. Graduating cadets were given a cautionary lecture called, "A Second Lieutenant's Pay Divided by Two." Their salary would be two hundred dollars a month.

"I can arrange the trip," my father said, "but what about Narcissa?"

"We'll take her along. I want her to see the world."

"You're going to take one daughter out of school because the other is engaged to a man you don't want her to marry?"

"You don't want her to, either. Narcissa will learn more in three months of traveling the Pacific than she ever would in three months of school."

And thus my off-the-wall education began.

My mother's motto was "Ask, don't tell." She did not tell Julia; she asked. "Which would you rather do, get married or go to the Orient?"

Julia did not hesitate a minute. "Go to the Orient. You can get married any time."

My father was not about to let his best girls travel alone. He ordered a lieutenant to be our courier. In the old Army you could do that. Lieutenant Don Rogers was fifteen years older than Julia, but, as she pointed out, a wonderful dancer.

For the trip, Mother's Japanese seamstress made me a new outfit. I can see it now. The tomb of Tutenkhamon, a fourteenth-century pharaoh, had just been discovered, and King Tut was the rage. My lavender dress was covered with miniature pyramids, hieroglyphics, fox-headed goddesses, sleek Egyptian cats. It was smocked to the waist in purple and had bloomers to match. I wore silk knee socks and black patent leathers with ankle straps. Julia said I looked like the cat's meow. I thought so.

One of my mother's friends said, "You are going to take two girls on a three-month trip to the Orient without your husband? How do you dare?"

My mother, who would dare to do anything, just laughed. "Women are on the move," she said.

Mother, Julia, and I stood at the rail of the USAT *Thomas*, throwing pennies into the water for brown *kanaka* divers. I waved an excited goodbye to my father and Fred on the dock. The white ginger-flower *lei*s around my neck smelled sickeningly sweet. As the ship pulled away, the band played "Aloha, Oe," and we threw our *lei*s in the water. If the tides carried them back to the beach, we would return to Hawaii. I certainly hoped we'd do that. I was crying, but not because I was sad to set out for adventure on the high seas. "Aloha, Oe" makes everybody cry.

We could hardly wedge ourselves into the tiny stateroom, which was full of flowers. In Hawaii people say it with flowers, over and over. Our big steamer trunk took up the rest of the space.

The *Thomas* was made of wood and sailors swabbed its decks twice a day. All day and night, black smoke billowed from its twin stacks, as men grunting and sweating in the engine room below the water line shoveled coal.

Up on the promenade deck we didn't give the firemen a thought. Filipino stewards brought trays of sandwiches and pitchers of hot broth to sustain us until the next delicious meal. We had been invited to sit at the captain's table. Captain Andersen, a fine seaman, was a friend of my father's. The captain's other guest was a tall congressman from Indiana. Like many a U.S. representative, Congressman Moore, a widower, was on an "inspection trip" of far-flung U.S. outposts (read joy ride). He soon became entranced with my mother.

A shipboard ritual was the daily siesta, and it was not optional. Every day after lunch, Julia and I lay on our berths while Mother read aloud. Her idea of fun was reading to her children. Mother's choice of book for the trip told a lot about her. *The Go-Getter: A Story That Tells You How to Be One* was a new bestseller by Peter B. Kyne. The tale of a scrappy kid who made it as a red-hot salesman conveyed lots of "how-to" in its driving narrative. If women had worked, my mother could have been a red-hot saleswoman. In fact, late in life, she sold real estate with gusto.

The *Thomas* took thirty days to go the 1,500 miles from Honolulu to Manila. Today the flight takes twelve hours. What's the hurry, I wonder? Psychologists say we rush around to stave off fears of dying. Doubtful. People have always been afraid of dying, but they haven't always been jet propelled. All I know is, I never again experienced the leisurely pace of that long voyage across the wide Pacific. Even a seven-year-old felt out of touch with the bustle of life.

All of the passengers were browbeaten by Carlos, the bath steward. He'd knock and say, "Mrs. Reeder, your bath is at 3:30 sharp." Mother would trot dutifully down the long corridor in her gold silk kimono to climb into a tiny tub full of hot salt water.

With me, Carlos was less accommodating. "Miss Narcissa, your bath is at 6:30 A.M." I resented the fact that Julia was "Miss Reeder," while I was called by my first name.

"I'm going to skip it tomorrow, Carlos."

"You haven't had a bath for three days. I'll meet you there at 6:30." Like everyone else, I stood in awe of Carlos. I was there at 6:30.

On board the *Thomas* was a couple far more famous than the congressman. All eyes were riveted on the handsome General Douglas MacArthur and his sexy new wife, Louise Cromwell Brooks. She looked like the "It Girl," Clara Bow, the raging star of Hollywood. They were moving to Manila with the bride's two children, Louise and Walter Jr. Louise was about my age and we became shipboard playmates. The MacArthurs dined in lonely splendor in the captain's quarters. They were the talk of the ship.

Everyone knew that the general's mother, Mrs. Arthur MacArthur, known as Pinky, had refused to attend her only child's wedding. She announced, "Of course, the attraction is purely physical," and took to her bed.

Our deck chairs were next to the MacArthurs' on the promenade deck and we enjoyed MacArthur-watching. As soon as the *Thomas* put to sea, the general began his deck-circling walks, his aide following three paces behind. My mother observed that Douglas MacArthur spoke to his bride once in seventeen days.

Louise lasted two years. When she moved out, Mother MacArthur moved back in. In his memoir, General MacArthur gives Louise one sentence: "My first marriage ended in divorce." Louise disposed of him, the second of her four husbands, more deftly: "Sir Galahad conducted his courtship as if he were reviewing a division of troops."

Another celebrity was Chef George, one of the first male models. In his chef's hat and red bow tie he posed for the smiling picture that still adorns the Cream of Wheat box. George became my buddy by converting the awful canned milk Mother forced me to drink into a delicious concoction of sugar, vanilla, and hand-crushed ice.

The trip was pepped up by Congressman Moore's fascination with my mother. The ship had to stop at Guam for more coal before steaming on to Manila. The Congressman was the guest of honor at a luncheon given by the governor of Guam, and he invited Mother to go with him to the governor's mansion. "Oh," she said sweetly. "I never go anywhere without my daughters." The four of us were the only passengers allowed to go ashore.

My memory of the luncheon is an excited blur, but I can recall in detail our return to the *Thomas* in the captain's gig. The ocean was running high. As we approached, we saw people standing at the rail with angry faces. How could we have known we were holding up the ship's urgent departure?

We had to hoist ourselves out of the small rocking boat to climb up a swinging ladder. Mother went first to show us how. She could do anything. Julia was next, as agile as a monkey. I inched up, hanging on to the slippery metal rungs with white knuckles. I was worried about getting saltwater on my new Mary Janes and terrified of drowning.

Captain Andersen was waiting for us. "Thank God you're back. I was about to leave without you. The barometer has hit bottom. A huge storm is coming. We must put to sea immediately. It's suicide to be at anchor during a typhoon."

It's not so great to be at sea during a typhoon, either. Julia, a terrible sailor, was actively ill. Even in the calm weather after Honolulu, she threw up during the day and got well at night. I was proud that I had never been seasick. At least there was one thing I did better than my sister.

Our ship began to roll dangerously. The captain came to our stateroom (no intercom, of course). "It will get rougher. Put on your life preservers, get in your bunks, and stay there." Wind and water whiplashed the small ship. This *was* my scariest moment. When the storm hit full blast, the *Thomas* would go up, seem to stop, plunge downward. Two life boats were washed away. The wireless telegraph was ripped out. We were on our own.

Our stateroom was on the top deck. Mother, Julia, and I lay flat in our bunks, holding on to the sides. I was in the upper berth; Julia was beneath me; Mother was on the side. My mother repeated Miss Mediera's mantra, "You are to function in disaster and finish in style." (We were immobilized in disaster and would finish in oblivion.)

Waves smashed against the glass porthole. They pounded the door, and saltwater began seeping into the cabin. Our steamer trunk slid back and forth in the water. Death by drowning—thanks to Fred's swimming lesson, I already knew how that would feel.

Mother: "Are you afraid, girls?"

Me (small voice): "Yes."

Julia (full throat): "No, I am not afraid."

Mother: "Julia, don't lie to me at a time like this. You must be afraid. What are you thinking about?"

Julia (long pause): "I'm thinking how in the Bible Jesus said, 'Peace, be still.' And the waters grew still."

Pause for Julia's vomiting. Silence.

(Julia was big on the Bible. When they were little, my mother overheard my siblings proposing toasts with ginger ale. Red said, "Here's how to George Washington." Fred said, "Here's how to Joan of Arc." Julia raised her glass and cried, "Here's how to Jesus!")

Slowly the storm began to subside. Eventually the waters did grow still—or stiller. Wearing my heavy, solid life preserver, I ventured out on deck. I was surrounded by wet, gray mountains—the waves were higher than the ship. Gripping the mahogany railing, I vomited. My one-upmanship over Julia went overboard.

Captain Andersen said the typhoon was the worst he had ever faced. Chef George tried to tempt the wobbly passengers with his best dishes, but it was a long time before anyone felt like eating.

Forbidden to use the contaminated water, we were a mess when we reached Japan. Our hair was stringy, our faces dirty. My mother was infuriated by what we saw on the docks of Nagasaki: women bent double, hauling sacks of coal onto a freighter. It hurts now even to write the word Nagasaki. Twenty years later our country would destroy the ancient, bustling city in a matter of hours, killing 39,000 people with a power beyond imagination.

At the hotel, we soaked in baths fragrant with sandalwood. Sipping steaming green tea, we recovered our equilibrium.

When we moved on to the Philippines, we stayed at Fort Corregidor with the commanding officer, General McCrea. Like all generals' quarters, the McCreas' house was elegant and spacious, with many guest rooms and several houseboys cleaning and polishing. I remember Manila as all white, splashed with purple bougainvillea. The buildings were white, everyone wore white, and tropical moonlight turned the nights white.

We did not see much of Julia in Manila. Many young officers danced attendance on her. The Jazz Age was raging and Julia could do the Black Bottom. Mother kept saying, "Men are crazy about Julia because she doesn't smoke, drink, or bob her hair. She's no flapper like that Louise MacArthur."

On the side Julia told me, "I'm going to dance every night we're here and not come home until the sun is up." And she did, too. In those days my mother was a heavy sleeper.

The thing I remember best about China was holding my nose. The odor of garbage and excrement in the streets was sickening. We rode in a Chinese rickshaw pulled by a man in a peaked straw hat. "Imagine making men do what horses should do," Mother said with disgust.

Of course we went to the Great Wall, where I had my picture taken pulling up my silk socks. I read recently that only one object on earth is visible from outer space: the 1,500-mile wall built by 300,000 Chinese in the third century B.C.

We could hear guns booming in the distance. The Chinese were at war again. We were supposed to spend a month in Kuangchou visiting old friends—General Miley was the American *Chargé d'affaires*—but our plans were canceled by Captain Andersen. "It's not safe here. We're leaving for San Francisco." Suddenly, California was added to our itinerary. That was fine by me.

We came back via the northern arc of the Great Circle, following the jetstream to California, a quicker trip. Docking in San Francisco, everybody stood at the rail to watch our celebrity, Chef George, depart, a *Thomas* tradition. Dressed in a white suit and straw boater, the King of Cream of Wheat sauntered down the gangplank. A uniformed chauffeur opened the door of his black Pierce Arrow. We all waved and cheered as our chef drove off to his other life.

We stayed at the old St. Francis Hotel—lots of red plush and gold trim. In the lobby I spotted a poster of the great Russian dancer Pavlova. I planned to become a ballerina, even though Mother said it would ruin my feet. I had to see Pavlova dance. Our courier Don Rogers, by now in love with Julia, moved heaven and earth and got four tickets. I certainly hoped she would marry him.

Pavlova was the essence of glamour and grace in a close-fitted pink feathered cap, pink satin toe slippers, and flesh-colored tutu. She seemed suspended in air; then, fluttering her long hands, the dying swan settled gently to earth. The audience jumped up, shouting. I yelled the loudest.

My father and Fred were waiting on the dock in Honolulu. We hugged and kissed and my mother shed tears. Fred said, "I'm sick of rice pudding." My father said, "The phone rang twice while you were gone. Both times it was wrong number." I said, "You'd better watch out for Congressman Moore, Daddy. He's in love with Mother."

My mother pronounced the trip a howling success. Julia came back engaged to marry Don Rogers (she didn't marry him, either). But it was no success to me. Thanks to my sister's romance, I missed the seven and eight tables—and never caught up.

⅋ 3. Women Can Slay Dragons

M y mother was an "old married lady" of twenty-five in 1904, when Anna Taylor went over Niagara Falls in a barrel. Anna wanted to prove that a woman can do anything a man can do. The newspapers reported her daring deed on the front page, adding: "Miss Taylor took a lot of the credit that belonged to the barrel."

"Typical," Mother fumed. "Men are threatened by brave women."

This was news to me. "They are?"

"Men go out and slay dragons. Women should stay home and tend fires."

"Don't you think women belong in the home?"

"Some do. Some don't. One role does not fit everyone."

My mother was a hundred-percenter. She believed in the Bible and it sustained her. "How can you doubt that Jesus could turn water into wine? That's nothing compared to turning water into electricity."

My parents were married in Little Rock, Arkansas, on April 10, 1901. I treasure the picture of my mother on that spring day, a twenty-two-year-old southern belle with upswept hair and a wasp waist. She has on a lace-trimmed satin dress with a spread-out train and carries Easter lilies. My father, twenty-eight, is a dashing lieutenant in a high-collared blue uniform with red artillery stripes down the trousers.

It was a Capulet and Montague match. Two of my grandfather Martin's brothers (my mother's uncles) were killed fighting for the Confederacy. The Reeders fought for the Union. The Martins were leery of the damn Yankees from Ohio.

Lieutenant Reeder took his young wife to Fort Riley, Kansas, the frontier cavalry post where he was stationed. Following army tradition, the bride and groom were met at the main gate by a horse-drawn *caisson* and pulled around the reservation, while the regimental band marched in front of them, playing "You're in the Army Now."

In those days the popular wedding present was cut glass. My mother was thrilled with the cut-glass vases, pitchers, bowls, and decanters they received. "Our cut-glass gifts were packed into a large barrel and shipped to Fort Riley," she told me. "I knew where I'd put each piece to brighten up our drab quarters." She paused. "When the barrel finally arrived, it sounded like a keg of nails."

"Oh Lord!" I cried. "How awful. Weren't you heartbroken to have your beautiful gifts smashed to smithereens? Did you cry?"

"Oh, no." My mother shrugged. "They were only things."

In 1909 my father, by now a captain in the Coast Artillery, was ordered to Fort Worden, Washington, on Puget Sound, his fourth post in seven years. My mother, who followed him west, was exhausted by the endless train trip across the country with Red, seven, Julia, five, Fred, three, and baby Nathaniel.

They had just settled in on the new post when tragedy struck our family. It happened eight years before I was born, but I feel as though I was right there.

One morning our Japanese cook, Masako, accidentally bought unpasteurized milk. She gave it to little Nat and by nightfall the baby could hardly breathe; his fever skyrocketed. For twenty-four hours, neither Mother nor Daddy left his bedside. The next day little Nat was dead.

Masako, dressed in her black kimono, walked behind the little white coffin. Julia always remembered the clack-clack of the cook's wooden clogs and her gasping sobs. Everybody cried, even my stoic father.

In his memoir, *Born at Reveille,* Red says he thought Mother would not survive the funeral. "They placed little Nat in a white casket that had white gingerbread work about its top. He looked like wax. His golden-blond hair was combed more carefully than it ever had been in life. I was frightened."

Sobbing, Mother put her arm around Red and led him to the casket. "Kiss little Nat good-bye, Russell," she said. Red was petrified, but all his life he would do what Mother told him. He leaned into the white coffin and touched his lips to the cheek of the tiny body. Years later he told me, "I wish I'd never done it. Nat's icy skin was the coldest thing I ever felt."

Red's account of little Nat's funeral chilled me to the bone. "Mother's consuming grief and the look of Nat lying in that white casket filled me with a horror of the dead that took long years to overcome, and even now I am not hankering to see any dead people."

Today the death of a young child is blessedly rare, but many of my mother's friends had to endure it. Disease was to her generation what car crashes are to mine.

The death of her baby opened my mother's heart wide. She volunteered at the hospital, caring for dying children. My father finally stopped her; he was afraid she might break.

Every day my mother prayed for little Nat. I used to gaze at the picture of him in her Book of Common Prayer, a blond toddler in a starched white dress and high-buttoned white shoes. I wished so much I'd known him, but in a way I did. My mother kept Nat's memory green.

❦ 4. Sibling Revelry

In her eighties my mother made a startling discovery. "I've been reading about something called sibling rivalry. I'm thankful we never had that in our family."

I was glad my mother did not know about my eagerness to beat my sister at everything, even seasickness. But how did she miss the running battle between Julia and Fred or between Fred and Red? Or my resentment that only Julia was called "Miss Reeder?" How did she ignore her own intense rivalry with her sisters, Susie and Honey?

Red, the first child, was my mother's favorite. And he was the guinea pig. As a little boy, he enriched his vocabulary hanging around the post stables. One day our mother heard him cussing a blue streak. She grabbed a bar of yellow soap, jammed it into Red's mouth and swished it around. He gagged. Then she hugged him. "You must never use those words again."

Later, Chaplain Easterbrook came to call on him. Red was stunned. The chaplain, Mother's spiritual guide, was dressed in his blue uniform, with silver crosses pinned on his high collar.

"Russell, I hate to hear of little boys who swear. It's very, very bad indeed."

"Swear? You know some boy who swears?"

"Yes, I do. Don't you?"

"Maybe."

"Russell, do you know what happens to little boys who swear?"

"No, sir."

"When they die, they go to the bad place." Chaplain Easterbrook let that sink in. "The devil heats up a pitchfork until it is sizzling red hot. He sticks it into boys who swear and broils them over a slow fire. Then he dips them into a vat of boiling oil and pitches them headlong into the fire."

Red jumped up and shouted, "Why that son of a bitch!"

Fred and Julia fought over everything from evolution to the telephone. One year, Fred's list began: "For Christmas, I want a one-way ticket to Hawaii for my sister Julia." Julia's fickleness drove Fred up the wall. "Make up your mind who you're going to marry," he growled, "or you'll be a has-been."

She just laughed. "Better a has-been than a never-was-er."

Julia enjoyed it when Daddy exploded at her younger brother. "You're not dumb, Fred. Why are your grades so terrible?"

"What parents don't know," I said to myself.

Fred had been invited to join the Outrigger Canoe Club of Waikiki, a huge honor for a high school student. Elated, he used to get on the bus to Punahoe at Fort Shafter, get off at his club, and spend the day surfing. If the heavy wooden surfboard bopped him, he'd be dead. Fred didn't care. He was a daredevil.

In the afternoon, he'd climb back on the school bus and go home.

I cringed when Daddy demanded angrily, "Young man, what do you expect to do with your life?"

"I'm going into the navy. I won't be stuck in some dusty old army post. I'll go to Annapolis and see the world."

"With your grades you won't get near the Naval Academy. Find another career."

Daddy's hot indignation would have reduced me to jelly. Fred remained cool. "I've sent for a correspondence course. I'll get into Annapolis that way." Who could have guessed that one day that maverick Fred Reeder would be an admiral in the U.S. Navy?

That summer, Cadet Charlie Summerall, only child of our next-door neighbor, the imposing General Summerall, came to Hawaii on furlough. Charlie, handsome, shy, reliable, gentle, serious, fell dead in love with Julia. Julia enjoyed the attention; mother was transported. Charlie Summerall was the very thing she was looking for.

The next summer Mother decided she'd take Julia and me to West Point to visit Cadet Red Reeder, whom she sorely missed. She also wanted Julia to have a fling with cadets. How else would her daughter realize what a splendid fellow Charlie Summerall was? A "fling" meant flirting, not kissing. At least that's what Julia told me.

Once again the three of us, layered in sweet-smelling *leis*, stood on the deck of an army transport. Crying, I tossed my *leis* on the water. I knew they would not reach the shore; my father had been ordered to Fort Monroe, Virginia. As we steamed past the rocky crest of Diamond Head, I wished we were heading to the Orient.

How I hated to leave Oahu, my beautiful birthplace.

It took seven days to reach San Francisco. Then we boarded the Union Pacific for my first train ride, the eight-day trip to New York. In the twenties trains were posh—white linen tablecloths, heavy silver, fresh flowers, delicious food—plus shocking jolts when the train stopped.

I slept in the upper berth, leaning down inside the green plush curtains to whisper to Julia in the lower. The game was to guess which men went with which shoes, left out for the porter to shine.

One morning my mother heard news: one of West Point's most famous graduates, General George Goethals, was six cars ahead of us. A brilliant engineer in the class of 1880, General Goethals did what the French could not: he joined the Atlantic and Pacific Oceans with a canal. Julia remembered the wild celebration on August 15, 1914, when President Teddy Roosevelt cut the ribbons to open the Panama Canal.

We got all dressed up to call on the great man: Julia in a silk pongee suit, with her beautiful auburn hair hanging down her back; me in a dumb white sailor suit, my hair cut like a boy's; Mother in her "traveling outfit," navy blue with a white collar, white gloves, and a navy straw hat. In those days, people dressed up for a trip. Today they seem to travel in their underwear.

I was scared of crossing the creaking, jolting couplings between the cars. What would keep us from falling through?

General Goethals, with his bristling mustache, white hair, and jaw like a bulldog was intimidating. He enjoyed my mother's attention, but he was shy. "Look," he said, changing the subject from himself, "there's Great Salt Lake. The salt content is so high, if you try to dive in, you'll just float on top." I longed to try it.

Wobbling back to our car Mother, still beaming, told us, "Girls, you just met an American hero."

Excitement was running high when we climbed on the Weehawken train to go up the Hudson. All three of us were seeing West Point for the first time. Its rugged beauty bowled us over—the broad blue Hudson winding below, the great, gray chapel, like an eagle, hovering above. My mother was also dazzled by her oldest child, a yearling, class of 1924, in his gray uniform with brass buttons. "It's sinful how closely my pride and love are linked," she sighed.

My mother's delight in Cadet Reeder was shortlived. Red was "turned back," cadet lingo for "found deficient in math and turned back to the next class." Mother and Daddy acted as though there had been a death in the family. I was shattered. How could my adored brother fail? I went into my room and cried.

Red must have been brilliant to get in to West Point in the first place. He was educated in post schools by old sergeants, some of whom knew less than he did. Mother finally got him an athletic scholarship to a military school in Alabama. The headmaster kept Red on the football and baseball fields and allowed him to graduate without touching a book.

Daddy hired experts to tutor Red. He passed a re-exam and entered the class of 1925. Great relief all around. Then he failed what the cadets call "thermogodamics"—and was turned back again. My mother and I were reduced to tears. My father said Red's military career was over. My mother said Red would be heard from again. The optimist was right.

Red's graduation in June 1926 was the most thrilling event of my childhood. Even our taciturn father was glowing with pride. His son was now a West Pointer. Julia's eyes were sparkling, not for Red but for Cadet Maxwell Taylor. He was her current beau, though Charlie Summerall still hovered in the background. The only thing that kept me from turning cartwheels was my starched white dress and new straw boater with long ribbons.

We sat on wooden chairs in front of Battle Monument, gazing at the sapphire Hudson in the distance. Up Thayer Road came the West Point band, playing "Stars and Stripes Forever." Behind marched the Class of 1926 in full dress: gray coats with brass buttons, starched white trousers, black shoes that shined like mirrors.

As the cadets clattered into the bleachers, Red came right past us. His red hair was hidden by his black-visored cap, but I could see his freckle-faced grin. My mother was wiping her eyes. Red cupped his hands and called, "Mother, after my trouble getting through, you wouldn't cry about my graduating, would you?" Everybody laughed.

Of course she cried. We all did; even Daddy had to take off his glasses and polish them.

When the adjutant called out "Russell Potter Reeder Jr.," wild cheering erupted. It went on and on. Not only had Red been captain of the baseball team, star of the swimming team, star of the basketball team, and star drop-kicker on the football team, but he had been a cadet for six years.

We were all there cheering, except poor Fred. He was a plebe at the Naval Academy. Like Cain and Abel, Romulus and Remus, Castor and Pollux, Red and Fred enjoyed brotherhood—up to a point. Fortunately, they didn't experience the same dire results. The year Fred entered, Red had kicked a last-minute field goal to clinch the Army–Notre Dame game. He got a big press, which did not help Midshipman Reeder. A first-classman sneered, "Who will you root for in the Army-Navy game, Mr. Reeder?"

Fred gave him a nervy answer. "Army, sir. Blood is thicker than uniform, sir." He was a long time living that down.

Their competitiveness played out on the golf course. They bought a sterling silver cup with handles on both sides and had it engraved "REEDER BROTHERS TROPHY." The winner got to keep the cup; the loser paid for the champagne. I can't remember who won the most, but I remember Fred lifting the big cup and saying, "Here's to sibling revelry."

Fort Monroe, Virginia, was another world. I was ecstatic over snow, even though it melted the same day. In summer, juicy fresh figs grew in our yard and the smell of crab hung in the air. Hampton was crab central. Mother made deviled crab every week, the best dish I've ever eaten.

To make money for new clothes, Julia started "Miss Reeder's Ballroom Dancing." She hired three enlisted men from the band to play piano, trumpet, and drums. They were loud and relentless. The reception hall at headquarters, an imposing salon with polished floors and gold-framed portraits of generals, made a dandy dance hall.

I was ten and had to wear my old dimity dress (the other girls wore taffeta). The boys wore navy suits with shorts (never long pants), and we all wore white gloves. Julia blew her whistle, the "band" blared the "Grand March" from *Aida,* and we paraded around the room in pairs. I was glad I didn't tower over the boys the way some of the girls did.

Boys sat on one side, girls on the other. "Ladies!" Julia cried, "Never cross your legs, just your ankles. Gentlemen, when you invite a partner to dance, remember the magic words, please and thank you."

Since I was sister of the Boss, I thought I rated special status. I did, but in the wrong direction. "Nardi, stop looking at your feet. Look into your partner's eyes when you waltz."

How can you look into your partner's eyes when he's looking at his feet?

At home I complained that she picked on me. Julia smiled sweetly. "I want you to be perfect, that's all."

Dancing classes came to an abrupt halt when the teacher got engaged to marry Charlie Summerall, now a second lieutenant. I hated the way they made moony-eyes at each other. I hated having to move out of my room when Charlie visited. But I liked Charlie—he treated me like an adult.

At the dinner table, I said crossly, "Why can't Charlie stay in Julia's room?" I hated their laughter. What was so funny?

I loved the wedding presents. One day, a huge box arrived. What could possibly be so big? We all stood around watching Julia struggle to open her gift. There were boxes within boxes. When she finally undid the last one, out jumped my dog Teddy.

Julia gasped, "Isn't that nice, somebody sent us a dog. Why he looks just like Teddy!" Red, home for the wedding, had concocted the hoax. Julia's naive reaction made his day, and mine, too. I loved to see her outwitted.

As we were dressing for the wedding, Mother sent me to get a gold piece from Uncle Nat. Daddy and his brother were the picture of sibling revelry, sipping bootleg whisky that Uncle Nat and Aunt Jean Reeder had brought from New York hidden in the trunk of their Rolls Royce. Uncle Nat, president of the Pressed Steel Car Company of America, had a pocket full of gold pieces. He handed me one the size of a dime, worth ten dollars.

On a golden October afternoon in 1926, Julia and Charlie were married in the post chapel, the Church of the Centurion, and I finally got a taffeta dress. Jane Sunderland and I were "junior bridesmaids." Our pale blue dresses were copies of the gowns worn by Julia's six bridesmaids. But they wore high-heeled silver slippers and we had to wear Mary Janes that my mother had painted silver.

Julia's creamy satin slippers were decorated with lilies of the valley. She wore a hidden blue lace garter, a souvenir for the groom. Her short white satin wedding dress, trimmed in *pointe de venice* lace, had a long tulle train. As the twenty-year-old bride walked slowly down the aisle on Daddy's arm, my mind kept tune to Mendelssohn's wedding march: "Here comes the bride / Short, fat, and wide / Ain't she a fool / Ain't she a fool / When she could have a good job / A-teaching school."

Except that this bride was short, slender, and beautiful. She carried a bouquet of large white pom-pom chrysanthemums. The rest of us carried bronze and yellow pom-poms. Nervous during the ceremony, I shredded mine, leaving behind a little pile of yellow petals when we exited to the joyous *Lohengrin* wedding march.

As Julia and Charlie left the church, the uniformed ushers drew their sabers and made a gleaming arch for the bride and groom to pass under. To me they looked like a prince and princess in fairyland.

After Julia and Charlie drove off for their honeymoon in the Blue

Ridge Mountains, I felt bereft. I was surprised how much I missed my sister. But not for long. I went right out and ordered calling cards for myself.

Now I was "Miss Reeder."

⅗ 5. The Great Book Escape

Suddenly I felt like an only child. After enjoying, if that's the word, five parents, I was down to two, who were older than Methuselah. Mother was forty-seven, Daddy was fifty-three, and they bugged me. Like my father, I escaped into books. "Outside of a dog, a man's best friend is a book," he'd say. "Inside of a dog, it is very dark."

My father was a library. After marrying him, my mother became a Reeder in more ways than one. "Never go on a trip," she instructed her children, "without a sweater and a book."

My mother was a communicator; my father wasn't. She could talk to anyone about anything—and did. Unlike most talkers, she listened as well. For my mother, listening was the essence of communication. Ask, don't tell.

I was a mix. Being a born chatterbox, I thought I was more like my mother. Years later I was surprised to discover that I was more like my father: I kept my true feelings in a lockbox.

School in the States was a shock. I wanted to go to the Catholic school. I loved the name, St. Mary's Star of the Sea. It was for girls only, and they got to wear blue uniforms. Instead, I was sent to Phoebus Grammar School, just outside the post, and wore gingham.

The village of Phoebus existed for two purposes, poles apart: Fort Monroe and Hampton Institute. The Institute, established after the Civil War "to teach Negroes a trade," might as well have been in Siberia. The "colored" college students were invisible.

The town had one stop light, one bank, and two restaurants. (There must have been one for "colored" people, too.) We went to Richardson's, which featured crab cooked eight different ways and had a sign in the window that said "EAT DIRT CHEAP."

The Phoebus grade school was a brick building surrounded by a dirt playground. The "colored" school across town was "separate but equal," a peculiar equality with overcrowded classes and no playground. Every morning in assembly, the principal led us in the Lord's Prayer, the Pledge of Allegiance, and "Carry Me Back to Ole Virginny."

After the joyous Hanahou'oli School, I was miserable there. The teacher, Miss Carmel, was a ramrod. I still feel the sting of her first report card. All A's except for a D-minus in arithmetic, but in deportment Miss Carmel checked "Whispers in class," "Talks too much," and worst, "Annoys others." I couldn't believe it.

My mother offered to straighten Miss Carmel out. My father said dryly, "Why don't you straighten Narcissa out first?"

At that time, my mother was reading *Self-Mastery by Conscious Auto-suggestion*, a bestseller by a Swiss doctor, Emile Coué. She had me chant "Every day, in every way, I'm getting better and better." Nothing happened. I still talked too much.

If one of her children felt blue, my mother's solution was to get a pet. I already had Teddy. He was the image of the dog listening to his master's voice in the Victrola ad. He slept on my bed or curled up in my lap when I read.

My mother knew I was still lonely. She got me a kitty, then a goldfish, then a yellow canary.

My parents did not know that I had an imaginary twin. Nat was always ready for anything. I talked to him before I went to sleep, and I could tell him everything; my perfect brother told me whatever I wanted to hear.

Sometimes Nat and I walked in the woods, looking for fairies. Bridget, an Irish girl at school, told me that she had seen little people in County Cork. Bridget said Irish fairies can be mean. They even kill people.

One summer day Nat and I saw a fairy. No bigger than your finger, she was pirouetting on a carpet of green moss. She had gauzy wings and a wispy bluish dress, like the Arthur Rackham drawings in my fairytale book. She vanished instantly. We never told anyone.

Every Saturday, Nat accompanied me to the movies. It cost me a nickel, but he was free. They weren't talkies but my, they were wonderful—

Lillian Gish tied to the railroad tracks, freeing herself just before the locomotive barreled over her; Charlie Chaplain dancing bowlegged and twirling his cane; the U.S. Cavalry slaughtering Indians (when I was little, I thought the U.S. Cavalry crucified Jesus).

Black children were always funny. When Buckwheat in "Our Gang" was scared, his hair shot straight up. Blacks were figures of fun in books, too. In Booth Tarkington's *Penrod* the twins who can't talk straight are named Herman and Vermin.

My mother never tired of reading me *Diddie, Dumps, and Tot, or Plantation Child-Life*. I still have her copy, published in 1882, when she was three. It's all about the happy lives of happy slaves on the happy plantation. Mammy and Uncle Snakebit Bob spoke a thick dialect that only my mother could pronounce. She made *Uncle Remus* come alive, too. Every time Br'er Rabbit escaped by pleading, "Whatever you do, *please* don't throw me in the briar patch," Mother laughed hard. "Joel Chandler Harris understood motivation."

At night from 6:00 to 6:15 we sat by the Atwater Kent, laughing at Amos 'n' Andy. It never occurred to us that they were white men caricaturing blacks. Amos 'n' Andy were funny and we loved them.

Looking back, it's hard to see anything good about race relations in the twenties. From my point of view, there weren't any. Army posts were segregated. There were no blacks in school. The only black I saw regularly was our striker, Hamilton, a black enlisted man who did chores. I loved him; we all did. When Hamilton came to tend furnace or shovel snow, his smile lit up the house. My mother, brought up to believe in segregation, taught me to have admiration, respect, and affection for black people.

When we read "Br'er Rabbit's Laughing Place," she'd say, "Everybody needs a Laughing Place. Mine is any place Fredrika and I get together." Fredrika was my mother's younger sister, our Aunt Honey. One of my strongest memories is my mother laughing with Aunt Honey until tears ran down their cheeks.

They didn't do that when Daddy and Uncle Forrest were around. It was as though the two Martin sisters belonged to a secret society. I loved it when the men rode off on maneuvers (mock warfare conducted on horseback). It was girls' night out—all night. I would sit at the top of the staircase and listen to Aunt Honey and Mother playing bridge with Mrs. Westover and Mrs. Arnold. They played all night. By 3:00 A.M. they were giddy with laughter, and their wild shrieks would wake me up. I wished my sister Julia and I could laugh like that. We never did. I thought that nobody ever laughed the way those two did.

I was wrong. The man I married could dissolve into helpless laughter, and it was contagious. Sometimes Tom and I would get laughing and couldn't stop. He said laughter is the sensation of feeling good all over.

My mother liked to read funny books. She thought *Billy and the Major* was hilarious. So was *Elsie Dinsmore*, but for the wrong reasons. *The Bobbsey Twins* and *Elsie Dinsmore* were outlawed—too trashy. I read them on my own, of course, and loved them, except when Elsie Dinsmore's chum stuck a knitting needle into Elsie's ear. Mother did not believe in censorship, except at home.

I can remember my mother, deep into *Middlemarch*, laughing as she quoted the bumbling Mr. Brooke: "Dorothea may read anything she likes, now that she's married." She may have laughed, but in her heart she agreed with him. Later she forbade me to read the book everyone was talking about, *The President's Daughter* by Nan Britten. I could hardly wait to get hold of it. What a letdown. The only juicy part was when President Harding seduced Nan in a broom closet at the White House.

A broom closet? My imagination wasn't up to it.

Even as I grew older, my mother kept reading aloud. To improve my tiny mind, she decided we'd do *Pilgrim's Progress*. "It's an allegory," she informed me.

"What's an allegory?"

Not a moment's hesitation. "An allegory is an earthly story with a heavenly meaning. John Bunyan got arrested for being a Baptist preacher."

"That's bad?"

"In seventeenth-century England it was a crime. He spent twelve years in a London prison studying the Bible. Maybe that's why *Pilgrim's Progress* is one of the most widely read books in the English language."

What I called "Pill's Prog" might have been widely read, but not by us. John Bunyan's eighteenth-century prose put my mother to sleep every time. We never got to Christian's rescue by the appropriately named Help.

She didn't doze over her childhood favorite, *Little Women* (published four years after the Civil War). How we admired Jo, scribbling in the attic where "genius burns." How we grieved when Beth died. How we rejoiced when Meg and John Brooke had twins. "We've never had twins in our family," Mother said wistfully. "Twins must be fun."

To her, everything was fun, especially dress up. In his eighties, Red was still talking about the lion suit she made him, with a long tail bushing out at the tip. I not only wanted to hear *Peter Pan* over and over, I wanted to be Peter Pan. So she made me a Peter Pan costume, complete with a black gauze shadow attached to my shoulders.

Emily Dickinson wrote, "There's no Frigate like a Book / to take us Lands away." I say there's no glue like a shared book to bring us together.

When we played the family game "What is your favorite children's book?" I insisted on four answers: *Sara Crewe or The Little Princess, Heidi, Anne of Green Gables,* and *The Secret Garden.* I see now that they have a common theme: a lonely orphan whose love of life brings joy to others receives happiness in return.

"You're never alone when you have a good book," my father liked to say. A pseudo–only child, I spent a lot of time reading and learned to relish it. Without books, I would have been lonely. Instead, I grew up as a happy bookworm.

❧ 6. The Undiscovered Country

Nobody forgets the first encounter with death. I was four years old. My mother and I were sitting on the porch swing at Fort Shafter. My father came slowly toward us, his blue eyes full of tears. He sat down beside my mother and put his arm around her. A terrible telegram had come from Arkansas. Fred Martin, "Bocker," her adored father, had died suddenly of apoplexy. My mother sobbed in my father's strong arms.

I was panicked. Not by grief, but by a little child's helpless fright when her mother weeps. What should I do? What was apoplexy? Nobody told me and I was afraid to ask. I had a vision of Bocker sitting on a bench in an apple orchard, suddenly felled by a deluge of apples.

My mother couldn't even go to her father's funeral. It would have taken three weeks to get from Honolulu to Little Rock. "I know I will see Papa again," she said between sobs, "because the Bible tells me so. I couldn't survive if I didn't know that after death we will be reunited with those we love, in some mysterious form beyond imagination." Faith was her life preserver.

Death came closer when I was ten and we were living in Fort Leavenworth, Kansas. We had moved there because my father was made dean of the Command and General Staff School. He ranked next to the general and the commandant, so we were given spacious quarters on a bluff overlooking the Platt River.

To me, Kansas was wonderful. After Hawaii and Virginia, I rejoiced in the extremes, bitter cold in winter, red hot in summer. Our first winter we had an early snowfall. After school, all of the children grabbed sleds and headed for a steep hill nearby.

I was a fifth grader in the post school. I had taken my first thrilling run on my new Flexible Flyer and was about to go again. Suddenly, there was a commotion at the bottom of the hill. Looking down, I saw people running toward a black tree. They looked like dark blots on the white snow. An ambulance roared up. Soldiers carrying a stretcher ran toward the tree; they picked up a small body and put it on the stretcher. The ambulance sped off, siren screaming. I felt sick.

Somebody said, "That's Elizabeth Andrus." She was a dark-haired fourth-grader with eyes like coffee beans. When you talked to her, she looked you right in the eye and really listened.

At suppertime we learned that when she crashed into the tree Elizabeth had ruptured her spleen. I didn't know what a spleen was, but my father said it was serious. The entire post hung in suspense. The next morning Elizabeth Andrus was dead.

None of the kids could understand it and no grownups talked about it, except my mother.

"One of the most obvious facts about grownups to a child," the poet Randall Jarrell wrote, "is that they have forgotten what it is like to be a child." We were forbidden to go to Elizabeth's funeral; it was "too upsetting." What was too upsetting was not being allowed to go.

My mother understood my panic.

"Remember that death is part of life," she told me. "*Everybody's* life."

"I don't want to think about it."

"That's just the point. Nobody wants to think about death, much less talk about it." My mother's eyes filled with tears. I knew she was remembering little Nat. "We are all going to die, Narcissa. But if we really thought about that, we would have to do things differently."

Consumed with curiosity, my class stood at the school windows to watch the funeral procession enter the post chapel. Officers in dress uniform carried the small white coffin. Could that happen to me? Emily Dickinson's "Zero at the bone is what I felt." There is a big difference between "We are all going to die" and "I am going to die." I could not even get my mind to consider such an outrageous idea. Yet pretty little Elizabeth Andrus was gone. Gone where?

Soon after her death, my Aunt Honey's father-in-law died. Mother's beloved younger sister, a curvaceous blonde with a dazzling smile, had married Forrest Williford, West Pointer (Class of 1906), an international fencing champion, and now a major stationed at Fort Leavenworth. They lived near us on Sherman Avenue.

To nobody's joy, Uncle Forrest's father lived with them. Known as Old Man Williford behind his back, he always wore the same black wool suit, stiff collar, and purple bow-tie. Old Man Williford talked with a twang and talked all the time. Listener or no listener, it didn't matter to him, which was lucky, because he repeated everything. My father called him Mr. Victrola.

The garrulous old fellow nobody wanted to listen to got pneumonia and died. As was customary, he was "laid out" in an open casket in the Willifords' living room. I was stunned when my mother asked, "Would you like to go with me to see Mr. Williford?" (Ask, don't tell.) Death had promoted him from Old Man to Mister.

"I would not."

"I think you should, Narcissa. Death is part of life. I want you to understand that. To live right, we have to accept death head on, and keep on accepting it." (Ask, and if you don't get the right answer, tell.) I had to go to the Willifords'. I would rather have gone to sea in a typhoon.

A black crepe bow hung on the door and the shades were drawn.

Uncle Forrest opened the door. He was wearing his dress uniform, with a black armband sewn on the sleeve. Tears filled my mother's eyes as she hugged him.

Across the living room, I could see the mahogany coffin on a metal stand. Aunt Honey's silver candelabras, six candles burning in each, stood on tables at the foot and at the head of the coffin.

The dark room smelled sickeningly sweet. There were tall vases of white lilies, smaller vases of red roses. Gladiolas were everywhere. To this day I hate gladiolas. I thought about what my grandfather put in my autograph album. "A kind word said to the living," Bocker wrote, "is worth a ton of roses sent to the dead."

I wanted to turn around and run, but my mother held on to my hand. We walked slowly across Aunt Honey's blue Chinese rug. We stopped beside the big coffin and stood perfectly still. I could hear myself breathing. I wanted to shut my eyes, but I wanted to look, too. What did death look like? I had to know.

The coffin was lined with quilted white satin. Mr. Williford seemed to have shrunk. He had on the same black wool suit, stiff collar, and purple bow tie. To my relief, his eyes were closed. I was sure he would be staring at me. His skin was chalky white, his cheeks rouged, his lips pink. Weirder yet, he was silent. I had never seen him when he wasn't talking.

My mother put her arm around me and hugged my shoulder. When she prayed the Twenty-Third Psalm, her voice quavered. "Yea, though I walk through the valley of the shadow of death, I will fear no evil: for Thou art with me . . ." I added, with feeling, "Amen." I tried to picture myself lying in a coffin in my blue taffeta dress. Impossible.

We hugged Uncle Forrest and Aunt Honey and kissed them. I felt like crying but Mother didn't, so I didn't. The two of us walked home in silence. We sat down on the porch swing, and my mother took my hand. "We honor Mr. Williford's body," she said, "but you do know he's not there, don't you?"

"How can you be so sure?"

"Because the Bible tells us so. The body stays, the spirit departs. Your body is temporal; your spirit is eternal. I want you to remember this always, Narcissa. We have just celebrated Mr. Williford's birthday into eternity."

Forty-five years later I was to hear my mother's voice saying those words as I stood next to her coffin, crying.

❧ 7. The Bent Twig

My mother had a thorough knowledge of the classics. One of her favorite literary allusions was, "'Tis education forms a common mind: / Just as the twig is bent the tree's inclined." Or she'd say, "'Children begin by loving their parents . . .'" Then she'd add, "That's Oscar Wilde. I can't remember the rest."

Years later, when I read *The Picture of Dorian Gray*, I gasped when I got to chapter 5. Wilde wrote: "Children begin by loving their parents; as they grow older they judge them; sometimes they forgive them." No wonder she couldn't remember it.

My father bent the twig forcibly. My mother pushed it gently. I liked her way better. She didn't think her children were the best. She knew they were. Never again will we find somebody who thinks we are as wonderful as our mother does.

Of all of life's connections, psychiatrist Theodore Reik said, "the relationship of parent and child, less noisy than all others, remains indelible and indestructible, the strongest relationship on earth."

But how do you free a child from the addiction of a parent's adoration?

When I asked a therapist, he shrugged. "Who knows? Making a child self-propelled is not simple, but discipline helps. Take a stand—be sure you're comfortable with it—hold the line and take the heat. That's one way to loosen those ties that bind, and keep on binding."

My father didn't need to consult a psychiatrist about discipline. He knew his mind and he made us toe the line. But we never doubted his love.

At Fort Leavenworth, the best fun of the year was the Halloween Party. It was an all-out event that raised money for the boy and girl scouts. Everyone on the post participated, selling chances, running the shooting gallery (pop guns only), the knock-'em down kewpie dolls booth, the guess-the-number-of-beans-in-the-bottle game. There was also a vaudeville show and anybody who could perform anything did.

Admission was ten cents. I loved the odor of hot buttered popcorn and sticky cotton candy, mixed with laughter and music.

The whole post turned out for this raucous event. It was the only time that enlisted men and officers mixed socially. The "colored" detachment had their own events, of course. This was 1929.

At the Halloween Party, everybody got into the act. My mother made brownies that sold for a penny apiece. My girl scout patrol ran the ducking-for-apples and the eating-donuts-off-a-string booths. I was jealous of my friend JoAnne Darby, who was going to sing a solo, "All Alone by the Telephone," and of Jimmy Muir, who did a juggling act. A born show-off, I longed to solo, too.

Suddenly I had an idea. I could dance the hula in the vaudeville show. I had the grass skirt, many-colored *leis*, a hibiscus crown (both made of paper), a recording of "Aloha Oe," and I could do a mean hula. I volunteered my "talent" and was accepted. I was twelve and I knew I was going to make a splash. I could hardly wait.

Then my father lowered the boom. "No," he thundered. "You are not going to get up there and wiggle your hips for the enlisted men." He was a man of few words. No more explanation. Just no.

I begged. I cajoled. I stamped my foot. I cried. I appealed to my mother. I think she was on my side, but she didn't dare cross him, either. "Your father knows best," she said.

"Oh yeah?"

I ran upstairs, slammed my door, and stayed in my room. That would teach them. Hours later I came out and announced, "You can go to the party without me."

No reaction.

Of course, I did go to the party, my eyes puffy, my lips pouting. In the car Mother said, "I'll bet you can stick your lips out further than that, Narcissa." I laughed and the crisis passed. Chalk one up for my mother's motto: the best relaxer is laughter. I enjoyed the Halloween Party, but not much.

Growing up, most kids find another family more fun than their own. Mine was the Godfreys—they would have loved my hula. Major and Mrs. Godfrey were the polar opposite of my parents. Mrs. Godfrey was a concert pianist, immune to housekeeping. Her concert grand piano was wedged into their small living room. Schubert was her speciality. I can see her pounding the piano, singing of the *Erlking* riding into the night, his infant son clutched to his breast. She ended: *Das Kind war todt.* The child was dead. I cried. For the first time I began to feel just a little of what my mother must have felt the day little Nat died.

Major Godfrey, a brilliant, absent-minded engineer, was immune to reality. I often saw the two of them smooching, something you'd never see at my house. One day I saw him put his hand on her breast. Shocking! They had spent their honeymoon in Paris. I thought they were glamour incarnate.

Their daughter Hope was my best friend. An unbent twig, she could do anything she wanted. We shared everything—and I mean everything—our sweaters, our diaries, our secret loves, chicken pox.

Hope had two brothers: Bobby, who was as smart in math as his father, and Pearce, who was as musical as his mother. Mrs. Godfrey (children never called adults by their first names) used to play "The Golliwog's Cakewalk" and little Pearce would dance for us. Where did he learn those steps? No television—it must have been in his genes.

The Godfreys were always launching Projects. One hot September day I helped them put up brandied peaches. We peeled a bushel of peaches, stuck cloves in them, put them in mason jars, and poured brandy to the brim. The fumes made us giddy. Mrs. Godfrey had found the recipe in a French cookbook. "Bury the peaches in the ground and wait six months. *Delicieux.*"

Six months later, I went to the Godfrey's. It happened to be April Fool's Day. Their dug up front yard looked like the Grand Canyon. An April Fool's joke, I thought. It was no joke; it was a crisis. Nobody could remember where the peaches had been buried. The Godfreys never did locate them, though they kept trying. It was the talk of the post.

I finished eighth grade at the Fort Leavenworth School. At last, I would put post schools behind me and attend Leavenworth High with civilians. I wanted to know kids who weren't army brats.

High school was fun but studying was not. The only course I was interested in was English. Algebra, General Science, and French left me cold. My English teacher's first assignment was to write a descriptive paragraph. I didn't think I could do it.

That night the moon was full. I lay on a bank above the river, gazing at the full moon until I felt transported. I tried to put my hypnotic trance into words, but I could not do it. All I could manage was, "The moon looked like a crystal ball on blue velvet." My paper came back with that sentence underlined. Miss Geiger had scribbled in the margin, "It seems, Narcissa, that you may be able to write." Seventy years later, I still cherish her comment.

The thing I liked best about Leavenworth High School was that it burned to the ground.

One night I dreamed that the school was on fire. In the morning, I told my mother about my dream. She gasped, "That's exactly what happened!" She held up the *Leavenworth Times*. Black headlines screamed "HIGH SCHOOL BURNS!" Excited, she told me I had a psychic gift. It was a rare trait, inherited from her side of the family.

This was good news. Who could say where my psychic powers might lead? I saw myself on stage, swathed in gold brocade robes, gazing into a crystal ball and predicting the future.

My father had no time for psychics. He told me the sirens wailing in the night had penetrated my dream. How could he fall for such an ordinary explanation? It was clear to me I had occult powers. After all, I did see a fairy.

The balance between my no-nonsense father and my nonsense-loving mother produced a creative tension. Sometimes my mother would win out; sometimes my father would prevail; but always I knew that what both of them cared about was me. That provided an indestructible safety net.

At age fourteen, when I was invited by a graduating midshipman to be his date for June Week at Annapolis, that safety net was put to the test.

How far could this twig be bent?

❧ 8. The Girl with the Glass Eye

In the spring of 1932 my father, now a colonel, was ordered to Panama to command Fort Amador on the Pacific side. How my mother hated packing up and moving every three or four years. It was backbreaking, and the enlisted men who helped us always broke things. Streaks of brown glue scarred Grandfather Reeder's white marble statuette of Venus de Milo and her grandmother's blue and white Delft teapot. My mother wanted to see the world, but she did not want to take our stuff.

I was ready to move. One year at Leavenworth High School had been enough. Kansas did not offer what Anne of Green Gables called scope for imagination. But when I went to the Godfreys' to say good-bye, I choked up. How could I leave the family I wished were mine?

Hope's house, as usual, was in an uproar. The smoky living room reeked of burning chocolate. Mrs. Godfrey was at the piano, head back, eyes closed, playing Schubert's *Serenade*. Major Godfrey was plotting God-knows-what on his drawing board. Hope was sketching Bobby in charcoal while Bobby, reading *20,000 Leagues under the Sea*, was posing, naked except for a G-string. Pearce was in the kitchen burning chocolate chip cookies.

I hugged and kissed each one, tears running down my cheeks. Then I ran out the door. At the corner, I looked back. Hope was on the porch, slowly waving her open palm. I felt that I was leaving half of myself behind. She was crying, too. I never saw her again. I still miss her.

The other wrenching good-bye was to Sergeant MacDowell, my beloved riding instructor from the "colored" detachment. Saturday mornings for five years I had attended Mac's classes in Fort Leavenworth's huge riding hall. Horses were a vital part of every post. We knew their names and the serial number branded on their necks. My favorite was a roan named Maybe, number XL473829, a beautiful jumper.

Mac's instruction in jumping and drill was so expert that we competed annually in the American Royal Horse Show in Kansas City. Had I known the word charisma, I would have said Mac was born with it. We all adored him. He was strict but fair; an approving word from Mac could make your week.

When I said good-bye, he held out his hand, but I hugged him and began to cry. "Farewell, Mac." I kissed his smooth cheek and ran to the car. My mother said, "You didn't have to do that, Narcissa."

Oh yes I did, I said silently.

About the same time that my father received his orders, I was invited to June Week at the Naval Academy, an all-out celebration culminating in commencement.

My mother's friend, Mrs. Camp, was horrified. "You're going to let Narcissa go to Annapolis at age fourteen?"

"Why not? She'll be fifteen at the end of June—and she'll be chaperoned." Like most mothers, my mother invested unlimited trust in chaperones. "Harry Hull's mother is going, too. I want my girls to see the world."

"If Nardi starts going out now," Mrs. Camp raised her voice, "by the time she's twenty she'll be a has-been."

In the next room, I mumbled Julia's motto, "Better a has-been than a never-was-er."

I had met Midshipman Harry Hull on the tennis courts that fall. Tennis was my passion, Helen Wills my idol. My white flannel eyeshade and knee-length pleated skirt were copies of my idol's outfit when she beat Helen Jacobs at Wimbledon.

I was sitting on the grass, watching the post champions, when Adonis appeared. "My name is Harry Hull," he said, holding out his hand. Impossibly blond, blue-eyed, and tall, Adonis was wearing white flannels and a white sweater with a V-neck outlined in blue and gold. He turned out to be a first-classman home on September leave.

His blue eyes looked into mine. "Would you like to hit a few balls?" Would I? I caught my breath. We took the court. It became evident that he was closer to Bill Tilden than I was to Helen Wills. We assumed the tutor/tutee position. Stimulating. Soon, I was receiving daily lessons.

Every evening, not to my father's delight, Harry came to our house to play checkers or parcheesi and make goo-goo eyes at me. I could handle those high school boys, but Harry was my first real beau. Who knew where the affection of a sophisticated man of twenty might lead? The more stand-offish I became, the more interested he became.

My mother was captivated by Harry. "Try not to win too often," she instructed me. "Men don't like women who seem smarter than they are."

By the time Harry's September leave ended, I was making goo-goo eyes at him. But I still wouldn't let him kiss me. My brother Fred, that suave ensign-about-the-fleet, told me (more than once): "I've kissed a lot of girls, but the ones I remember are the ones who wouldn't let me kiss them." Looking back, I'm pretty sure Mother put him up to that. As Harry was leaving for Annapolis, though, it dawned on me that I'd miss him. Still timid, I finally let him kiss me. On the cheek. Was that my heart fluttering?

My father frowned on my going to June Week. He wasn't worried about my age; he was worried about my education. Leave two weeks before the term ends? He was appalled.

"Listen, Daddy," I said, "they've already sent my transcript to Panama. LHS will never miss me and I won't miss it."

"Russell," Mother said quietly, "do you want Narcissa's education confined to books?"

My father turned to his best friend. "Come on, Teddy, let's go for a walk."

Although our family never had much money, my mother brought us up like rich kids. Wherever we lived, she found a good dressmaker. By far the best was Yvonne, a Parisienne who married Sergeant Heflin during World War I. When she met Haf-LEEN, as she called him, she was working for Valentina, a famous *couturier* in Paris. Yvonne could copy any gown in *Vogue* magazine.

For the 1932 June Ball Yvonne made me a long yellow tulle gown, trimmed to the knees with yards of rainbow-colored ribbon, made for swirling. She didn't have to copy a picture. She copied the dress in Julia's trousseau that I had been coveting for six years.

On the Greyhound bus going to Annapolis I entertained Mrs. Phillips (Harry's mother had remarried after his father died) by describing how I used to sneak out on full moon nights, after my parents were asleep. In the bright moonlight, I would climb out on the red tin porch roof, my heart racing, and slide down the drain pipe. Hope and I would meet by the flagpole at midnight and roam around the post feeling wicked. She was my first love. Now we'd be called gay; then we were bosom buddies. At first, the M.P.'s questioned us. Later they'd just laugh and wave. Shinnying back up the drain pipe, I'd grip the gutter with sweaty palms, thinking, "If I let go now, it's all over."

Just as I had hoped, my tale shocked Mrs. Phillips. "What would your parents say if they knew what you were doing?"

"That's half the fun, taking risks," I boasted. Conversationally I was a risk-taker. Actually I was a mouse. I never took a real risk until I went away to college.

Harry had borrowed a car so I could get around Crabtown (midshipmanese for Annapolis). One of Harry's pals, a mechanical genius, had rehabilitated a 1920 Model-T Ford. For reasons unknown, he called his jolly car Jo-Jo.

I saw no reason to mention the fact that I did not have a driver's license. Fred, who had taught me to play poker, had also taught me to drive. Annapolis streets are narrow and I dented Jo-Jo's fenders, but nobody seemed to care.

Frequently, Jo-Jo stalled. To get him going, someone had to crank his engine. I discovered that if I stood next to Jo-Jo with the crank in my hand, gallant midshipmen would appear. The more the car broke down, the giddier I became.

I knew I was pretty, because my mother told me so. She was a born builder-upper. I would take inventory in the mirror. Red, smiling lips beneath a slightly hooked nose, bright hazel eyes, and thick, flowing blondish hair braided around my head. Harry kept talking about the sparkle in my eyes. Mother used to say, "Watch out for people whose eyes never light up." Yes, I would think smugly, I guess I'll do.

The June Ball was held in Dahlgren Hall, the armory, which inexplicably had a polished dance floor. Harry had filled in his friends' names on my hop card, keeping quite a few dances for himself.

Colored lanterns glittered above white tables decorated with dogwood and lilacs. Inside, the sophisticated young women in sleek satin dresses made me feel S.S.G., Leavenworth High shorthand for sweet, simple, and girlish.

The orchestra played "Who? Who Stole My Heart Away?" and "I'll Be Loving You, Always." The over-poweringly sweet smell of the gardenia corsage from Harry made me lightheaded. It was either that or love.

The most fun was the stag line. Dick Mandelkorn, who had cranked Jo-Jo, cut in several times. Dark-haired, dark-eyed, and handsome as a prince, he asked me if I would go out with him when his ship came to Panama. I was delighted. As they say in Dickens, "Little did I wot."

Harry was puzzled by my popularity. "How come you know so many guys?"

"It's Jo-Jo," I said. "They all know how to crank."

When you're young, what to talk about with the opposite sex can be a problem. I remember getting ready for my first dance when I was an eighth grader. Putting on the blue taffeta with the puffed sleeves from Julia's wedding, I asked my mother, "What do I talk about with the boys?"

"You don't talk, Narcissa," she said. "You listen. Remember the magic words: ask, don't tell."

"O.K., O.K., ask what?"

"Find out what they're interested in. You might even learn something. When *you* are talking, Narcissa, you aren't learning anything."

At Annapolis, I was abashed at being so young, and I wanted to say something the older girls would not say. On an impulse I tried, "I have a glass eye. Can you tell which one it is?"

My ice breaker worked well with the future admirals. Harry could hardly contain his laughter when a second-classman asked, "Have you danced with the girl with the glass eye? I couldn't even tell which one it was."

When the band played "Smoke Gets in Your Eyes," Harry held me close and we swayed cheek-to-cheek. I felt myself melting inside. Harry was affectionate and smitten and I was almost carried away. It was delicious. At midnight, they played "Good Night, Ladies," and Cinderella with the glass eye rattled home in her magic Model-T, dreaming of becoming Mrs. Ensign Harry Hull.

After the graduating midshipmen tossed their white caps into the air, Mrs. Phillips and I pinned ensign's insignias on the shoulders of Harry's starched white uniform. Midshipmen were not permitted to marry until they graduated. That afternoon, Harry and I attended six nearly identical weddings of his classmates in the Naval Academy Chapel. I watched the laughing couples march under the flashing crossed sabers and thought, "My, wouldn't that be fun."

Weddings are contagious and Harry began to talk matrimony. Suddenly, the big risk-taker was running for cover. I had inhaled the fragrance of romance wafting around the chapel, but being tied to one man? What a terrible idea. I wanted variety.

"Harry," I said, "I hope your ship will come down to Panama." When we parted I kissed him good-bye, but not really. My mother had made me leery of sex. For me sex meant "male" or "female" on your driver's license.

My mother could talk openly about death but only obliquely about sex. On the transport going to Panama she asked me, "Did you let Harry kiss you?"

"Oh, yes. He gave me lots of big juicy kisses." Mother just laughed. She knew I was lying.

⅋ 9. The Little Princess of Fort Amador

At Fort Amador, my parents let me practice-drive our black Pierce Arrow around the post. Jo-Jo had whetted my thirst for driving legally; getting a driver's license was the most important thing in my life. I was so green my mother said, "Narcissa, a stop sign means pause, not park." Even when I was driving alone the MPs never questioned me; the car belonged to the commanding officer. I began to have delusions of grandeur, thinking of myself as the privileged little princess of Fort Amador.

I was strictly forbidden to drive through the post gate into the Canal Zone. One day I decided to chance it. I can't even remember now why I did that. I suppose I was testing the waters. After a little spin around Balboa, I tried to turn around in someone's driveway. I struck a little white fence. I panicked. Instinctively wanting to flee, I backed up—and dragged the fence with me. It was stuck under the fender. I felt the rush of heat that comes when you know you're dead wrong. My temples throbbed; my stomach churned.

A woman rushed out, yelling at me. They called the CZ police. I broke out in a sweat. The police demanded my driver's license. I just shook my head. I had lost the power of speech. The policeman rolled his eyes upward and wrote out a ticket. He made me get in his cruiser while his partner climbed into our car. They drove me home.

I had to walk into the house and try to tell my parents what had happened. They were sitting at the dinner table with Julia and Charlie, eating coconut ice cream, my favorite. Everybody stopped eating. Ah-Linn, our Filipino houseman and my good friend, was refilling the water glasses. He froze in place. They stared at my burning face. I tried to explain what I had done, but I burst into tears. Tossing the ticket down in front of my father, I ran upstairs. I threw myself down on my sleeping-porch bed. Gasping with sobs, I buried my head in the pillow. My life was ruined. I knew that.

First my father came up. I braced myself for a lecture on disobedience, but his tough exterior hid a softness. "Don't cry, Narcissa. The most important thing is to learn from your mistakes." I only wailed louder. My father gave up and soon my mother appeared. "Narcissa," she began, "letting yourself go to pieces is much worse than having a small accident." That really made me howl. I moved from misery to melodrama. She said firmly, "Pull yourself together," and left. I kept sobbing.

Later I was aware of somebody else. I raised my head. Charlie Summerall, my strong but gentle brother-in-law, was sitting beside me. He and Julia were stationed nearby at Albrook Field. Punch and Judy, their three-year-old twins, were at home with their Jamaican nanny. I always thought Charlie, who did not have an aggressive bone in his body, was miscast in the military.

Charlie, bless him, didn't say a word. He just patted my back and murmured, "Now, now." Soon, I was taking deep breaths. He must have stayed beside me for an hour. His quietness permeated the room. For the first time I experienced the solace of shared silence.

Much to my surprise, I began to recover. My twenty-five-cents-a-week allowance wasn't up to the whopping fifteen dollar fine, plus the cost of that crummy little fence. I had to earn the money from my mother by polishing silver. (Much to Ah-Linn's amusement.) The luster of "little princess" had been sadly tarnished.

The greatest day of your young life is when you get that driver's license. But not for me. All the fun had gone out of it.

I thought Balboa High School was beautiful. White concrete with a red tile roof, it formed a square around an open, flower-filled patio. I loved to stand on the second floor, inhaling the overpowering fragrance of the frangipani trees, and gaze down on palms, purple bougainvillea, and pink oleander. To a kid from Fort Leavenworth, Latino architecture was exotic. I certainly wasn't in Kansas anymore.

One of the best things that can happen to anyone is a great teacher. Miss Jessup was a great teacher. In the Canal Zone in the thirties, the teachers were "Miss." If they got married, they lost their job. How could a woman pay attention to husband and home and teach, too? Miss Jessup was a faded blonde of forty-five, tall and overweight. Her blue eyes saw life romantically, but I doubt she ever had a beau.

She gave her students a lifelong feeling for the power of words. When she quoted Rupert Brooke—"the cool kindliness of sheets" and "the rough male kiss of blankets"—her blue eyes sparkled. The spinster vanished.

Miss Jessup took us straight through a thick red anthology, *Adventures in English Literature*. For me, traveling at top speed from *Beowulf* to H. G. Wells was a glorious journey. She hit a bump when we got to Keats. "'On First Looking Into Chapman's Homer,'" she said, "shows Keats's lack of education. He didn't even know Balboa discovered the Pacific." She read the end of the sonnet:

> Or like stout Cortes when with eagle eyes
> He stared at the Pacific—and all his men
> Looked at each other with a wild surmise
> Silent, upon a peak in Darien.

Everybody laughed. *We* knew Balboa discovered the Pacific. We were smarter than John Keats.

"You cannot live in Panama," my mother declared, "without going through the canal." Like Robert Frost's Bluebird, she wanted her children to "do everything." So at six A.M. we boarded a tramp steamer in Balboa. A trip through the canal cost five dollars (now one hundred).

We were dazzled by the engineering feat. To connect the Atlantic's one-foot tide with the Pacific's twelve-foot tide, Mother's "friend" General Goethals created Gatun Lake, eighty-five feet above sea level. Huge cement locks lift ships up on the Pacific side and lower them on the Atlantic side. Fantastic—but who needs eight hours of watching water ooze into cement chambers?

My mother and I sat on the deck in the stifling heat, nibbling avocado sandwiches and sipping sarsparilla. She read from a guidebook, as was her wont. "For 300 years men searched for a way to connect the Atlantic and the Pacific. The trip around the tip of South America was 7,873 miles. Goethals's Canal cuts through forty-seven miles of jungle."

"Boring, boring," I muttered.

"Boring!" she exclaimed. "There's no such thing as boring. There's only lack of imagination."

The train back took four hours to go forty-seven miles. It kept stopping to let natives on and off. Hot air blew in the window as the green jungle slid past. We chugged to the summit of the mountain and rattled down into Balboa. Whistles screaming, bells clanging, we finally pulled in to the station. Mother sighed. "It has been a long day, but weren't we lucky to be able to go through the Panama Canal?"

Wellesley College

"I know you're only sixteen," Major Seibert said, "but I've watched you ride. Somebody brought you up right. Would you be willing to jump both my horses in the annual show at Fort Clayton?" Wow. I wanted to call Fort Leavenworth and tell Mac.

On Horse Show Day, the sun was hot and the sky blue, and the air crackled with excitement. Sitting in a box with my parents was my hero, Fred. He had flown his open-cockpit plane over from Coco Solo, the naval base on the Atlantic side. My brother, one of the first fliers in the U.S. Navy, had earned his wings at Pensacola in 1932. The planes he flew looked as though they were made with matchsticks.

Riders from all of the posts in Panama competed. Maybe I had the best horses; maybe Sergeant MacDowell was the best riding instructor; maybe I was lucky; probably all three. Anyway, I led both horses to the judges to collect two silver cups. I stood there in my white cork helmet, white polo shirt, wide canvas polo belt, starched white breeches, and mirror-shiny boots and felt as dashing as Rudolph Valentino. My ego zoomed out of control.

Fred gave me a big hug. Nobody loved to win more than he did. "I'm giving you another prize—your first plane trip." He knew that ever since he got his wings, I had dreamed of flying.

My father was dubious. "I'm not sure you should fly alone." My mother protested. "If Narcissa shares her first plane trip, it will only be half an adventure."

Today, children fly before they walk. My first plane ride at age sixteen was awesome (the real meaning of the word). When our twelve-seater roared down the runway I gripped the seat until my hands hurt. Rising into the air was scarier than jumping a horse over a four-foot fence.

The roar was deafening; my ears popped and my heart pounded. Trying to calm myself, I focused on my tiny window. I could almost touch the mountainous white clouds. Below, red roofs, blue water, emerald hills—it looked like Oz. Imagine peering *down* on the Panama Canal. Imagine looking *down* on the setting sun. Even Fred would have given that sunset an A-plus. There is no twilight in the tropics. The hot copper coin just drops, leaving an orange glow. As though someone has thrown a switch, the sky turns deep blue and stars shine.

Savoring my perfect day, I realized two things about myself. First, I craved independence. Even though my first flight terrified me, I was glad to be alone. Second, I was born competitive. That isn't all bad—when you win. It wasn't to be all good, either.

Fred had lots of ideas about my future. Numero uno: college. A scary idea—who knew what perils lurked there? But, having tasted independence, I wanted to get the hell out of high school.

High schools didn't have counselors for girls, just for boys. Behind my parents' back, I went to Mr. Spalding, the principal, and told him I wanted to skip a year. He was shocked. "Do two years in one? You will miss a lot."

"I'll pick it up later," I said airily. "I want to be on my own." We argued for a while. My heart was in it; his wasn't. I combined junior and senior year.

"It was bad enough when you dropped Latin for household arts," my father said. "Now this." Fred said, "Just be sure you get enough credits for college."

My education continued apace at the Union Club, an elegant old Spanish colonial in Panama City with a roofless dance floor extending out over the Pacific. At the Saturday night dances I learned to rumba and to tango. The best dancer was Tony Zubieta, a suave, swarthy Panamanian. I was crazy about him, but I kept that quiet.

One night I was dancing in the moonlight with Fred when Tony cut in. Later Fred said, "You let me down."

I was stunned. "What did I do?"

"We were interrupted and you haven't asked me to finish my story."

"What story?"

"You were just pretending to listen, Narcissa. If you want to make a dent on a man, any man, learn to listen." The lesson lasted.

The Union Club was a happening place during Carnival, the wild celebration that precedes Lent. Holding out the full skirt of my costume, I danced the pollera. In the streets, everybody was your friend. Marimba bands and shaking maracas filled the air. One night, I overstayed my curfew. When I got home, all lights were on and the door wide open. My parents had called the police. They were sure something terrible had happened to me. Something terrible had happened to me all right: them.

After Carnival Mother took Julia and me to Tobago to ease us into Lent. Julia gladly left her four-year-old twins with Charlie and their *aymah*. Tobago Island, a two-hour boat trip across glassy Panama Bay, was cooler, less rainy, and far from the madding crowd. As we strolled paths of crushed shells beneath the lime trees, ragged Panamanians greeted us politely. "*Buenos dias*." We stayed in the army guest house, a vacation retreat for officers and their families.

One evening we joined a procession led by a Catholic priest shaking holy water. Four strong men were carrying a glass coffin. In it we could see a highly painted statue of Jesus. We entered the candlelit church, the center of the ancient plaza and watched the priest cover Jesus' coffin with black veils, to be removed ceremoniously on Easter morning.

I inhaled the heavy incense and considered switching from Episcopalian to Roman Catholic. The three of us knelt for a long time, praying. I prayed for an opportunity to run my own life.

During *siesta*, Mother read aloud *Anthony Adverse*, a fat Napoleonic novel whose eponymous hero swashbuckled around the world. I don't think she knew why it was a bestseller. In 1934 *Anthony Adverse* was a sexy shocker. She read fast when she got to "Then he was completely aroused. He noticed he did not care whether he had any clothes on or not . . . Faith stirred slightly and put out her arms in the semi-darkness." Mother forged ahead. Julia nodded knowingly. I put my head under the pillow.

When we returned from Tobago, the big news was that the fleet was coming. Prosperity at last. Panamanian bartenders, prostitutes, and shopkeepers would soon be rolling in money. For me, the fleet meant seeing

Harry Hull again. He and I carried on a heavy correspondence. In those days, a girl collected beaus the way some people collect stamps.

I was elated when Harry brought three shipmates to swim at Fort Amador. I swam in my new one-piece bathing suit made of white rubber trimmed with pink rubber roses. It fit tighter than a bathing cap. The cove was protected by a shark net. Danger lurked, but it wasn't from a shark. Suddenly, my suit ripped down the side. I couldn't stretch the remnants to cover me. What to do?

"Harry!" I yelled. "All of you have to get out and face the other way. I'm not decent." Laughing, they obediently swam to shore and stood with their backs to me as I ran to my towel, clutching shreds of the rubber suit.

My mother arranged an *al fresco* dance at Fort Amador. A bandstand stood in the center of the plaza in front of our house. Beyond the palm trees rolled the Pacific, with the lights of Panama City in the distance. Japanese lanterns were strung above a temporary dance floor and the post band was converted into a jazz combo. Naval officers in starched white uniforms arrived by bus. Other buses brought giggling girls in long dresses.

My new dress was a flowing pink organdy with a boa made of hundreds of pink organdy "feathers." I stuck six fresh frangipani blossoms in my braid and smelled like a funeral. I knew a few of the ensigns on Harry's ship. When his classmate, Dick Mandelkorn, invited me to dinner on the cruiser *Richmond,* I was flattered; Harry was jealous.

I told my mother I had a date with Dick Mandelkorn and she said, "He sounds Jewish."

I replied, "He is Jewish."

Years had passed since she took Julia and me to the Orient, but inherited prejudice was intact. "One thing leads to another, Narcissa. If you married into a different culture, you'd be miserable."

"I'm not going to marry him," I said. "I'm going to have dinner with him."

"I don't think so," she said. I called on my father for help. No discussion. Just no. I burst into tears. I knew they were wrong, but I couldn't do anything about it. When Dick called, I had to say, "I'm sorry. I can't keep our date. I've got a terrible headache."

I had a headache all right. I was sick all over. I knew Dick knew what the problem was. Both of us were angry, for different reasons. I loved my mother and father, but I couldn't stand their intolerance. I told myself prejudice had been drummed into them in the nineteenth century, when they were young. I cried myself to sleep.

Later, I confided my shame to Harry. His answer shocked me. "Don't worry, Dick Mandelkorn has coped with worse than that. He was ostracized at the Naval Academy."

"How?"

"He was the only Jew in the class of 1932. In our yearbook, roommates appear next to each other, on the page. Dick Mandelkorn didn't have a roommate. Next to his picture, the editors put a crude cartoon of a Jewish midshipman. It didn't help that he graduated first in the class."

By now I knew too well what pre-judging meant. But I didn't know any Jews, except Dick. And he was off limits. I decided I would do something about that. And I did.

Trying to get along with my parents made college attractive. None of the girls I knew went to college. Women who sought higher education in the early days were heroines. By the thirties it didn't take heroism, but you had to be willing to be "different." Again I sat opposite Mr. Spalding. His resistance had collapsed.

"What college are you interested in?"

"How would I know? I've only seen one. When we lived in Kansas my parents took me to a football game at K.U. The coeds looked like kewpie dolls. I want to go to a place that takes women seriously."

"There's a new women's college in Vermont," he said. "It's called Bennington. Like you, Nardi, it's unconventional." Wow, if only the Godfreys could hear that.

While I was struggling with the College Question, an alternative presented itself. One night, as Harry and I were leaving the Union Club after swaying in the moonlight to "Smoke Gets in Your Eyes," he said, "Let's go for a ride in one of the carriages." As our horse clop-clop-clopped over the cobblestones, Harry put his arm around me and kissed me. My first real kiss. By the time our carriage returned to the Union Club, we were both murmuring "I love you." Then, Harry dropped a bomb.

"Will you marry me?"

"What are you talking about? I'm only sixteen. That's too young."

"You'll get older," he laughed. "I'll wait if I have to."

"I guess you'll have to." Suddenly, it all came clear. "I am going to college."

"Don't do that. Being a navy wife will be more educational."

"Thank you for asking, dear Harry, maybe later." I was in love with love, but I didn't want to settle down.

My parents did not like the thought of my going away. But Daddy was for education and Mother for new experiences. She said, "You're absolutely right about a women's college." She was back in her chaperone mode. Or was it "Votes for women?"

The 'rents gave in. Now the question was, which college?

My father said flatly, "Bennington is too new; Vassar too social; Smith is a hot-bed of socialism. How about Radcliffe?"

Mr. Spalding spiked that. "I think you might get into six of the Seven Sisters—Smith, Vassar, Mt. Holyoke, Barnard, Wellesley, and Bryn Mawr. You'd better forget Radcliffe—it's in the stratosphere with Harvard."

Years later I asked Bill Wilson, legendary dean of admissions at Amherst College (men only), the secret of his success.

"C.Q.," Bill said. "For me C.Q. is more important than I.Q."

"C.Q.?"

"Curiosity Quotient. If a student has curiosity, there's no stopping him. If he doesn't, there's no way he can get it." Then Bill added, "Women too, of course."

I may have had a poor educational preparation for college, but I was long on curiosity. At least I thought I was, until I met Tom Campion. He had more curiosity than anyone I ever met.

In the end, Hope's family tipped the balance. Colonel Godfrey's sister, Helen Godfrey Mansfield, was alumnae director of Wellesley College, which I couldn't even spell. I had never met her, but the Godfreys went to bat for me and my shaky credentials (A in Latin American history, A in household arts, D in geometry).

You can change your name, your hair color, your weight, your home, or your husband, but there is one thing you can never change: where you went to college. That's all right by me.

The Wellesley catalogue was hard to decipher—but the pictures! Oh, those gothic buildings, towering oaks, and the blue, blue lake. I knew I'd be happy—if I could just get there.

But it cost so much. Due to the Depression, all army and navy officers had received a pay cut. My parents were caught in the pinch. In 1934 a year's tuition at Wellesley College was $500, room and board were another $500, a cool $1,000 a year for a Wellesley education. (Did anyone ever get a better bargain?)

Fred to the rescue. He said he'd give me $500 each year. At that time, his salary as a lieutenant, junior grade, was $125 a month, plus an $18 food allowance. How could he afford to help me? I think it had something to do with gambling. He was an ace poker player.

Thanks to Helen Mansfield's efforts, eventually a letter came from Wellesley. I ripped it open. I knew they had rejected me on account of my glaring math gap. What I didn't know was that the Depression had all the colleges scrambling for live bodies.

I was a live body all right. Wellesley accepted me.

My attendance depended on getting a scholarship. I can recite the letter verbatim. "Dear Miss Reeder, Because of your peculiar credentials, it is with some trepidation that we are awarding you a $500 scholarship for your first year at Wellesley College. We are taking you as an experiment and we hope you will prove us justified."

❧ 11. A Yearn to Learn

In September 1934 I traveled alone on a U.S. Navy transport from Panama to New England. I left a warm world of palm trees, pelicans, hibiscus, iguanas, and gardenias and set sail for a place I'd never seen called Wellesley College in a foreign country called Massachusetts.

Ah-Linn wrote me a note that brought tears. "Dear Miss Nardi, Someday I see you it is great lady, Farewell." I started to sob on the dock and my father tried to comfort me. "In Boston they have the right values," he said. "Up there they don't care what you have—it's what you know that counts."

I sobbed harder. I didn't know *anything*.

My mother, the southern belle, said, "Don't study too hard. Men don't seek out smart women." Then, inexplicably, she added, "I hope you can visit Amy Lowell's grave in Mount Auburn Cemetery." I later decided it was not only Amy Lowell's poetry but the cigar that attracted her. My mother cherished the oddball.

Our six-day voyage included exotic stops at Port-au-Prince and San Juan and energetic games of shuffleboard with young officers. The most dashing figure aboard the *U.S.S. Henderson* was Lieutenant Jack McCain, who worked hard all day and played hard all night. He swore a lot, drank a lot, and was the life of every party. Jack specialized in inventing new cocktails and bewitching new girls. (Unfortunately, at seventeen I was "too young to consider.") Who could have guessed that the father of Senator John McCain would command three submarines in World War II, become a four-star admiral, and at sixty-one, in the middle of a homecoming party, drop dead? As I strolled the deck with him in the moonlight, I tried to confide my fears about entering Wellesley. He didn't get it. Fear was not in the McCain vocabulary.

Ensign Harry Hull met the boat and drove me to Wellesley "under orders from Mrs. Colonel Reeder," he said. I was happy to see him, but he talked matrimony and I talked matriculation. I was even more afraid of marriage than I was of Wellesley. We parted with a big hug and a small kiss. After he left, my spirits plummeted. I felt like someone from back of the beyond. Not even the Frederick Law Olmstead tree-shaded campus, nor blue Lake Waban, nor medieval Tower Court could divert me.

I was swamped in homesickness.

I found New England cold and the people my mother called "Northerners" bone-chilling. Most of the good things in my life—my education, my friends, my husband—I owe to Wellesley College, but at first I was utterly intimidated by it.

As a pea-green freshman, I went to Green Hall "Information" for help. Suddenly, I was engulfed by a strong, sweet fragrance. "What are those blue things?" I exclaimed.

Information Lady: "You've never seen hyacinths? Where are you from?"

I felt like saying, "Another planet." Instead I muttered, "Panama." She was impressed. In 1934 diversity at Wellesley was dim. In our class of 450, Kitty Baldwin (my roommate) represented the South and I represented Latin America. We had one black classmate, Jessie Fitzgerald from Baltimore. She kept to herself. I don't go in for regrets but one time

I wrote Jessie to apologize for not being friendly but got no absolution. She had died.

As ravishing as the fragrance of hyacinths were murals in glowing blue, purple, and gold. "What are those?" I asked.

"They illustrate "America, the Beautiful," composed by Katharine Lee Bates, Class of 1880." She pointed. "Those are the amber waves of grain. That one's the purple mountain majesties and this is the alabaster cities."

Years later a therapist asked me, "What makes you cry?"

"'America, the Beautiful,'" I blurted out. Then, to my surprise I added, "and the smell of hyacinths."

I adored from afar President Ellen Fitz Pendleton, who hummed around campus in an electric car with a rod instead of a steering wheel. It was known as the fishbowl. In her academic robes, white hair piled high, rimless spectacles glinting, Pres. Pen stood at the lectern in Houghton Chapel and read the Bible with a New England inflection. I had never seen a woman like that: intellectual, poised, a born leader. Pres. Pen read Matthew, chapter 6, verses 19 to 21, so often she didn't look at the Bible. "Lay not up your treasures upon earth where moth and rust doth corrupt, and thieves break in and steal. But lay up your treasures in heaven where neither moth nor rust doth corrupt, and where thieves do not break in nor steal. For where your treasure is, there will your heart be also."

"Wellesley College," she told us, "is the place to begin laying up your treasures."

"How?" I wondered.

My English professor, Miss Annie K. Tuell, was Head Intimidator. The self-appointed guardian of the English language and all of its literature, Miss Tuell was an aging spinster in crepe-soled shoes and a wool cape. She fed on medieval romance. She was particularly devoted to the courtly world of Edmund Spenser's *Faerie Queene,* where "roses red and violets blew" tokened "immortal bliz," and I didn't understand any of it. Miss Tuell wrote on my Knight of the Red Cross theme, "Miss Reeder, your timorous attempts to express yourself in writing are lamentable." Ouch.

In 1934 Wellesley "girls" were required to attend daily chapel at eight A.M. and to take Bible—Old Testament, first semester, New Testament, second. Given an option, I'd have skipped both. And I would have missed the words that still sustain me.

I was not, as it happened, intimidated by Miss Seal Thompson, my Bible teacher. I loved her. Miss Thompson was five feet tall, with graying blonde hair and rimless glasses that hung from a shoulder pin. A devout Quaker, she wore floor-length, high-necked dresses that reached her high-buttoned boots. Miss Thompson would hold up her forefinger and ask in her soft voice, "Hast thou done thy homework?"

She gave me advice I still heed. I complained to her about Miss Tuell's assaults on my diminishing ego. "Thou art fortunate." She smiled beatifically. "God sends us every day an opportunity to experience humility. Count thy blessings, Miss Reeder."

I recall only four male professors, one of whom, Mr. Sheffield in the English department, struck us with awe. His brother-in-law was T. S. Eliot. "Tom," Mr. Sheffield confided, "loves practical jokes such as whoopee cushions and button-hole flowers that squirt water."

J. Alfred Prufrock is a clown?

The Wellesley faculty was female, erudite, eccentric. They all had Ph.D.'s, so why were they addressed as "Miss," not "Professor"? Their wisdom still reverberates in my head. Dean Frances Knapp stressed the college motto, *Non Ministrari sed Ministrare*—Not to Be Ministered Unto, but to Minister. That precept, she informed us, guides a Wellesley woman throughout life.

Years later, when I was president of the Wellesley College Alumnae Association, an alum who was slightly tipsy told me, "Our motto means everything to me, 'Not to Be Administered Unto, but to Administer.'"

Miss Knapp told us, "You cannot write a good theme in a room with an unmade bed." The college had excellent maid service in those days, so we translated it into unmaid bed.

Miss Sophie Hart dealt only in aesthetics. She would waft into the classroom, trailing chiffon scarves, and say in her deep, thrilling voice, "Young ladies, civilization is merely a matter of making order out of chaos." Quoting Tennyson's *Ulysses*, she recommended "living life to the lees." I wanted to do that, even after I learned that "lees" means dregs, as in wine.

Mrs. Mallory, our erratic psych prof, explained why a horse cannot play the piano. "We could build a piano that horses could use," she said confidently, "but nobody can make a horse *want* to play the piano."

To me, New Englanders talked funny and dressed funny. They preferred old clothes. "Use it up, wear it out, make it do, or go without," they said. A Harvard man took me to Sunday dinner (boiled beef and cabbage) at his family's home on Beacon Hill. I looked at the old pine furniture, the bare floors, the worn orientals, the beaten-up pewter plates, and thought, "These people are really hard up."

My roommate from Montgomery, Alabama, was appalled by Yankees. "Down South," Kitty drawled, "we try to make people feel good. Up here, they try to shape you up."

In January of 1935 the thermometer fell to twenty below. After a huge blizzard, Kitty refused to get out of bed. I had not seen snow since I left Kansas and I couldn't get enough of it. The minute it started snowing, I went out. I loved walking miles in the silent falling snow, a delight I would one day share with my husband, the snow man.

The biggest influence in my new life was my father's cousin, Roger Williams Bennett, Harvard 1914, who had fought in the trenches in World War I. Stunned by that searing experience, Roger was an impassioned pacifist. He went to divinity school, and became an Episcopal minister. He had a church in Wellesley Hills, so he came regularly to take me to lunch and work on my conscience.

Between Miss Thompson's devout Quakerism and Roger's turn-the-other-cheek pacifism, my military background became unacceptable. I turned into a pacifist, which had a double dividend. It allowed me to talk endlessly with the two people I most admired, Roger Bennett and Seal Thompson, and it upset my parents. My father wouldn't even discuss it. My mother shook her head. "Over-educated already."

Four years later, when World War II broke out, Roger was rector of St. Mary's Episcopal Church in Newton Lower Falls. The vestry tried to get rid of him because he refused to display the American flag in the church. Roger never gave an inch, and the situation got ugly. "Why would I stop being a pacifist just because a war has been declared?" he asked.

One day Wellesley's radical professor Vida Scudder, stopped him on the street, exclaiming, "Oh Roger, I so envy you."

He gasped. "You envy me, Miss Scudder?"

"All my life I've wanted to be persecuted for my faith. Stand your ground, Roger." He did—and the vestry gave way.

I never did get to Amy Lowell's grave, but her poetry helped me adjust to my new habitat. I learned to enjoy "the sight of a white church above thin trees," and to vibrate, as Amy did, to the "roots of lilac under all the soil of New England."

❀ 12. Something Only a Real Friend Would Do

My mother set great store by friendship, but she didn't always approve of my friends. She used to say obliquely, "Your best friend is the one who brings out the best in you." At Wellesley, my friend Rachel Rosenthal brought out the best in me, but it wasn't fun. Over sixty years later it still hurts.

The kids I grew up with were "army brats." We had everything in common, including a permanent feeling of impermanence. When I left Panama to go to Wellesley my father had said, "Sometimes the most valuable part of college is education by friendship."

I had no idea what he meant then, but I do now.

I never had any Jewish friends until I went to Wellesley. The Jewish girls I met at college delighted me. They were not "different," except for one thing. They were up in arms about Hitler and I'd barely heard of him. This was 1935.

Sophomore year, I met Rachel Rosenthal—a turning point. She had long dark hair and big dark eyes. I connected her with the only "Jewess" I knew, Rebecca in *Ivanhoe*. We had little in common—Rachel grew up on an estate in Westchester—but we connected through golf. She belonged to a posh club in Scarsdale and was coached by a pro. Army bases always had golf courses; my brothers were my coaches. Our frequent golf games on the nine-hole Wellesley course were always competitive (a nickel a putt), and often hilarious.

Rachel and I took long canoe trips on the Charles River. Munching peanut butter sandwiches and sipping Coke from glass bottles, we discussed such intellectual topics as which is a better date, the physical athlete or the mental athlete? Which band swings better, Glenn Gray or Glenn Miller? Sometimes we'd stretch out on the grass and read poetry aloud. Our favorite, naturally, was the *Rubaiyat of Omar Khayyam*.

> A book of Verses, underneath the Bough,
> A Jug of Wine, a Loaf of Bread—and Thou
> Beside me singing in the Wilderness—
> Oh, Wilderness were Paradise enow!

At that time I was head over heels in love with West Point. My brother Red, my sister Julia, and her husband Charlie were all stationed there. I visited as often as possible—but not to see them. "Thou" for me meant cadets. I went to see the cadets—the more cadets, the better.

I persuaded Rachel to go with me to enjoy the unlimited supply of cadets. I thought the U.S. Military Academy was *the* place and I talked of little else. A classmate would say, "How many cadets did you hear from today?" Oblivious to the edge in her voice, I'd launch into a discussion of my "beaus." If I gave her an attack of mego ("my eyes glaze over"), I was blissfully unaware of it.

With 20/20 hindsight, I would say that I was as self absorbed as one could get. My conversation was limited to two topics, me and the Corps of Cadets. Then one day, like George Minafer, the pampered young snob in *The Magnificent Ambersons,* I got my comeuppance.

In junior year Rachel and I lived with six others in the tower of Shafer Hall. One evening I heard laughter exploding in the next room. The murmur of low voices would erupt into peals and shouts. Something was very, very funny. I paid no attention, though the uproar continued a long time. I was packing to leave the next day for the Army-Yale game in New Haven.

Late that night Rachel came in to my room. She didn't say anything; she just stood there. Then she almost whispered, "Do you have any idea what all the laughing was about?"

"Not the slightest," I replied, snuggling under my black, gold, and gray West Point blanket.

"You," she said. "They were making fun of you."

I sat up straight. "That laughter was at *me?*"

Rachel sat down on my bed. "They've been swapping stories about your West Point obsession and how easy it is to get you to make a fool of yourself. I wasn't going to tell you. Then I decided you needed to know." My third grade report card—"talks too much" and "annoys others"—flashed before me.

I spent the whole night crying.

My mother had tried to tell me I talked too much. She kept repeating "Ask, don't tell," but I didn't get it. Now it was too late; I was a mess. The more I thought about it, the harder I cried.

I opened my swollen eyes in the morning, feeling limp and forlorn. I didn't want to see anybody, ever. I sent a telegram (those were the days) to my date saying I was sick, which I was. I could not bear to go to breakfast in the dorm. Putting on dark glasses, I walked to the village, head down, scuffing through the dry leaves. The scrambled eggs in an alley cafe tasted like cardboard.

A blank weekend loomed ahead. I wasn't going to the game, and I wasn't going back to the dorm. Where could I go to escape my humiliation? I thought of "my father the library." Why not hide out in the library? Then I had a novel idea—why not throw myself into my studies?

There were almost no students in Wellesley's marble book sanctuary that golden October Saturday. I had the place to myself. What a relief. For weeks I had been avoiding an art history paper on *Mont St. Michel and Chartres* by Henry Adams, which was heavy going. Now I would face it.

Hour after hour I immersed myself in Henry's ponderous sentences and brilliant insights. During that long library weekend, a new world slowly unfolded and I gradually began to lose myself. For the first time, I encountered the discipline and joy of difficult learning.

Sunday morning I stopped working long enough to go to chapel. I remember every detail of that service. The preacher was the Reverend Charles O. Taylor, dean of Harvard Divinity School. He seemed to be talking to me. "College is a time for friendship," he said, "and friendship is the elixir of life." That sent me scurrying back to the library for a dictionary.

To the Greeks, I discovered, an elixir was a powder for drying wounds. To medieval alchemists, an elixir was a compound said to change base metal into gold. For us, an elixir is "the quintessence or the underlying principle."

All weekend I studied, hard. Intense concentration was strange to me. I knew I was onto something when I began to lose track of time. I had come seeking refuge, but instead I had found a focus. By Sunday night I was almost, not quite, "singing in the wilderness," and "thou" had become Wellesley College.

Years later I found a passage in T. H. White's *The Once and Future King* that hit home. "The best thing for being sad," Merlyn advised the despondent young Arthur, "is to learn something . . . Learn why the world wags and what wags it. Learning," Merlyn said, "is the thing for you."

By Monday I was back on an even keel. Being made fun of wasn't the end of the world after all. I raised my sights and at the end of that year had only A's and B's, a first for me.

As I struggled to hold my tongue and *listen,* the moral of my shattering weekend slowly dawned on me. It wasn't discovering the life of the mind. It was discovering friendship.

Rachel did something only a real friend would do. She took the risk of telling me the truth. Leveling with me about the ridicule of my "friends," she didn't exactly turn my life to gold, but she did turn me around.

I had never discussed these appalling events with anyone, not even Tom. Then one day, on an impulse, I sat down and wrote the whole story to Rachel, now living at Rancho Mirage in California. I thanked her, sixty years late, for the most valuable lesson that I learned in college.

Rachel answered by return mail: "Your letter was a total surprise. I never dreamed I had any impact on your life. Thank you for writing. I've just been diagnosed with breast cancer and your letter gave me a lift."

Friendship is the elixir of life.

❧ 13. Two Great Teachers: Failure and Orson Welles

One day I got a letter from Hope Godfrey, postmarked San Francisco. I ripped it open and was stunned. Collapsing on a window seat, I stared out at the Green. Hope's note was short and to the point. "I met Steve at a Longshoreman's Dance and the next day we got married. He is big and strong and beautiful and marriage is better than you and I ever imagined." Hope married! And here I was, stuck in a nunnery.

I had read in *Les Miserables* that "the supreme happiness in life is the conviction that we are loved." I felt like crying.

It was February 14th and everybody had a sweetie except me. Shafer Hall was awash with valentines and roses, but not for me. I thought about Lloyd Sherman of Kentucky, the heroine of the best series in my book-saturated girlhood, *The Little Colonel's Knight Comes Riding.* Would a knight ever come riding for me?

Again I wandered lonely as a cloud in the Wellesley Library. On the bulletin board I found a valentine Gertrude Stein composed for Sherwood Anderson. Stein was a big deal in the thirties and I enjoyed her incomprehensibility.

> Very fine is my valentine.
> Very fine and very mine.
> Very fine is my valentine very mine and very fine.
> Very fine is my valentine and mine, very fine very
>   mine and mine is my valentine.

At last, a Stein quote I could understand.

Despite my newfound love of learning, Mother need not have worried about my being too smart. Kitty Baldwin, my best roommate ever (except for my husband) had flunked out at the end of freshman year. Kitty was smart but morning assembly in her Alabama finishing school had opened with the song "I'll Follow My Secret Heart."

I lived with the "Goon Girls," a goofy group who excelled at not studying. I was sitting at my desk one miserable, rainy November night, trying not very hard to learn French verbs. Jane Tracy, ringleader of the goof-offs, stuck her head in the door. "Whatcha doin'?"

"Nobody's doing nothing," muttered Rachel. "We've got the glooms."

"That's just it. Want to see Spang swallow a goldfish?"

"A *what?*"

"You heard me," Trace said, "a goldfish. Meet me in the john in ten minutes and bring money. It'll cost you a quarter."

Goldfish swallowing—where do ideas like that come from? This was

1935 and nobody had ever heard of such a thing. Word spread through the dorm like wildfire. At last a gloom-chaser.

Christmas vacation was coming, and we had to dispose of all pets and plants. After Virginia Spangler and Jane Tracy cleaned out Spang's fish tank, one goldfish was left. (They'd already hidden the turtles in friends' beds.)

"What'll we do with him?" Tracy asked.

Spang never missed a beat. "I'll swallow him. The kids will pay good money to see that. Round 'em up—you and I are going to make a bundle."

The john was a long, bleak room with white porcelain sinks along one wall and brown wooden stalls along the other. It was jammed. Patty Dyar stood at the door collecting quarters. Mousemeat Matthews was holding Spang's almost empty fish tank. In it swam one medium-sized, red-gold, unsuspecting fish. "Where did the turtles go?" I asked.

"Never mind," whispered Tracy, then loudly: "Can everybody see? Move in closer." We all inched forward. She scooped out the fish and, holding it by the tail, advanced slowly toward Spang. Spang clapped her hand over her mouth and ran into one of the stalls. Her vomiting was loud and distressing. We were stunned. What to do? Patty took the fish, dropped it in the tank, and started toward the door.

"Wait!" cried Tracy. "I'll do it!" Everybody cheered. "Bring me the fish." Mouse held out the tank. Silence—except for Spang's gagging. "The moment has come," Tracy announced. Nobody breathed. She stretched out her arm and reached into the water. She grabbed the fish. Holding it by the tail, she raised it above her head and intoned slowly, "Bye-bye, little goldfish." She threw back her head, opened her mouth, and paused dramatically. The fish's body was thrashing back and forth. Slowly, Tracy lowered the goldfish into her mouth. We didn't know whether to cheer or scream.

GULP!

Goldfish was gonzo and so was gloom. Trace faced us, bugging her eyes, sucking in her cheeks, pouting her lips, opening and closing them like a fish. Wild cheering. She took a bow, then another, then another. Spang applauded weakly. Mouse counted out the money—ten dollars. Tracy clapped. "That'll get me to Bowdoin's Christmas house parties."

The Boston Globe (who told them?) headlined "WELLESLEY'S NEWEST

FAD." "Fame at last!" Tracy crowed. The Associated Press picked it up and soon Tracy's "goldfish gluttony" swept all of the colleges. (After that came "How Many Can You Get into a Phone Booth.")

It's hard to be serious when you live among goons. Shafer Hall was distraction central. "After you leave home," I thought, "everything is fun and games." I had to fail a course to get the news. Elizabethan Drama, taught by T. H. Vail Motter, an Oxford intellectual who looked like Leslie Howard and acted like Attila the Hun, was my undoing.

My well-prepped classmates had no trouble with Elizabethan prose, but for me Christopher Marlowe was a sleeping pill. I read in *The New York Times* that *Dr. Faustus* was playing in a New York theater. It seemed easier to take a train to the city than to read the damned play—and I could go up the Hudson to West Point for a hop as well.

I stayed by myself at the Barbizon Hotel for Women (bathroom down the hall) and taxied to Greenwich Village, a long way, for thirty cents. The Federal Theater was one of FDR's unemployment relief projects and the price was right: eighty-five cents a ticket. Dr. Faustus was played by a heavily made-up, bearded actor with a sonorous voice named Orson Welles. Welles was the works: producer, director, and dazzling star. His physical presence was palpable and I fell for him, flat.

That show had everything—smoking cauldrons, thunder drums, unearthly music, and Bill Baird puppets as the Seven Deadly Sins. The bare stage was walled in black velvet. Shafts of white light made actors appear and disappear. When sinners climbed up out of hell (fifteen trap doors), furnaces flared red and orange flames.

I was riveted. From his opening intoning of "What will be shall be" to the end, when Faustus, waiting to pay down his soul to Lucifer, listens motionless to the slow striking of the clock, Orson Welles was overpowering. He was twenty-one.

On the train back to Boston, I memorized the Deadlies, just in case: pride, envy, wrath, avarice, sloth, gluttony, lust.

Unfortunately, neither *Dr. Faustus* nor the seven sins made the exam. All the other plays I had, shall we say, skimmed. Mr. Motter pierced my bluff and gave me an F for the term. I hated him. He (not I) had endangered my all-important scholarship.

I was stunned. I had never failed anything. What would my father say? Rachel took long walks with me around Lake Waban, listening to my tirades against "T. H. Vail Attila." How did she know that the way to help a friend in crisis is to keep them talking? That wasn't hard. Even if she had spoken, I wouldn't have heard her.

Second semester I threw myself into Renaissance Drama, just to show that man, and my education took off. The B-minus I got at the end of the term felt like an A-plus. I am forever grateful to T. H. Vail Motter for turning me around—and for unwittingly turning me, with a little help from Orson Welles, into a lifelong theaterphile.

A year later my new heartbeat, Orson Welles, staged *The Cradle Will Rock* by Marc Blitzstein—or tried to. It was denounced as subversive because it was militantly pro union, and the U.S. Government actually closed the show. Many rejoiced. My father may have been a conservative Republican, but he grasped the big picture. "Hitler is shutting down theaters and publishers all over Germany," he said. "That's how it begins. The words 'free speech' mean free speech."

Fun and games with the "Goon Girls" turned out to have great value. Tracy, who had been a friend of Tom Campion's since their Andover/Abbott days, was the one who introduced me to Husband. Years later, Tom read an article in *Harvard* magazine that referred to our era as the "goldfish-swallowing generation." It called Jane Tracy of Wellesley "a pacesetter who in 1935 tripped off a national fad."

"Just think," Tom laughed, "if you hadn't messed things up, I might be married to a national pacesetter."

II. With Tom

Marriage, Kids, and
The New York Times

❦ 14. The Little Colonel's Knight Comes
Riding (in Joe Kennedy Jr.'s Car)

Tom and I met in 1938, when we were both seniors. He drove out from Harvard in a roadster borrowed from his classmate Joe Kennedy Jr. to see my friend Tracy. She took one look at her old friend and summoned me. "You've got to take a look at this guy." Tall, blonde, handsome, Tom had on a loud, green plaid grouse-shooting suit his roommate had bought in Scotland—tight trousers, belted jacket, matching fore-and-aft Sherlock Holmes hat. He looked like something out of the 1890s.

We looked into each other's eyes. His brown ones were lit with laughter. He was intriguing, but Tracy had first dibs.

That night he telephoned. "How'd you like to go to the Ringling circus?"

"I thought you were Tracy's friend."

"Tracy wants me to get to know her friends." This fellow is quick, I thought.

Our first date at Ringling, Barnum, and Bailey's Circus was memorable for three things. (1) Gargantua, the enormous, lethargic ape who slept in his white cage as they wheeled him in to a smashing crescendo of Ravel's "Bolero." (2) Tom's tribute to Shakespeare. (3) Tom didn't try to kiss me. That was news when I got back to the dorm.

After the circus he took me to Jacob Wirth's, Boston's hundred-year-old tavern. Over hot bratwurst and cold beer, he remarked, "How do you feel about Shakespeare?" He pulled out a piece of paper. "I copied this after I heard Copeland recite it in his last class."

"Who's Copeland?"

"Charles Townsend Copeland. He's only one of Harvard's most famous English professors, that's all." Tom handed me the paper. "I memorized all fifty-seven lines. Test me out. 'Oh what a rogue and peasant
slave am I . . .'" He recited the whole speech, with gestures, ending in
a dramatic whisper, "'The play's the thing wherein I'll catch the conscience of the king.'"

"Perfect," I laughed. Then he took the paper, folded it into a water
bomb, filled it with beer, went out, and tossed it down the street.

I was aghast. "Why did you do that?"

"Because it's springtime and you and Shakespeare are here and I feel
good." This guy's cuckoo, I thought—definitely, delightfully cuckoo.

That spring, Tom came out to Wellesley as often as he could borrow
Joe Kennedy's car, which was often. When I met Joe he flashed his famous smile and said, "My mother wanted to go to Wellesley but her father sent her to a convent." Joe Kennedy majored in friendship. "Joe's old
man," Tom told me, "says Joe is going to be president."

"President of what?"

"United States, what else?"

My gimmick was that I wouldn't let a boy kiss me. It drove them up
the wall. I learned this from my mother (via Fred). She was a romantic
southern belle who broke a lot of hearts. She wanted her daughters to
break hearts. But she also wanted her sons' hearts to stay intact. When
I came home after a date, she would be waiting up to hear about my
evening. "Did he try to kiss you? Did you let him?" I hated that.

In the blossoming New England springtime I wondered if my no-
kissing policy would hold up. Tom and I spent a lot of time canoeing on
Wellesley's Lake Waban or sitting on the bench at Tupelo Point. I was
too unsure of myself to tell him about the Wellesley tradition. If a
Wellesley woman takes her beau to Tupelo Point and he does not pro-
pose, she throws him in the lake. We called it the Tupelo Point of No
Return. I couldn't have lifted him anyway.

How can you play the no-kiss card if a man doesn't try? I'd been dating (old sense of the word) Tom for several months and I seemed to be
the only one interested in kissing. Finally, as we sat in silence beneath

the white cloud of an apple tree, he put his arm around me. He gave me a kiss, a real kiss. It darted through me with the speed of an arrow.

"Do that again," I said. Warmth spread through my body. We murmured sweet words. It was delicious.

I grew up in the Age of Innocence, and I mean innocence. My grandmother was even apprehensive of the Bible: too much sex. My sex manual was *National Geographic.* I knew a lot about anatomy as displayed in New Guinea, but closer to home I was on shaky ground.

Our dating grew more intense. He took me dancing at Norumbega Park, a mecca for the big bands: Guy Lombardo, Glenn Gray, Tommy Dorsey. We imitated Ginger Rogers and Fred Astaire, dancing cheek-to-cheek. "If music be the food of love," he whispered, "play on . . ." Our sexy swaying was far more romantic than today's dirty dancing. I still remember a sign on the wall: NO DANCING UNLESS MOVING YOUR FEET.

Shortly before finals, Tom invited me to have dinner with his father and stepmother at the Commodore Hotel in Cambridge. I couldn't understand why he was so jittery about taking me to meet his parents. Years later, I learned that they came to Boston because Tom had written his father: "I've met the girl I'm going to marry." In a panic, his parents hopped the train. We got along famously. According to stepmother Marie, Pop told Tom, "You're much too young to think about marriage. You have to finish graduate school first. But don't let that girl get away."

Harvard, Yale, and Princeton expelled even graduate students who got married. In the thirties, if a Wellesley girl married she had to leave college. Too much carnal knowledge loose in the dorms. We all knew about the Wellesley senior, Class of 1935, who confessed to President Pendleton that she had eloped during spring vacation. After serious deliberation, Pres. Pen handed down her verdict.

"When you got married, you broke a cardinal rule," she told the sinner. "But since graduation is two months off, and you came to me with the truth, I will allow you to graduate *provided* you give your word of honor you will not cohabit with your husband—until after commencement."

The bride, vastly relieved, promised.

Cohabiting, the thirties euphemism for sex, never came up in my relationship with Tom, but don't think we didn't think about it. One night we sat alone in Wellesley's Greek amphitheater, white with moonlight. I wanted to tell him, "Sex is Greek to me," but I didn't dare. No matter, he would find out anyhow.

Wellesley College took a dim view of sex. Only one of our teachers was married, charming Mrs. Mallory in the psych department; she even had children. We were mesmerized by her.

Most of the girls I knew were virgins, with the possible exception of two racy characters. Two of our other classmates vanished overnight. We learned later that they were lesbians. As shocking as it was incomprehensible.

The rest of us were eager for information that young women now seem to be born with. We wanted the facts, but we were leery of the experience.

Harvard protected its young men with ironclad rules called Parietals: *Women only allowed in rooms Weekdays: 1:30 P.M. to 4 P.M. Fridays and Saturdays: 1:30 P.M. to 11 P.M.* Webster's says *parietal* means "pertaining to a wall." Punishment ranged from first warning to severance of connection to "expunging student's name from Harvard records." Tom said, "*Parietal* and *expunging*—only Harvard talks like that."

He said that in psych class they studied Freud's dreams and Krafft-Ebing's nightmares, but who could relate to men that wanted to sleep with their mothers or fell in love with chickens? Kissing under the apple tree, that's what Tom and I could relate to. With each kiss my curiosity increased.

Wellesley freshmen were required to take Hygiene, as sex education was then called. After we worked our way through the reproduction of the amoeba, the paramecium, and the white rat, we were ready for Dr. Mary De Kruif's famous forty-minute lecture on sex, known as the Organ Recital. The divorced wife of the famous author Dr. Paul De Kruif, she was an ample figure in heavy tweeds, wool stockings, and ground-gripper shoes, about as unsexy as you could get.

The Organ Recital was a damp firecracker. She raced through it, light on detail, heavy on warning. "Never wear red satin," she told us. "It arouses men." We all raced to Filene's to look for red satin dresses. I kept mine for years. Whenever I wore it, Tom's brown eyes sparked.

Dr. De Kruif's final sentence was arresting. "Young ladies," she warned, "remember—dancing leads to babies." (In my case, she was right. I tangoed with Tom and we had five children.)

The most risqué thing I ever did in college was to sign out, just before graduation, for a chaperoned overnight—and then go on an unchaperoned all-night swim with my Harvard beau, sans nudity (we swam at dawn in our underwear). Hoping to impress Tom, I quoted Juliet, "'Night's candles are burnt out . . .'" He came right back with "'jocund day stands tiptoe on the misty mountain tops.'" Unlike the lovers of Verona, our tryst was sans sex, unless you count a lot of enthusiastic kissing.

In those days, a person knew when to stop, a lost art. The fact that Beau turned out to be Husband makes my naughty escapade tamer than Gargantua dozing to the beat of "Bolero."

The sun was high when he took me to the Copley Hotel for breakfast. By now neither of us wanted to be apart, ever. After giggling over our bacon and eggs, we fell silent. He was headed to graduate school in Cambridge; I back to Virginia with my parents. When would we meet again? Suddenly, Tom pulled out his wallet and took out a five dollar bill. He held it up with both hands. "Watch," he said. Slowly, he tore the fiver in half. "What are you doing?" I gasped. "That's illegal."

"Here's your half." His brown eyes looked into mine. "I want to be sure we meet again."

❦ 15. If You Come to a Fork in the Road, Take It

To graduate from Wellesley, English Comp majors had to write a novel. Mine, *No Guts, No Glory,* was about (what else?) West Point. Miss Elizabeth Manwaring, my Victorian professor, wrote on the outline, "Your title is in poor taste." I couldn't think of another, so I kept handing in installments labeled *No Guts, No Glory.* On the second she wrote, "Questionable title." Then just: "Title?" On the completed manuscript she wrote, "This title grows on one."

"Persistence," Calvin Coolidge said, "is omnipotent."

Having used up my persistence to get my degree, I never pursued publication. A case of no guts and no glory.

Are all commencements a blur? Mine was. My clearest memory is the pride in my father's eyes. "No one can ever take that B.A. away from you, Narcissa," he said.

Wanting to please him, I had applied for a teaching fellowship at Wellesley so I could get an M.A. in English. When it came through, I wobbled. Was I up to that? Doubtful. So what if I'd be near Tom Campion, who was at Harvard Business School? I wouldn't admit that I was afraid of intimacy. I told myself my parents needed me and back to Virginia I went.

In the thirties most college women had three career choices: nursing, teaching, or secretarial school. My classmate Cookie Lovejoy talked her way into med school and stunned us all.

I got a job teaching sixth grade at the public school in Fox Hill, a fishing village whose main street ended at Chesapeake Bay. The small town had three Baptist churches, and if children misbehaved, parents prayed over them. I had one rebel, Harvey Maker, with big eyes and ears, who looked like a turtle. I'd say, "Will you read, Harvey?" and he'd say, "Oh God, Miss Reeder, do I have to read again?"

I went to call on Harvey's mother, who ran the penny arcade at Buckroe Beach Amusement Park. She had on a captain's cap and reeked of gin. Harvey was reading *Captain Billy's Whiz Bang*. "Mrs. Maker," I said, "I don't want to upset you, but Harvey is using bad words." She wheeled around. "God damn it, Harvey, have you been swearing again? Jesus Christ, where do you hear them words? Not from me and I know Goddamned well not your old man."

The next year I moved on to teaching English at Newport News High School, and my salary jumped from sixty-nine to seventy-three dollars a month. After being independent, living with my parents was a drag, but I couldn't afford rent. I was trying to pay for my new old (very) Ford coupe.

Like Elizabeth Barrett and Robert Browning, my romance with Tom flourished by letter. Unlike the Brownings, we talked on the phone, too, although long distance cost four dollars a minute. Unfortunately, our telephone—which my father hated and refused to answer—was just outside his study. "That young man is the last of the wild spenders," he growled.

Then Tom invited me to New York for a weekend. Some excitement. My mother made sure I stayed at the Barbizon Hotel for Women. I had forgotten how handsome Tom was—and how much fun.

He took me to see the hit play *Our Town*, Thornton Wilder's master-piece about the extraordinariness of ordinary things. We both cried when Emily, who died in childbirth, returns briefly from the dead. Unable to bear how she once lived—as though she had unlimited time—she asks Stage Manager, "Do any human beings ever realize life while they live it—every, every minute?"

"No." He pauses. "The saints and poets, maybe—they do some."

Later, sipping frozen daiquiris in the Biltmore Bar—that was the place to go—we were still in Grovers Corners. I said I liked the Stage Manager saying, "There's something way down deep that's eternal about every human being."

Tom nodded. "I liked it when Mr. Gibbs said that before he got mar-ried, he was afraid they would run out of things to talk about. That's one trouble we'd never have, right?"

What's he getting at, I thought. Out loud I said, "If you ran dry you could always quote Shakespeare." He chuckled and ordered two more daiquiris. Suddenly, he pulled out his half of the five dollar bill. "Where's yours?"

I fished it out of my wallet. "They still match," he laughed. "Hang on to it." What did that mean?

We parted with a long kiss. On the way back to Virginia, rattling along in the upper berth, I said to myself, "That Tom Campion may be a knock-out, but he'll never be serious. There are lots more fish in the sea."

At Julia's suggestion, I borrowed money to go to Europe. Tom had been twice, but I never. "You really ought to see Europe," Julia said, "be-fore there's a war." She said it lightly. Nobody realized Hitler's horrible agenda.

In the summer of '39 I went to Europe with three army girls I grew up with. We pinched our pennies but hit the high spots—dancing at the American ambassador's Fourth of July reception in Paris, meditating in Chartres Cathedral at sunset, skiing on summer snow in Zermatt, watching the Duchess of Windsor watch the Duke build sandcastles at the Lido, chatting with Cary Grant in Harry's Bar in Venice. I kept sending Tom postcards. He thought I was making it up.

In Heidelberg, young Nazi officers gave us a rush. They were handsome, not sinister. When one of them began vilifying Jews, I said naively, "That's not Christian." He shot back, "Mein Gott, we're not *Christians*." Our train was stopped at the German-Netherlands border and a Jewish family had to get off, but nobody imagined the atrocities later discovered.

War clouds loomed, but my chums wanted to see Britain. I couldn't go because school was starting. I came home alone on the last trip of the beautiful French liner *Normandie*. (Moored to a dock in New York, she was burned by saboteurs.) We were in mid-ocean when Britain and France declared war on Germany. Everybody was scared. After that it was daily lifeboat drills and peering over the Atlantic for enemy periscopes.

A week later, my pals headed home on the *Athenia*. Off the coast of Ireland their ship was torpedoed and sank. Once I knew they had escaped in lifeboats, I was consumed with jealousy. They spent a week being wined and dined in Galway. All of their possessions had gone down with the ship, and the Irish wouldn't let them pay for anything.

I now had to teach to pay off my debt. I was required to teach *Ivanhoe* to sons of Slovak shipyard workers in Newport News. They said, "What's with this broad Rowena?" Jewish students said, "How come Sir Walter Scott calls Rebecca 'the Jewess?'" I was over my head in more ways than one.

Suddenly, things brightened up.

In the spring of 1941, Tom was working for Procter and Gamble in Cincinnati. He kept calling to tell me he missed me. I had the same problem. I was going out with other men, but I connected Tom to Cole Porter's hit: "You're the top, you're the Coliseum. You're the top, you're the Louvre Museum."

Tom announced that he was coming to see me. He wanted to meet my parents. I pretended I didn't know why. He alarmed me by saying he was going to hitchhike. In those simpler times, heavily influenced by Claudette Colbert and Clark Gable in *It Happened One Night*, we all hitchhiked. I had been pretty good at it in college.

"Tom!" I exploded. "Don't you dare let my parents know you're a hitchhiker." He obliged by hitchhiking as far as Hampton, the town next to ours. Then he hopped on the C & O and ten minutes later Mother and I welcomed him at the Phoebus station. He kissed me, but not really. That came later. "I'm glad to be here," he said with a twinkle. "It was a long trip."

Not only was Tom a hitchhiker; worse, he was a Democrat. "Whatever you do," I instructed him, "do not say anything nice about the Roosevelts." At dinner the first night, I choked on my soup when he announced, "I've been reading a wonderful book. It is called *My Day* by Eleanor Roosevelt." I kicked him under the table. He smiled and said, "Eleanor Roosevelt is a great woman." Silence. People either loved or hated the Roosevelts. There was no middle ground. My father's comment: "Harvard men have radical ideas."

The next night, Tom borrowed our car to take me to the Williamsburg Inn for a tête-à-tête candlelight supper. We ate a little and laughed a lot. On the way home, he stopped in Yorktown at what the British call a "lay by." It was a warm night and the moon was rising out of the mist. He turned off the ignition and said, "Remember what Thornton Wilder said?" I shook my head. "'People were made to live two-by-two.'" I nodded. Then he asked me to marry him. Before I could answer, he pulled a white box out of his pocket, took out a diamond ring and slipped it on my finger. "I had my mother's engagement ring reset," he said. For once those merry brown eyes were grave. What could a girl say?

Tom always called the evening when I decided to turn Campion "Yorktown's second greatest surrender." I'm still mad because driving home he threw my ring box out the window, like it was a water-bomb full of Shakespeare.

The next day he bearded my father in his booklined study to ask for my hand in marriage. Daddy knew what was up but refused to help. He had zero interest in having his last chick fly the coop. He launched into a discussion of our new Delco heating system. Finally, with great trepidation, Tom interrupted. "Sir," he said, "I want to marry your daughter."

Silence. My father was big on silence. Finally: "And how do you plan to support Narcissa?"

"I've got a good job in the production department at Proctor and

Gamble. I'm already making eighty-six a week and they tell me my prospects are good."

Too much for Daddy. He veered right back to Delco.

When I told my mother we wanted to get married, she was dubious. "He seems so happy-go-lucky, Narcissa. Is he a playboy?"

"I'll let you know," I said. She never said any more about that because she fell for him as hard as I did.

Mother and I waited in the dining room. Typically, she had a bottle of cold champagne all ready. When the men came out, looking a bit worn, Tom winked at me. What a relief. My father recovered enough to raise his champagne glass. "Here's to the bride and groom," he said with a small smile.

To get a marriage license in Virginia, you had to pass a Wasserman test proving you had no venereal disease. Our wedding was almost derailed because husband-to-be sent bride-to-be a wisecracking telegram and by mistake it was delivered to her father. It read: "How did you make out on your Wasserman test?" Daddy was not amused.

With the prospect of a wedding, new questions hovered on the horizon. I had never heard the word condom. For me, birth control was a pre-condom-conundrum. But not for Tom. A month before the wedding, his father actually took him, a newly minted Harvard MBA, to a drugstore and "introduced" him to Trojans. They were both embarrassed.

Some mothers dispensed a little sex instruction to their daughters just before the wedding. Others thought that was the bridegroom's prerogative. I knew one mother who wrestled hopelessly with the topic, then said, "Well, dear, just remember, if your hairdo is perfect, your sex life isn't."

My own mother believed in learning by doing, as long as you had a marriage license. The night before I was married she told me, "Enthusiastic cooperation works better than anything else."

Instead of a rehearsal dinner, we had separate bachelor and spinster dinners. On the way to his party, Tom stopped by our house and said, "Come outside. I have something to give you." The moon was shining on the Chesapeake and the air was heavy with the sweetness of Daddy's gardenias. Tom gave me a deep kiss. Then he pulled out his half-a-fiver. "Go get yours." When I came back he clipped the two pieces together and handed me the whole bill. "Here's your marriage insurance," he said. We both laughed, but underneath we knew this was serious.

On July 5, 1941, I became Mrs. Thomas Baird Campion. The idea of a married woman keeping her own name was twenty-five years in the future. "Mrs." was big in those days. Most women, especially my mother, preferred it to "Ph.D."

Twenty-five members of Tom's family came, traveling from Columbus, Ohio, to Phoebus, Virginia, via sleeping cars on the grand old C & O, a bit longer than Tom's C & O trip. All of my family showed up, but for once we were outnumbered.

Our wedding at St. John's Episcopal Church in Hampton was at eight P.M., because I thought you only went to bed with a man at night. There were complaints about the hour, but the candlelit church, decorated with ferns and white camellias, was beautiful. Tom's beloved brother Frank, a sophomore at Yale, was best man. Men wore white dinner jackets and bridesmaids wore droopy pastel chiffon dresses they hated. I wore a lace jacket with a standup collar, a full tulle skirt, and a long veil fastened with a halo of orange blossoms. I carried a bouquet of white orchids and had a ten-inch waist.

I processed slowly down the aisle on my father's arm to Wagner's "Here Comes the Bride." I glanced at Daddy. That strong jaw was set. I was transported; he was not. I only had eyes for the best-looking man I ever saw. For once he looked serious.

"Who gives this woman to this man?"

Daddy came through. "I do." Later I wondered who gave me the groom. Tom and I actually had a debate over "love, honor, and obey." Finally he agreed to drop "obey." People were shocked—wifely obedience was expected—but they were impressed when we recited our vows from memory. We knew them by heart—in more ways than one.

We sailed out to the rousing music of Mendelssohn's "Wedding March," followed by a crash of thunder and zigzag of lightning. We were drenched by a proper Wagnerian cloudburst. "This is a good omen!" exclaimed Tom, the born optimist. "Arabs say, 'Rain on your wedding day, long and happy marriage.'"

Our reception was held in the Casemate Club at Fortress Monroe, a relic of the war of 1812 surrounded entirely by a moat full of seawater.

Tom and I waltzed alone, gazing into each other's dancing eyes, to "Let Me Call You Sweetheart" (my mother's favorite).

I'll never forget what Tom's father said as we were leaving in a borrowed car for our honeymoon at the old White Sulfur Springs Hotel. Pop put his arm around me. "Be good to her, Tom," he said.

And he was. My first and last husband was an enabler of "enthusiastic cooperation."

❦ 16. Pregnancy and Pearl Harbor

Tom had good news for me on our honeymoon. "I've rented an apartment for us in Clifton, near the University of Cincinnati. It's really nice—our first love nest—not one of those cold modern places. It's Victorian. It has character."

It had character all right—all bad. I walked around our first home—two rooms separated by sliding golden oak doors, a big butler's pantry stuffed with unopened wedding presents, a nineteenth-century kitchen with a gas stove on skinny legs. And an icebox, literally. Our refrigerator required a daily ice man and an ice pick. I took it all in, marched outside, sat down on the steps, and cried.

Tom suffered from an excess of empathy. His eyes filled with tears. Suddenly he began to laugh. "Vas you effer in Zinzinnati?" It was the slogan of a local beer. I laughed in spite of myself. We made do.

I cried again three months later when Dr. Crudginton said, "Yes, my dear, you are pregnant."

We'd only just been married. I didn't want a honeymoon baby—I thought. I cried again when I told Tom. He was ecstatic over the news—but puzzled. "My mother died young and I never had any sisters. Do all women cry a lot?"

"Yes," I lied, "a lot."

The good news was that we had outgrown the icebox apartment. We found another on Zumstein Avenue with a tiny second bedroom, an electric fridge, and a shared backyard. Open and sunny, it felt like a palace.

I felt like crying when Tom's parents insisted on giving a tea dance at their Rocky Fork Club in Columbus to introduce "the bride and groom." The bride's stomach protruded unmistakably beneath her lace-trimmed black velvet. "I can't do it," I said. "Yes you can," Tom said, "you can do anything you put your mind to." When he flattered me I always fell for it and he knew it. I was embarrassed by our instant, learn-about-birth-control-by-doing baby, but I needn't have worried. People would remember only one thing about that party.

Tom and I were swaying to Irving Berlin's "I'll Be Loving You, Always." Suddenly the club president stopped the music. Our party came to a screeching halt. In a stentorian voice he announced: "Japanese aircraft have bombed Pearl Harbor. Our country is at war." Shocked almost speechless, people left quickly.

I was beginning to grasp my father's oft-repeated conviction: "There is no way to escape suffering." I used to cry about things that went away. No longer. Where would the next bomb hit? Everybody had the jitters—blackouts, guns on rooftops, searchlights cutting night skies, air raid sirens. The Japanese never came but the draft did. Tom and I were glued to the radio when President Roosevelt drew a number out of a glass bowl. "One-five-eight," he announced, and 6,175 unmarried men across the land were drafted into service.

Everything changed. Women put on pants (a shocking innovation) and took men's jobs. Three million teenagers pitched in on farm and factory. We collected animal fats for glycerin, gave up butter, saved tin cans (remove both ends and smash flat), ate vegetables from Tom's victory garden. I did my part: first I lost the food ration book, then the gas ration book. Tom found both of them.

Radio was our Bible; Edward R. Murrow our prophet. And how grounding it was to hear the rolling tones of Winston Churchill reverberating across the sea. "I have nothing to offer but blood, toil, tears, and sweat."

"With one sentence," Tom said, "the world found a new kind of leader."

Procter and Gamble switched Tom from making Ivory Soap to making glycerin for explosives, which deferred him from the draft. His hours were long and he came home exhausted, but we knew we were lucky—he came home. When our brothers went off to war, we both struggled to stifle tears, saying, "They're doing what they were trained to do." But that wasn't true of Frank, Tom's brother. He was graduated early from Yale and enlisted in the Field Artillery. In France, Frank Campion would receive a rare honor: a battlefield promotion from sergeant to second lieutenant. Surely Frank was the only soldier with a copy of Chaucer in his knapsack.

My brother Fred, one of the first fliers in the U.S. Navy, would be executive officer of the *USS Bataan*. Under extreme stress his ulcer flared up; he had a massive hemorrhage at sea, spent five months in a navy hospital, and was retired as a rear admiral at thirty-nine. Our brother-in-law, Charlie Summerall, would earn the Silver Star for gallantry at the Kasserine Pass in North Africa. Red would lead—and that is the word, *lead*—the three thousand men of the 12th Infantry regiment onto Utah Beach in Normandy. He was awarded five medals, including the Distinguished Service Cross.

They all came home. But when they went off to war, who could predict the future? We tried to imagine just what they were experiencing. Impossible. I cried bitter tears—we all cried—when Red's leg, shattered on D-Day plus six, had to be amputated.

Into this uncertain time, the baby I didn't think I wanted was born. (Tom, of course, knew better all along.) Tommy weighed an incredible eleven pounds. I took one look at him and was hooked for life. The proud father peered through the glass partition in the hospital nursery and exclaimed, "What's my son doing in there with those infants?"

Both of us were mesmerized by Wonder Baby. When he was three months old, I took him to Reederhaven to show him off to my parents. Tommy and I shared a lower berth and spent the night peering out at the lights.

My parents were also mesmerized by Wonder Baby, who was mesmerized by Fritzie and Noodle, Daddy's dachshunds. My father's dogs were his safety valve. After his mandatory retirement from the army at age sixty-four, he became depressed. Feeling fit as a fiddle, he was suddenly shelved. The dogs sat on his lap and he talked to them. What was he telling them? We wished we knew.

Tommy was a welcome diversion for my father, who was obsessed by "that psychopath Hitler." Having fought the Germans in World War I, and now watching his sons go off to war, all he could say to express his inner turmoil was "I feel useless." I hated that. I longed to comfort him but I didn't know how. Every night my mother and I sipped sherry and watched him pour himself stiff drinks. We knew alcohol increases depression but we never spoke of it. Ours was a family where a lot went unsaid. You were expected to rise above problems, not discuss them.

After we returned to Cincinnati my father wrote, with what was for him a flood of feeling, "Today I went into Tommy's room and Tommy wasn't there."

Three months later Julia called. She began bravely, "Narcissa." Her voice broke. "Daddy had a stroke. I found him—his eyes were open but he wasn't there." Now she was sobbing. "He's dead, Narcissa. Daddy is dead. Only Fritzie and Noodle were with him." Our father was seventy years old.

I could not cry—I couldn't even take it in. He had looked so well when he took us to the train in his straw gardening hat. He'd been picking fresh corn from his "raccoon patch." He kissed Tommy good-bye and passed him to me, his blue eyes swimming. "Come back soon," he had said.

I tried to pack to go back but I couldn't even find my black dress. I shuddered with dry sobs in Tom's arms but hardly knew where I was. Even a loving husband and a wonder baby could not penetrate my loss. Tom understood. "I was fourteen when my mother died. I felt cut off from everybody."

He was unable to leave, but he borrowed money from a friend to get a nurse to care for Tommy and to give me the luxury of a lower berth. When he kissed me good-bye, those brown eyes were swimming, too. I was numb. I didn't feel anything.

All alone on the train, I said aloud, "He died. He is dead. I'll never see my father again." I still didn't believe it. I still couldn't cry. This was my first experience of a death in my heart. An invisible curtain had dropped between the world and me.

Sleep was impossible. I rang for the porter. "Could you give me some writing paper?" He brought me a yellow tablet and I started to scribble about my father. I wrote all night. My mother later had my thoughts put into a little booklet for the family. It began:

Do not mourn for Russell Reeder. His life was complete. Mourn if you must for us who will miss him forever but do not mourn for him. He came all the way around the circle, and in fine style, too. He died suddenly which was right. In all my life I never saw him sick in bed. If he had lived to be an invalid, he would have willed himself dead and his will was so strong he would have died on purpose.

By morning the dam had burst. I wasn't just crying, I was sobbing. I loved him so much. But I was coping. I had discovered, the hard way, that writing is therapy.

My mother was the brave wife of a soldier. She put her arm around me and took me to the coffin in front of the fireplace, just as she had at the Williford's in Fort Leavenworth when she explained that death is part of life. I could accept it then, but this was now. I looked at my father in his uniform with the battle ribbons from the Spanish American War and World War I, I looked at his white hair and mustache and translucent waxy skin, and gasped, sobbing. I felt frightened and alone, as though I had been abandoned in a vast desert. I'd lost my compass. He didn't tell me much; he showed me the way.

I sobbed when we drove slowly through the pale November sunlight of Arlington Cemetery. Yellow and brown leaves sifted slowly down as the army band played Chopin's Dead March. When the bugler blew taps, I thought my heart would break.

Back at Reederhaven in Phoebus, my father's absence spread over everything. I said to myself, "Now! I'll read his diaries and understand my father." No such luck. Mostly weather reports and political comments. I turned to the time when Tom had asked him for permission to marry me. "*Now!*" Still just facts, no feelings. But on the day after we got engaged, Tom and I had played golf in Hampton. When we returned he had put his golf shoes on a shelf in the garage, rather than take them inside. I couldn't believe what I read. It was utterly out of character. My father had written: "Tom Campion left his golf shoes for me to polish. What does he think I am, a shoeshine boy?"

I ran across the yard and threw myself down in the long grass on the other side of the seawall where no one could see me. I couldn't stop crying. *How* could my beloved father so misunderstand my beloved husband? I felt wasted by grief.

I couldn't even tell Tom—I never did.

Of course I overreacted. I had no idea what was really going on until years later when Tommy had a breakdown in college and saved us all. That was when Tom and I learned (among other things) about Freud's insight into those indelible ties that bind father to daughter, mother to son. One day it dawned on me that my father was swamped by unacceptable feelings about his daughter, feelings as old as Oedipus and Greek mythology, universal feelings that defy reason.

And I was swamped by grief.

Now I know grief is never a waste. The tears of grief are a flood tide sweeping us toward the mystery at the center of life. The Buddhists understand that. They teach that deep sorrow awakens the mind and opens the heart to the suffering of others—which might be why people die.

And my father was right: there is no way to escape suffering.

❦ 17. New York on $10

It is no accident that Tommy came as a surprise. I had grown up admiring Margaret Sanger but I could not imagine how birth control worked. My friend Betsy asked her mother, flat out, to explain it. "Birth control," her mother said tersely, "is deciding how many children you want. And then having that many." An older, streetwise girl was more explicit. "You won't have a baby," she told us, "if you only sleep with a man during the months that have an 'R' in them." But Tom was a good teacher.

Our first three perfectly spaced children—Tommy, Tad, and Toby (whatever made us think "T's" were a good idea?)—were born in "Zinzinnati," three years apart. In our little apartment on Zumstein Avenue, second son Tad lived in a baby basket behind the dining room door. When Toby was born, Tom bought our first house, a modest Victorian with a big stained glass window. "Can we afford it?" I asked. He said, "Us and the bank."

Our marital difficulties were mostly over money. (How typical; how boring.) Sometimes I overspent and then we had the Budget Talk. We both believed we should have a budget, but not very much. The dispute would heat up until Tom announced, "This is all about who's in charge." Nobody wants to talk about that. So he'd say "Fudgit the Budget," call our best friends Fi and Bob Keeler, and invite ourselves to dinner. That was one way to spend less.

One day Tom got a letter from Harvard Business School. *The New York Times* was looking for a production engineer. Would he like to be considered? Would he? The *Times* snapped him up (no surprise to me) and we drank a whole bottle of champagne.

Tom headed for New York in our old Chevy with the two older boys, then four and seven. Baby Toby and I luxuriated in a lower berth on the C & O Railroad. I was too excited to sleep and too nervous to read. I gazed at the passing lights and wondered what was ahead.

The transition to New York was swift and confusing. Where to live? Tom, a born go-getter, researched Manhattan, New Jersey, Long Island, Connecticut, Westchester. Too many choices. I took to my bed with psychosomatic flu. He picked Bronxville because of the famous public school and its nearness to the city. "I can get to Grand Central Station in twenty-seven-and-a-half minutes." I laughed at that. He said, "Listen, kiddo, to a New York commuter half a minute equals half an hour." We put all of our money into a white Dutch Colonial with squat pillars in Lawrence Park—worlds away from the apartment in Cincinnati that had reduced me to tears.

Wherever we've lived our church has been important. Tom had been a vestryman at Church of the Advent in Cincinnati. When we moved, we joined Christ Church, Bronxville. It was very Anglican, with incense at mass (communion to us) and a priest named Father Hohly. Too much for my mother. When she visited us she said, "Why not look for something that isn't high church?"

That was the first time Tom stood up to his mother-in-law. "We will stay at Christ Church," he said. "Period." I wish I had told him how much

I admired his strong resistance to an irresistible force, something I seldom achieved. She's still telling me what to do, although she is long gone.

All of the ladies in Christ Church wore hats, so I went to Best & Co. in Westchester to buy one. To my regret I never got into New York City. I took Toby, age three, with me. I tried on berets, broadbrims, but nothing worked. Then I found a cloche of pheasant feathers and gazed in the mirror. Perfect.

I looked around. No Toby. My three-year-old had toddled off while I looked at myself. Panicked, I ran up and down the aisles. "Toby! Toby! Oh God, I've lost my child. I've lost my baby!" Others called, "Toby! Toby!" My stomach churned. How could I be so interested in my face that I lost track of my little boy? Narcissus is the name. Vanity, vanity, all is vanity.

"Is this yours, Madam?" I swirled around. The floorwalker was holding my toddler. Toby was silent but tears rolled down his cheeks. Tears ran down my cheeks. "Forget the hat," I said, a sacrifice that did not ease my guilt.

Toby and I were relieved to get home. Tom listened to my horror story sympathetically but did not grant me absolution. He simply coined an adage. "There's nothing better than finding someone you've lost." Then he added, "But try not to make it a habit."

For the next twenty-three years, our address was to be 5 Paradise Road. Our neighbor, Brendan Gill of the *New Yorker,* called our place "The Pacesetter House of 1922." We loved the quiet, shady lane where Tommy and Tad could play across the street in the "bacon" lot.

One November day in 1950 I got a postcard from "Mose Who Loves Old Clothes." Mose offered "New Money For Old Clothes In A-1 Condition." What a jolly idea. We scurried around collecting a pile of things we thought we no longer needed. Tom refused to part with his Chesterfield with a velvet collar, but I donated a pink satin negligee and my mother's gray squirrel fur piece and muff, only slightly motheaten.

Mose arrived and cast a cold eye on our clothes. Silence. We held our breath. Mose lit a cigar, blew out a column of smoke, and said, "Ten dollars for the lot."

We could hardly believe our good fortune. Flushed with success, we decided to take our tenner and blow it in the city. "We won't take any other money," Tom announced. (That was easy—we didn't have any other money.) "We'll make it a game to find out what one couple can do in New York on ten dollars."

We studied the *Times* theater page and selected the prize-winning play *The Lady's Not for Burning* by Christopher Fry. I waited in a no parking place on Forty-fifth Street while Tom went into the Royale Theater.

He came out beaming. "I got two seats in the front of the balcony."

"Have we enough left for dinner?"

"Sure, tickets were two fifty apiece."

In those halcyon days it was easy to find free parking, even on Saturday night. We left the car on Eighth Avenue and wandered north in a light drizzle. We found a bistro with checked tablecloths and candles in chianti bottles. The *La Boheme* atmosphere looked inexpensive.

We read only the right-hand side of the menu—had to be careful not to eat more than we could pay for. Coq-au-vin came with rice and a green salad. With what we had left, should we order dessert and coffee or have a glass of wine? Decisions, decisions.

Our chic waitress said with a slight sneer, "It's *vin ordinaire*." It wasn't *ordinaire* to us. The total bill for two dinners and wine, tax included, was $4.75.

Tom said, "We only have twenty-five cents left. What will I give the waitress? I can't tip her a quarter." This was before credit cards. He called, "Mademoiselle!"

She sauntered over, a glum-faced brunette in a tight black dress. Tom smiled at her. "I'm afraid I don't know your name."

"Yvonne."

"Yvonne," his voice was confidential, "I have to tell you something embarrassing. We are out of money."

Rolling her eyes, Yvonne said, "*Tant pis.*"

Tom took her hand. "I promise I will come back Monday with your tip." She did not smile back. "Will you trust me until then? I work at the *Times* on West Forty-fourth Street."

Yvonne shrugged and walked away. Not a big hit.

We ran through rain to the theater. The play was billed as "a comedy in verse." Lots of verse, little comedy. Pamela Brown was a witch who longed to be burned at the stake, and John Gielgud was an adventurer who longed to be hanged. Not a barrel of laughs. They spouted Christopher Fry's poetry at top speed, which was impossible to follow, at least from the balcony.

But there was one actor whose every syllable resonated to the rafters, a young man we had never heard of named Richard Burton. We decided Burton was worth the whole $2.50.

We headed home in the Studebaker. We had bought two Hershey bars for dessert and still had a nickel left. I crowed, "What a good time you can have in New York City on ten dollars."

"Omigod."

"What's wrong?"

"We forgot the tolls." In those pre–Major Deegan Parkway days, you had to pay ten cents on the Henry Hudson Bridge and ten cents on the Saw Mill Parkway.

"Maybe the toll takers will trust us," I said hopefully.

"Not bloody likely. We'll have to go home the back way, through Yonkers."

It was a long, long trip in pelting rain. On a dark street in the dark town of Yonkers, Tom moaned again, "Omigod!"

"What's wrong now?"

"We're out of gas."

Chug, chug, chug. Stop.

"How much gas can you get for a nickel?" I asked. He didn't laugh. In those days friendly policemen roamed the streets. Almost immediately, an Irish face appeared at the window. "What with the wind and the weather, why would you be stopping at this time of night?"

"Officer," Tom said, "we're smack out of gas."

The cop chuckled. "No problem. I'll fetch you a can full in a trice." (What's a trice? I still don't know.)

"There—is—just—one—other—problem," Tom said slowly. "We're also out of money."

The Irish cop threw back his head and laughed. "You kids." He pulled out a dollar bill and handed it to Tom. "You can return this to Paddy O'Malley any time you get round to it."

On Monday, Tom took Yvonne sixty cents. He spoiled our New-York-on-$10 story, but he made Yvonne smile. When he took the dollar to Paddy, he was already smiling.

As Garbo used to say in that husky voice, "Dose ver de daze."

Bronxville was a square mile filled with conservatives. But the Bronxville School was surprisingly progressive, exciting, beloved by the children, and most of the parents. The principal, Miss Julia Ann Markham, was a dynamo who took the children's side in every discussion. One day she stopped Tom and me on the street, looked us in the eye, and asked, "Are you worthy of your children?" Of course not. Who is?

Our kids learned about sex in science class. The teacher told them that if their chosen animal did not reproduce, they would not get promoted to eighth grade. She introduced the topic by letting the boys and girls watch a pair of gerbils mate. All gathered round, eager to see what would happen when the male gerbil was placed in the female's cage. I don't think the teacher anticipated the results.

What happened was—as the children watched open-mouthed—the female ate the male. When Tom heard that, he said, "Lotsa luck to the psychiatrists who try to straighten those kids out."

The most sexually sophisticated youngsters in our neighborhood were the seven Gills. They talked a good game—casually reporting who was sleeping with whom at the *New Yorker*—but when young Rosemary Gill came to see our youngest, Russell, just born, she exclaimed, "What a cute baby! Is it going to be a girl or a boy?"

Brendan Gill believed in the good neighbor policy. One night when Tom was working late, he called to ask me to go to the Village to see *The Threepenny Opera*. I called a sitter, got all dolled up, and headed for Big City excitement. The show was as good as Brendan said it would be, with Jerry Orbach over the top as Mack the Knife. We stopped at P. J. Clark's for a beer and headed home.

This was before Hollywood morality. Ours was an innocent evening, unless you happened to be infested with "the green-eyed monster." When we got to the toll booth, the attendant leaned into the car, "You Mr. Gill?" Startled, Brendan said, "I'm Gill. Why? Is something wrong?"

"A Mr. Campion telephoned. He's looking for his wife. Is she with you?" Brendan was stunned. I slid down in the seat, wanting to hide. I couldn't believe it. Here I was, trying to be sophisticated, and Tom had tracked me down. I felt guilty—but what had I done?

Tom was waiting on the sidewalk when we drove up. He was angry—and relieved that I was okay. I was embarrassed—and flattered. Brendan Gill, perhaps for the first time in his life, was flabbergasted. He was also consumed with curiosity. "How in God's name did you get hold of the right toll booth?"

Tom, the Can Do Kid, laughed in spite of himself, "I just called them all."

❧ 18. From Magazine Article to Movie Contract

One summer afternoon Tom, my brother Fred, and I were sitting on our porch listening to Red tell Marty Maher stories. We laughed as though we'd never heard them before. Sergeant Maher—the Mr. Chips of the Military Academy—came to West Point from Ireland in 1896 and was successively a mess hall waiter, swimming instructor, gym custodian, general factotum, and greeter. An honorary member of the classes of 1912, 1926, and 1928, he was famous for his expertise in the rearing of future generals.

"One June Week," Red said, "a new second lieutenant invited Marty to have a graduation drink. After a couple of snorts, the shavetail said, 'I don't make a habit of drinking with enlisted men.' Marty has perfect timing. He took a long swig, then said, 'Me bye, to tell the truth, you are the lowest-ranking man I ever drank with.'"

Fred jumped to his feet. "By God, Red, you've got to write about Marty. He is an original. Marty Maher's life would make a great book, a great movie."

Red shook his head. "I can't. They put out an order that officers serving at the Military Academy can't earn money anywhere else."

"That's the dumbest thing I ever heard," said Tom. Sometimes our Harvard fellow had trouble with military logic.

Red got the bad end of another edict. In those days, anyone who lost a limb was forced to retire. His military career ended after the invasion of Normandy. This was hard for Colonel Red Reeder to accept, but West Point refused to give him up. They brought him back to the academy as an instructor and coach.

Both brothers zeroed in on me. "You have to do it, Nardi. You majored in English." I had never published anything, but I'd been conditioned, like Pavlov's dog, to do what my brothers told me. "I'll give it a try, but you have to help, Red."

"Help" he wasn't; co-author he was—and a brilliant one. Red was the source of all the best Marty Maher stories (except those Marty told himself). Red actually wrote half of the book. It was fun, but having a silent co-author was not. I'd never do that again. As time went by, undeserved credit sent my guilt-count zooming.

Red and I came up with a feature story about Marty. Red wrote the news hook: "A portrait of Sgt. Martin Maher, United States Army (Ret.), presented to the United States Military Academy, the anonymous gift of several retired graduates, was unveiled last Thursday. The portrait, which hangs in the cadet gymnasium, is arresting because the artist, Charles L. Wrenn, has caught the half-leprechaun, half-scamp character of his subject. But its real significance is as an example of the way the so-called caste system works at West Point."

Of course, the whole event was masterminded by Red. He dreamed up the idea of saluting Marty's fifty years at West Point with a portrait. He raised the money for it and he "found" the portrait painter, a well-known artist who just happened to be our cousin Charlie Wrenn.

Where to market our piece? That was the question.

Red: "I like to start at the top. How about *The New York Times Magazine?*"

Tom: "The editor, Lester Markel, is a friend of mine."

In those days the *Times Magazine* was full of thinkpieces by double domes like H. G. Wells and Barbara Tuchman. Red said they needed to lighten up. Tom provided the entré—a little influence goes a long way— but no one swayed Mr. Markel; he was law unto himself. Tom said everybody at the paper was afraid of him.

I didn't know articles should be mailed in, so I went to see Mr. Markel with ours in my hot little hand. Scared and ignorant (a bad combo), I said, "Could you read it right now?"

"*What?*"

I can't believe I said, "If you don't want it, I'm going to take it over to the *Herald Tribune*."

He actually read it that day and told me to come back later. "You can write," he said.

"Would you put that in writing? I want to show my husband." When he read the note, Tom laughed. "You said the right thing. Lester hates the *Trib*."

"West Point Salutes a Salty Sergeant" occupied a full page in the February 19, 1950, *Times Magazine*. Marty was overwhelmed. So were we. Our joy—and amazement—knew no bounds.

Two weeks later a voice on our phone said, "This is Louis Ruppel, the editor of *Collier's Magazine*. I want you to do an article for us about Marty Maher and his famous cadets."

I thought it was one of my jokester friends, maybe even my jokester husband. I answered, "Yes, and I am Queen Marie of Romania." Fortunately, Louis Ruppel had a sense of humor.

Red and I set to work unearthing more Marty stories. How Marty left Ireland at seventeen with the British cops hot on his trail, how he had an arranged marriage to Mary O'Donnell, an Irish maid on the post, how he taught generations of cadets to swim but couldn't swim a stroke. That fall *Collier's* published "The Old Sergeant."

Tom said, "Why don't you two go on and do a book?" We drew up a chapter by chapter outline that, with the two articles, landed us a contract with David McKay Co. (now deservedly extinct).

We were before tape recorders. Marty would propel his old Ford flivver from West Point to Bronxville for "working" visits. He'd settle on our sofa with a glass of Bushmill's Irish whisky to enjoy his hobby: talking. Tom adored him and so did our boys, Tom, eight, Tad, five, and Toby, two. No other guest came with his toothbrush in a vest pocket, high-buttoned shoes, long johns instead of pajamas—and knew the "Little People" personally. The boys were delighted to learn that Irish fairies did bad things.

Our "as told to" book was more "as told to" than most. Marty could read headlines and grocery lists, but actual book reading, no. Every time Red tried reading the manuscript to him, Marty fell asleep. "Mother of God, Red," he complained, "why should I listen to that stuff? Hell, I lived it."

Basically, I wrote the first half of the book, reading it aloud to Tom. "You are wonderfully patient." I said. "Aren't you getting sick of this stuff?"

"I enjoy what you write," he said, and he meant it.

Red wrote the second half. We edited and re-edited each other's stuff until it blended. Red cured me of exclamation marks and I cured him of the word "very." Unlike some collaborators, we still liked each other at the end. The book was completed in the maternity ward of the Bronxville Hospital, after the birth of Cissa. Tom asked, "Which is easier, a baby or a book?" I passed.

At Tom's suggestion, we had a family contest for best book title. Tommy won a baseball mitt by coming up with *Bringing Up the Brass*. Red and I differed over which of Marty's "byes" we'd ask to write our introduction. I wanted General MacArthur, but Red preferred the president of Columbia University. He said General Eisenhower was younger and might have a bigger future. Marty dictated a letter to his old friend Ike that ended, "P.S. How's your bad knee?" The general responded with gusto: "For Sergeant Marty Maher I am breaking a long-standing and inflexible policy by writing this little foreword to his book . . ."

Brendan Gill gave *Bringing Up the Brass* a big boost in *The New York Times Book Review*. "Here is a marvelous old man, bold and funny and full of sap . . . His voice roars and sings in your ears; his big hands, broken and tattooed, gather you in; you are embraced, beguiled, made drunk on talk of games and ghosts and good times not yet over."

The excitement snowballed. We were all giddy when our agent called to say Columbia Pictures wanted to buy our book for a movie. They offered not very much money. Tom said, "At Harvard Business School they taught us to say no to the first offer." Months of silence. It looked like, thanks to Tom, we'd lost our Big Chance. He stood his ground. "They're playing you like marlins. They'll be back." When they finally came back with another mini-offer, Red and I jumped at it. Tom just shook his head.

Homage to our new Chandler. Fred, Nardi, Red, Fort Leavenworth, Kansas, 1920.

Military formality: family Christmas portrait, 1928. (*Back*) 1st Lt. Charles Summerall, Mother, 2d Lt. Red Reeder. (*Front*) Julia Reeder Summerall, Colonel Reeder, Army Brat, Midshipman Fred Reeder.

All the women in Panama
dance the Pollera during
Carnival, 1933.

The Goon Girls—Jane Tracy, Patty Dyar, and NRC—return
from Dartmouth Winter Carnival, 1937. (Tracy introduced Nardi
to Tom Campion.)

SHE KNOWS HER MEN

NARCISSA 'NARDI' REEDER
Wellesley senior who gets tired, sleeps to win sophisticate crown

MOST SOPHISTICATED
Wellesley Girl Tells Secret

The way to be sophisticated is to get very tired and then walk around half asleep.

Or so, at least, says Narcissa "Nardi" Reeder, recently voted the most sophisticated Wellesley senior by classmates in a graduation poll.

Nardi can think of no other explanation for what she laughingly calls her "success."

"I don't drink hard liquor—only a little wine and beer—never smoke, and don't go out with anybody I don't know," she says, "so being tired is the only reason I can see. And the funny part is that I get tired from writing and studying and exercising and that sort of thing. I only go out occasionally."

But "occasionally," according to Nardi's classmates, is after all pretty often.

"Have I known many men?" she counters. "Oh yes, I've known a few."

She explains gaily that she knows "just about everybody in the army." Her father is an officer now sta- tioned at Fort Monroe, Va.

"But you can't learn much from cadets," Nardi says. "They are mostly just nice boys who don't know everything."

A large part of Nardi's success as a sophisticate, her classmates say, is due to her uncanny skill in make-up. She recently was head of the make-up committee of the Wellesley Barnswallows, student drama group, and achieved such fame there that she has received a job with a noted fashion concern.

The age of innocence—
engagement the old-fashioned
way. Phoebus, Virginia,
Easter, 1941.

"I do." Casemate Club, Fort Monroe, Virginia, July 5, 1941.

Mother and Wonder Baby No. 1 sunbathing. Zumstein Avenue, Cincinnati, Ohio, 1943.

Falling in love with Switzerland on our first trip abroad together. Zermatt, 1953.

"At last, a girl!" Cissa reading her mother's article in *American Artist* magazine on artist Nancy Ellen Craig, who painted Cissa's portrait. Bronxville, New York, 1954. PHOTOGRAPH CREDIT: Patricia Coughlan

Ready to elope again at eighty. My mother, Blacksburg, Virginia, 1959.

Celebrating the publication of
*Patrick Henry, Firebrand of the
Revolution.* Williamsburg,
Virginia, 1961.

Beach family Campion. (*Back*) Tad, the 'rents, Tommy; (*Front*) Toby, Russell, Firecracker, Cissa. Amagansett, New York, 1962. PHOTOGRAPH CREDIT: Frances Gill

Revisiting my birthplace. Fort Kamehameha, Hawaii, 1969.

President of Israel instructing NRC, president of Wellesley College Alumnae Association. Golda Meir came from Israel to celebrate Wellesley's centennial and receive an honorary degree, May 28, 1976.

NRC picked up speed when Bin Lewis, publisher of the *Valley News*, suggested she write a column. The first "Everyday Matters" appeared April 4, 1987—and it's still going. PHOTOGRAPH CREDIT: Donald H. Smith

The dance of life. Dartmouth, 1990. PHOTOGRAPH CREDIT: Nancy Wasserman

I fell for Bill Clinton at the reception after Dartmouth College awarded him an honorary degree. June 11, 1995, PHOTOGRAPH CREDIT: Elizabeth Crory

In Hillary's White House office, NRC with HRC: "To Nardi Reeder Campion with affection and respect from her fellow Wellesley alum—Hillary Rodham Clinton 1993." HRC treasures this watercolor that belonged to Eleanor Roosevelt.

The original Set: Russell, Cissa, Toby, Mater, Tommy, Tad, Pater. Thanksgiving 1998.
PHOTOGRAPH CREDIT: Medora Hebert

"Grandchildren are the real payoff." Missing Tom at wedding of Amy Thomas and
Peter Campion. Ned, Ashley, NRC, B&G, Maddy, Grady, Berit, Manolo, and Iris.
Strafford, Vermont, August 3, 2002. PHOTOGRAPH CREDIT: Peggy Campion

At Hemingway Memorial, Sun Valley, Idaho. "Above the hills/The high blue windless skies . . ./Now he will be a part of them forever." PHOTOGRAPH CREDIT: Ashley Campion

How could we know that the eccentric director John Ford, winner of four Academy Awards, had fallen in love with our book? Ford loved it because Marty reminded him of his Irish father, a yarn-spinning bartender.

Babes in the Holly Woods, we should have listened to Tom. Columbia would eventually spend over four million dollars on the movie, an astronomical amount in the early fifties. Had we known enough to hold out, we might have divvied up a wad, but our so-called agent was on Harry Cohn's side. (Harry Cohn *was* Columbia Pictures.) We happily signed for ten thousand dollars. Even in 1950, that was a pittance. Later, when my mother eloped (yes, eloped), we were able to give the bride and groom a honeymoon trip to London and Paris on the *Q.E. One.* That was fun.

Another compensation was seeing the book come to life with an all-star cast, brilliantly directed. John Ford, creator of such classics as *The Grapes of Wrath* and *The Quiet Man,* was a crotchety genius. The sentimental script was "creative fact." It invented a baby who died (Marty and Mary O'Donnell had no children); an adopted son; and an emotional World War I send-off from the West Point railroad station. The announcement in Cadet Chapel of the attack at Pearl Harbor is pure hokum.

You can't make a West Point film without official cooperation. Columbia pictures liked our title, but the Department of the Army did not. They said "brass" was pejorative. The decision went up to the army chief of staff, Red's childhood buddy General Matthew Ridgway. Tom said, "He'll reverse the decision." He read aloud General Ridgway's endorsement on the jacket of *Bringing Up the Brass:* "My lasting impression of Marty is not just of humorous anecdotes nor of escapades, of which there are many, but of the solid gold of his heart."

This time Tom was wrong. Gold was in but brass was o-u-t. Columbia's second choice was *The Long Gray Line.* Never mind that a poll showed people thought *The Long Gray Line* was a movie about (1) a prison, (2) the Confederacy, (3) a bus company. Tom said, "Maybe they could call it *Bringing Up What Used to Be the Brass.*"

When asked what directors appealed to him most, Orson Welles famously said: "The old masters . . . by which I mean John Ford, John

Ford, and John Ford." A riveting storyteller and a past master at framing scenes, Ford inspired Stephen Spielberg. Critics said they both suffered from the same weakness: oversentimentalizing.

John Ford, born John Martin Feeney, was the tenth child of Irish Catholic immigrants. He grew up in Cape Elizabeth, Maine. During World War II, he was in the navy. When he met Red, he did a double take. "Where were you when the German shell smashed your leg?" Red was too taken aback to answer. Ford went on, "It was by a convent wall in Normandy, wasn't it?"

"That's right. How did you know?"

"I'm the guy that got you the grapefruit juice."

"You did what?"

"On D-Day plus five I was evacuating wounded," Ford said. "I took one look at you and thought, this man is finished. The best thing I can do for an Irish mug like that is find his rosary. I started going through your pockets. You stirred from your coma and said, 'I'm no fisheater. Get me some grapefruit juice.' I got it, thinking that would be the end of you. Ten years later I walk into a room and find you here at West Point." To celebrate their reunion, John Ford and Red Reeder had a grapefruit cocktail and, to the dismay of Hotel Thayer, threw their glasses into the fireplace.

Ford wanted "the man I rescued in Normandy" in the movie. In the outdoor ceremony at Trophy Point, Colonel Red Reeder swears in the new cadets. But Red's voice didn't suit Ford, the perfectionist, so he had a deeper voice dubbed in. Years later Tad called us excitedly from Paris. "Guess what. We're watching *The Long Gray Line* on TV and Unk is swearing in plebes in French."

A busy Boswell, Red recorded Marty's befuddled reaction to watching his life in the movies. "First Mr. Ford introduced me to myself. I am Tyrone Power, a handsome Irish laddie with flashing black eyes and a back straighter than half the cadets. Ty is a broth of a boy, but in me movie he ages faster than whisky. My dear Mary is a beautiful colleen, Miss Maureen O'Hara. Maureen's Irish purr of a voice makes my heart miss like the engine in my car. Ward Bond, with his bristle mustache and tight blue uniform, is so close to my old boss I choked up. 'There's dead men walkin' the post tonight,' says I, and headed for Cohen's where they keep the spirits bottled up."

Marty was stunned when they picked an early 1900s gingerbread cottage near the Hudson to be Marty and Mary's home. "That's Dr. Appleton's house!" Marty cried out. "We never lived in such a grand place, Red. You can't trust movies. They've got me painting cannon balls at Trophy Point, doing plumbing on the post—*plumbing*—and going to the White House to see Ike—all phony baloney."

"Marty," Red said, "you have to be ready. These folks would redo George Washington."

"Everything in this movie is wrong as hell, Red," Marty complained. "I've just been up to the cemetery. It's more gussied up than Memorial Day—Mr. Ford ordered fresh flowers on all graves. They were burying my imaginary baby. Glory be to God, Mary and I never had any children. Where in tarnation did they get that baby they're burying, that's what I want to know."

The Long Gray Line ends with a flourish. White-haired Marty stands with the superintendent taking the review as the Corp of Cadets marches past in honor of his retirement, the West Point band booming forth "The Wearing of the Green" and "The West Point March."

Marty's final verdict on the film about his life was upbeat. "The first time I saw *The Long Gray Line* I almost collapsed. Holy cow, Mr. Ford promoted me to master sergeant. I've only been able to see the movie nine times but hope to go more often. It's a three-handkerchief weeper. Every time I see the show I get better."

The movie may have made Marty Maher immortal, but he never got a big head. "What's all the shoutin' about?" Marty asked. "All I ever done was try to help people."

❀ 19. My Husband the Jokester

"Are you sure this is the right night for the party?" Tom asked one October evening in the fifties as we donned our evening clothes.

"Have I ever made a calendar mistake?" I asked. He grinned and nodded like Harpo Marx.

Life with Tom, like life with anyone, had its ups and downs—only with him it was mostly ups. He was full of fun and it was impossible not to laugh with him. He loved to dream up practical jokes and could make a game out of anything.

To shorten car trips he invented the Life Saver Game. The five kids popped a Life Saver into their mouths. Blissful quiet. The winner: the one whose unbroken Life Saver lasted longest. The prize: another Life Saver, of course.

He'd bet on anything. Before he cooked lobsters, he put them on the floor so we could bet on whose lobster would make it across the linoleum first. Years later he and I got into an argument about which of two Dartmouth College professors was taller. That afternoon, I found a message on our answering machine: "My tall man is taller than your tall man. Hans Penner is 6′ 8½″. Roger Soderburg is only 6′ 8″. You owe me five dollars." You had to pay up pronto; his motto was "Fast pay makes fast friends." When Lord and Taylor sent a bill to Paradise Road as "5 Pair of Dice Road," Tad said, "Your reputation is spreading, Dad."

He won a lot of money from me, but I won most of it back when Nixon resigned. Tom had started the ball rolling a year before with, "I bet you five dollars Nixon won't go." We upped it almost daily from there. In the end he had to fork over five hundred dollars, our biggest bet ever.

Once I asked, "How come you always have time to play games but so little time for our so-called budget?"

"Games are a way to come closer to somebody; budgets are the opposite."

Tom went in for all games, except slapjack and old maid (overexposure with small children). He played a serious game of chess but I gave that up. I couldn't get the hang of those little horses jumping sideways. On our honeymoon he taught me backgammon (among other things). He and I lived together from 1941 to 2000. That's 3,068 weeks. A conservative average might be four games a week. We played approximately 12,272 games of backgammon. Of course we played for money, but nobody got rich.

Kids loved his riddle collection. How do you make pants last? Sew the coat and vest first. What did the hen say when she laid a square egg? Ouch. Why are hurricanes named after women? Because they're not himicanes. What does N stand for on the helmets of Nebraska football players? Knowledge.

Tom was at his best on long jaunts in the car. ("Just remember, kids, when I yell at you on this trip I don't mean it.") He invented License Plate Poker, which is too complicated to explain. And he perfected Find All Fifty. On one trip, it took him only two days to find a license from every state in the Union. His secret: "Study the backs of trucks."

Memory games were mother's milk to him. He'd start, "I packed my grandmother's suitcase and in it I put an apple, a baboon, a clarinet." He could zip through to "z" with nary a glitch.

He always had time for games with grandchildren. I excelled at Parcheesi but Tom hated "bored" games. He craved action, as in jacks, marbles, kites, touch football. He thought he was good at Memory—you remember, spread fifty-two cards face down and try to turn up pairs. But after six-year-old Maddy creamed him he told me, "You can forget Memory."

Best of all he loved a practical joke. If it required dressing up, so much the better. When Cissa was in Bronxville High, she got a Christmas job selling ladies' pocketbooks at a nearby Lord and Taylor's. Tom could hardly wait to go shopping. He disguised himself with a gray wig, a gray felt hat, and his long black Chesterfield coat, a relic of the thirties. Hobbling up to Cissa's counter on a cane, he addressed the pretty young clerk in a cranky voice. "Little lady, whatcha want for this purse?" He knocked three purses to the floor and shoved them with his cane.

Cissa was undone. She ran for the supervisor. What to do with such a freak? When he uncovered his disguise, she yelled *"Dad!"* Tom was so carried away with his new persona that when he got home he toddled around the neighborhood, scaring the children.

On that October evening in the fifties, we were dressing up for a black-tie party. Our neighbors the Ketchums had invited us to a dinner in honor of the cofounders of *American Heritage Magazine.* We felt flattered to be included. We got all dolled up in tuxedo and black velvet and strolled from Paradise Road to Plateau Circle, looking like the cat's pajamas. We thought.

Barbara answered the door, smiling graciously. She wasn't dressed up at all. When she saw us her jaw dropped. "Oh dear," she said. "The party is tomorrow night. But you look beautiful. Come in and have coffee and dessert with us."

The next night we got all dolled up in tuxedo and black velvet and strolled from Paradise Road to Plateau Circle, feeling only slightly stupid. "Hey, Mr. Campion," called Jimmy Turner, age five, "where's your wig?" Tom beamed, basking in his neighborhood fame.

The dinner was lavish, fifties style. Starched white linen, scarlet roses in silver vases, candles, crystal, bone china. Oysters, roast lamb, fresh asparagus, and for dessert, what tasted like straight whipped cream. At each seat, placecards in silver holders stood next to silver cups of cigarettes. All of us smoked because we were so sophisticated.

The next day Tom said to me, "Let's put on our evening clothes and go to the Ketchum's." Again we got all dolled up in tuxedo and black velvet and strolled from Paradise Road to Plateau Circle, now known as Dejavuville. Barbara answered the door. Her grin would have melted the polar icecap. Without missing a beat she said, "We were just saying we hadn't seen you since yesterday. Dick!" she called. "The Campions are here again."

On the way home Tom said, "That was my kind of practical joke. We amused ourselves; we surprised our friends; nobody got hurt; and I even got to dress up."

❧ 20. Father Knows Best?

A good father needs three things: a sense of humor, unlimited energy, and a feeling for what's important. Tom had all three. For me, raising kids was learning by doing. It came naturally to Tom.

One winter when he was reading Catherine Drinker Bowen's *Yankee from Olympus,* he reported, "Justice Holmes said, 'A true democracy creates opportunities for everyone to grow.' Maybe we don't have enough democracy around here."

"Weren't you taught that father and mother know best?"

"Of course, but these kids have a different mindset. I think we ought to give them more say. Why don't we hold a family meeting every month and let the kids bring up issues that bother them." It seemed a splendid suggestion. The kids, who were growing up in a benign dictatorship, jumped at the suggestion.

Six of us gathered around the dining room table for the first meeting. I was holding baby Cissa on my lap. (Russell wasn't even a gleam in his father's eye.)

"'Now sits anticipation in the air.' *Henry the Fifth*," Tom said.

"Nothing like starting on a high plane," I said.

He began with a hot topic: trash removal. Could the children take more responsibility for cleaning up? All eyes turned to Toby. The job of emptying the garbage had descended to number three, who was terrible at it. He was so forgetful that one night his exasperated father left a plastic bag full of garbage on his bed. We all agreed we'd try to help Toby improve.

I moved that everyone take Firecracker, our cocker spaniel, out more often. She peed on the dining room rug so regularly it was starting to smell. Tom seconded and the motion carried. Tommy moved that his siblings be required to keep quiet on Saturdays so he could sleep. There were no seconds so the motion was tabled.

The discussion period was more like it. Tad said Toby played his trumpet so loud he couldn't study. Toby asked plaintively, "Can't somebody stop Cissa from getting into my stuff? She goes up my bookshelves like a ladder."

After the meeting adjourned, the pleased father turned to the pleased mother. "Let's go for a walk, I feel good. I think we're onto something."

The next family meeting was short and snappy. Numero Uno kicked it off. "This is a democracy, right?" Tommy said.

"Indeed it is," his father replied. "Everyone is created equal." Pinkie, our live-in saint who was a second mother to us all, stood in the doorway rolling her eyes.

Tommy pounced. "I move that all allowances be tripled."

Tad: "I second it."

Toby: "I third it."

Before Tom or I could react to the mutiny, Tommy said, "I move the meeting is adjourned."

Toby and Tad shouted, "Second!" They all jumped up and ran outside. That was it, the meeting was over.

I was seething. I looked up at Tom. He stared blankly, shocked. Then he shrugged holding his hands upward a la Woody Allen, and started to laugh. Soon I was laughing, too. Tom's humor was a valuable solvent, yet again.

That was our last family meeting.

As the kids grew up, Tom drummed into them one lesson about money: "You can *not* solve money problems with money," he used to say to them. "If you go broke, it's bad planning." Tad and Toby got fifty cents a week; Tommy had been promoted to seventy-five cents. "If you want more money," he told them, "I'll help you get a job." They took it to heart. Our kids always worked.

Tad went door-to-door selling subscriptions. He kept winning the same bonus prize. Flimsy folding grills were stacked up in our garage; even the Salvation Army wouldn't take them. Tom said, "It's clear what Tad's going to be. He's a born salesman."

Russell, big for his age, excelled as a lifeguard. Cissa, after years of practicing on baby Russell, became a sought-after babysitter (twenty-five cents an hour). Toby played trumpet in several bands, but for love, not money. Tom said, "I think the profit motive was left out of Toby."

The big moneymaker was Tommy. Starting in sixth grade, he delivered Sunday newspapers for a couple of tough characters named Harold and Milton. He had to be at work by four A.M. to sort the papers, assemble the sections, and deliver the heavy bundles. He did it until he went away to school, amassing a small fortune and a coffee dependence.

His father was impressed. "Tommy's going to be a mogul." When he left for Andover, Tommy passed his job on to Tad. Tad was delighted to quit sales and join Harold and Milton. He not only earned big bucks; he earned the respect of big brother.

Early one Sunday morning, our phone jangled. I could hear Harold shouting, "Where the hell is Tad?"

"I dunno," Tom mumbled, staggering out of bed. He called back. "Tad is sick. He has a fever."

Harold yelled louder. "That's too God-damned bad. What am I supposed to do with Tad's route?"

Tom hesitated, just for a second. Then he said, "I have to get dressed. It'll take me fifteen minutes to get there."

I sat bolt upright. "You're not going down there in the dark to deliver Tad's papers?"

"Yes I am."

"I can't believe that. You're an executive at *The New York Times*. You can't deliver the Sunday paper." He stopped tying his sneaker and looked me in the eye.

"How will Tad feel if he's fired from the job his older brother got for him? "

That shut me up. When the front door closed, I got out of bed and made coffee. Sleep was impossible. I checked on Tad, dispensing my cure-all, aspirin, and sat down to worry. It's fine to put the kids first, but at the expense of your health? Lifting heavy bundles could give a man Tom's age a hernia, or worse.

Seven o'clock. Eight o'clock. Where was he? At Lawrence Hospital? It was 8:30 when a haggard Tom dragged in, holding both palms against his back.

"How could I ever have kidded Tommy about being overpaid? I'm going to bed."

"Are you all right?"

He grinned. "Better than all right. Harold told me I done good."

Tom knew how to prioritize. Family came first. His job was right up there, though. Since he assumed we were safe at home, he thought nothing of working late at the *Times*. One night the children and I finished our supper early. The setting sun was still glinting through the spring-green of an April afternoon. Toby, six, said, "Let's all go for a ride."

"Good idea," I exclaimed. Anything to promote togetherness among the quarrelsome crew. Tommy, Tad, Toby, and little Cissa piled into "Woody," our '49 Ford station wagon, for a spin around Lawrence Park. We drove slowly through the narrow, winding roads. Tulips were in bloom and white dogwood laced the woods. "My," I said, "aren't we lucky?" No answer. Not kid talk.

As we were heading home I had a bad idea. Trying to please Tommy, who at twelve barely tolerated the rest of us, I said, "Would you like to drive the car into the garage?"

Tommy almost smiled. "That'd be okay."

As we changed seats, I said, "There's nothing to it, Tommy. Push the pedal, pull this lever back, and step on the gas pedal slowly. Just go straight ahead." The other three kids were ominously quiet. Maybe I had more faith in older brother than they did. Tommy put his foot on the accelerator and the car bucked. Then it shot forward. I guess I should have instructed him in how to stop.

CRASH! We drove straight through the stucco wall of the garage. I yanked on the emergency brake. The boys in the back seat yelled. Cissa screamed and kept on screaming. All I could say was, "My God!" I switched off the engine.

Tommy's face was a study in woe. "You couldn't help it," I gasped. "It's my fault." No reply. He had lost the power of speech. I felt sick all over.

We had taken out a corner of the garage, so part of the peaked roof was hanging down. The station wagon, constructed of heavy duty steel, was just scraped. All it would need was a paint job. All Tommy and I needed was a total remake.

It wasn't hard to get the kids into their nice safe beds. I kissed each one good night with what I hoped were soothing words. Tommy turned his head away. Years later he confessed, "I didn't go to school for two days. I was too embarrassed. I hid in our fort and read *Mad* magazines. When I went back, I got a surprise. The kids thought I was totally cool."

I was the one who needed soothing. I went downstairs and dialed the *Times*. They located Tom in the noisy composing room. I opened my mouth to tell him what happened—and started to cry. I couldn't say a thing.

"What's the matter? Why are you crying? What's happened?"

"I've done something terrible," I sobbed.

"*What?*"

"It's so terrible, I can't even tell you."

"For God's sake, TELL ME."

"I was trying to teach Tommy to drive—and—and we went through the garage."

"What do you mean, you went through the garage?"

"I mean we drove into the garage and came out the other side."

Silence. A long silence, punctuated by my blubbering.

"Something's wrong with this phone. I thought you said you drove through the end of the garage."

"We did. Tommy was driving, but it was my idea. It's *awful.*" I began to cry louder. "It's my fault and Tommy feels so guilty."

"Was anybody hurt?"

"No."

"What about the car?"

"Okay—I think. I was able to back it out, but the garage is teetering."

"It's only the *garage?* Is that all?"

"Yes," I whispered, "but . . . but . . ."

"I thought somebody was dead. Who needs a garage?"

I took a deep breath.

"Where are the kids now?"

"They wanted to go to bed."

"I guess. Are you all right?"

I began to laugh.

He said, "Don't get hysterical."

"It's so terrible," I sobbed, laughing, "and so funny."

Suddenly he was laughing, too. "Listen," he said, "stop crying. Bad things happen. On a scale of one to ten, driving through the end of the garage is about five. Get some hot tea. Try to relax, I'll be right home."

He should have bawled me out. He never did. All he said was, "It shook me up to walk up our driveway and see the moon shining through the end of the garage."

P.S. Tom's predictions were way off. Tommy became a lawyer/professor; Tad, a physician/editor; Toby, a chiropractor/screenwriter; Cissa, a pianist/composer. Russell became the mogul.

❧ 21. Blizzard Baby

My brother Fred said, "You're not going to stuff your house with boys trying to get a girl, are you?"

We did.

Tommy was nine, Tad, six, and Toby, three, when Cissa was born. A girl at last! She got a huge welcome. Tom and I were so overboard about the change of pace I was afraid we might turn our three boys away from girls altogether.

We didn't.

About this time, Betty and Bob Saudek introduced us to Great Spruce Head, a Shangri-la island five miles out in Penobscot Bay. As Captain Jimmy Quinn steered his mail boat out of Stonington harbor, the only passengers were six Campions. We floated into a true blue world—the sky, the sea, even the sunshine. "You live in a paradise, Cap'n," Tom said.

"Ayuh."

That was their entire conversation, but they became friends. In Maine, communication does not depend on words.

We fell in love with Great Spruce Head Island. It's been in the Porter family since 1912, when the patriarch, James Porter, sold part of downtown Chicago and bought the island.

The Porters built seven houses on their isolated 250 acres, including two for caretaker/farmers. When we went there in the fifties, the Big House was occupied by Fairfield Porter, the artist. Eliot Porter, the photographer, had built his own house, as had his brother John, our kids' seventh grade master teacher at the Bronxville public school. John Porter, tennis fiend, had built a court hidden in the woods. Our tennis games were as serious as they were improbable.

Fairfield's unsold paintings were stacked on the porch. "Nobody will buy these," he told us glumly. "They're too large." Why, oh why, didn't we buy one? They now sell in five figures and hang in the Metropolitan Museum.

Eliot was a physician who did research at Harvard Medical School, but his true love was photography. We used to laugh at the way he would spend hours squatting on the beach, waiting for sunlight to strike orange lichen on gray rocks so he could snap a picture. A few years later, he abandoned medicine and became one of America's great nature photographers. His books *Summer Island* and *In Wildness Is the Preservation of the World* were conceived on Great Spruce Head Island.

Not everybody there was creative. Some of us went to loaf and restore our souls. Stretching out his long legs, Tom said, "On this island you don't have to do, you can just be." We were relaxing over hot clam broth on the cool screened porch. The kids had charged off to explore and the quiet was exquisite. "Listen," he said, "a cardinal." The clear whistle came again and again. Tom gazed at the sapphire bay and the peaked evergreens of the islands and said, "It doesn't take much to make me happy."

On the Fourth of July, everybody on the island, and friends from other islands, turned out for the annual clambake at the Double Beaches. It was a rip-roaring event featuring verboten fireworks smuggled from Canada.

The fifth of July was our anniversary. How to observe rounding the fifteenth buoy, that was the question. Tom said, "Let's go off by ourselves, just the two of us."

"You mean take the mail boat back to Sunset?" There weren't too many places to go.

"No, dumb-dumb, I'm talking romance. Let's pack a picnic and paddle over to Butter Island and celebrate fifteen years of wedded bliss, more or less."

We had always preferred intimate celebrations. This one turned out to be our most intimate. We picnicked in a secluded grove on deserted Butter Island. It was unusually hot for Maine, and we drank a whole bottle of cold chablis, lifting our glasses for goofy toasts. "Here's to my groomsman Joe Ellis, who hit his head on a toilet and missed the wedding." "Here's to our first car, The Smoker. It was worth more than $100. Maybe $100.75."

Then we fell quiet. Tom put his arm around my waist and pulled me close. A long deep kiss, then slowly, very slowly, he began to unbutton my blouse . . .

Late that afternoon, we were spread out on our plaid blanket, gazing at the sunset gilding the cream-puff clouds. Suddenly Tom began to laugh, hard.

"What's so funny?"

"Our fifth child—let's call it Question Mark—will be able to win the What's Your Earliest Memory game, hands-down. All 'it' has to say is, 'I can remember a hot July picnic—a hidden grove, chicken sandwiches, blueberries, raspberries, and cold chablis. I went with my father and came home with my mother.'"

Question Mark's arrival rivaled his origin. Born two weeks early, instead of being an April Fool, Russell arrived in the middle of a March blizzard that shut down the entire East Coast.

On Tuesday, March 20, 1956 *The New York Times* headline read "13.5-Inch Snow Paralyzes City." Tom got snowed in at the paper. Pinkie, our beloved housekeeper, got snowed in at her home in the Bronx. Enormously pregnant and lethargic, I was snowed in with four children, ages five to fourteen, who were highly excited by the raging snowstorm. By the time they all went to sleep, I was exhausted. At three A.M. I awoke with labor pains. I didn't even try the *Times*. I called our dear friend and next-door neighbor John Allen. "Johnny, can you take me to the hospital?"

He gasped. "I'll be right there."

"Hurry, Johnny."

I was getting too old for this. We had convinced ourselves that every couple needs a child for their old age. I was thirty-nine; Tom was forty. Who says that over the hill you pick up speed? Forget it.

As I was adding a book and a sweater to my already packed bag the phone rang. "The snow is too deep. I can't get the car out of the garage. I called the ambulance."

Paradise Road, a narrow, winding semi-cul-de-sac, was obliterated by snow. Could the ambulance find it? First came the police car, blowing a siren. Then a huge fire truck clanging its bell. Then the ambulance, blowing a louder siren. The only one who woke up was Toby, age eight. "What's happening?"

"I'm going to the hospital to have the baby."

"Okay," he said, heading back to bed. "I'll tell Dad where you are." Ho-hum, I thought.

As the EMTs carried me out on a stretcher, Johnny Allen trudged beside me holding my hand. "I'll stay with the children," he said.

In those days, obstetricians knocked the mothers out. When I came to, Tom was holding my hand. The spicy smell of roses filled the air. "It's a boy." He kissed me and I whiffed cigar. Three cigars were sticking out of his vest pocket. For Tom fatherhood was fun.

"Our kid's already on page one." He held up the *Bronxville Reporter* and read the headline in a booming voice: "Blizzard Baby Born at Lawrence Hospital."

"Now Cissa will have four knights in shining armor," I said sappily.

Tom hooted. "Four bosses is more like it."

Still feeling sentimental I said, "Honey, we'll never have another anniversary like our fifteenth."

"Let us hope. Five is a quorum—or should be."

The nurse brought in a small, sleepy bundle wrapped in a pink blanket. We were stunned into silence by the miracle. For life's big moments there are no words. Our communication was silent but intense. Tom, eyes swimming, called on Shakespeare as usual: "'The child's father so tenderly and entirely loves her.'" Then he added, chuckling, "Lear also called Cordelia 'our joy, although our last.'"

✲ 22. My Pen Pal E. B. White

Reading to children was big in our family, and E. B. White topped the list. Tom's favorite was *Charlotte's Web*, mine *Stuart Little*. I read it to Tommy first, and when Tad turned six I got to read it again. "The best part," Tad remarked, "is when Stuart gets rolled up in the window shade." He sat down and printed a letter to E. B. White at the *New Yorker*.

Dear Mr. White,

  I think "Stuart Little" is great, but I think ice skates made of paper clips is loony.

      Sincerely yours,
      Tad Campion

To Tad's joy, his favorite author replied immediately with a handwritten note.

Dear Tad,

  Thanks for your letter. I'm glad you liked the book about Stuart. I went skating yesterday, but not on paper clips. Got to go down cellar now and tend the furnace, so will say good-by.

      Sincerely yours,
      E. B. White
      North Brooklin, Maine

Mr. White got so many letters about Stuart that eventually his publisher sent out a canned reply: "Are my stories true? No, they are imaginary tales. In real life, a family doesn't have a child that looks like a mouse. But real life is only one kind of life—there is also the life of the imagination."

That year—1953—Tom took me to a balloon-festooned dinner dance given by Anne and Brendan Gill in the huge gym of their "Owl House." I couldn't believe my luck: my dinner partner was E. B. White. He was a thin man with a high forehead, white hair, a darker mustache, pointy eyebrows, and true blue eyes. His shy, boyish manner made him easy to talk with—and laugh with.

He told me he was the sixth and last child of parents who loved children. He grew up in nearby Mount Vernon and went from the local high school to the staggering sophistication of Cornell University. When the music started, Mr. White recalled the time he took a beautiful girl tea-dancing at the Plaza Hotel but was too embarrassed to ask her to dance. He didn't ask me to dance either.

Of course I told him how excited I was when my son got a reply to his letter. "Stuart first appeared to me in a dream," he said, "all complete with his hat, his cane, and his brisk manner."

E. B. had been christened Elwyn Brooks because Jessie Brooks White, his mother, admired the Welsh name Elwyn. He hated it. As a freshman, he was nicknamed Andy after the president of Cornell, Andrew D. (no relation) White, and it stuck.

Tom moved to our table as soon as he could. He was as charmed as I by Mr. White's hesitant, bemused conversation. Unbelievably, E. B. White had started out as copywriter in an ad agency. After Cornell he and a buddy drove across the country in "Hotspur," a Model T flivver. ("We only put the top up once, in North Dakota.") They financed themselves doing odd jobs. ("I won twenty-five dollars in a limerick contest.") One day a waitress spilled soup all over his only suit. He hurried back to his room and wrote up the calamity. The next day he sold the story to the local paper. Peering owlishly at us through spectacles Mr. White said, "That was when I discovered people will pay good money for clearly written accounts of other people's disasters."

After the party I wrote Mr. White a note thanking him for the fun. Like Tad, I received a rapid reply, this one home-typed.

Dear Mrs. Campion:

I had a fine time, too. And I'm not going to tell you why, either. I apologize for my failure to ask you to join me in the attitude of the dance, but I haven't improved any since the days of the Plaza and I thought I would spare you that ordeal.

My impression is that Brendan gives these parties two or three times a week, from the way he acts around the office.

    Sincerely,
    E. B. White

Tom, the *Charlotte's Web* addict, was dazzled, too. He said, "Maybe you could get Elwyn to talk to the kids in our school." I wrote and asked him. EBW replied in one paragraph, written in ink on North Brooklin, Maine, stationery.

17 October 1954
Dear Mrs. Campion,

Much as I would like to speak to the school children of Bronxville, I do not feel able to accept their invitation. I'm no good at public appearances—even in the comparatively mild and comfortable air of an elementary school—and so I just pass up all dates of this sort, for what I believe to be the good of the community. It cuts me out of much that I would like to see and enjoy, and builds walls around me that I wish were not there. I'm afraid it all goes back to another elementary school, very close by in Mount Vernon, and the dark, fear-ridden days of my childhood when they managed to scare the daylights out of me. I've not made a successful recovery.

    With many thanks and regrets,
    Sincerely,
    E. B. White

Mr. White had a passion for anonymity. Few people knew that for fifty years E. B. White composed the snappers for the *New Yorker's* newsbreaks (funny column fillers):

"New Sultan of Morocco Entitled to Four Wives: Prefers Mahogany" (*Omaha Bee-News.*) Snapper: *Our preference is for the bird's eye maple.*

"Gent's Laundry Taken Home. Or Serve Parties at Night" (*Pittsburgh Sun Telegraph.*) Snapper: *Oh, take it home.*

If they used your newsbreak, you received five dollars. In 1959 I sent him an ad from *Pointer View,* a newspaper at West Point: "*FOR SALE: Wedding Gown—Petticoat & veil; baby bassinet, and ironing board.*" White's snapper was *On to the sober years—the years of wash and wear.*

Dear Mrs. Campion:
  Sometimes weeks and weeks go by, and then along comes five dollars. Hope you enjoy this money, and thanks for sending the break.
    Sincerely,
    Andy White

"Onward and upward," Tom laughed, quoting another of White's "Departments," a handy expression he said he swiped from the Unitarian creed. My favorite departments were "Letters We Never Finished Reading" and "How's That Again?"

My correspondence with the Great Man lapsed for about twenty years. Then in 1977 Wilfred Sheed made snide comments in reviewing *The Letters of E. B. White.* Tom handed me the *Times Book Review.* "Time to write another letter to the editor." Writing letters to the editor is my hobby; some even get published. "I hate this review," I exclaimed. Tom shrugged; the only things he hated were bigots and black flies.

"In Andy's own words," he said, "Sheed should be 'marked for oblivion.' *White's Letters* is the best book I've read in years. Too bad the six letters he wrote to you aren't in it."

I followed Tom's suggestion.

30 January 1977
To the Editor,
  I don't know what Wilfred Sheed means when he says E. B. White did some "bloviating for the Human Spirit, before returning to what he does best: the hammering out of fine sentences about small matters." Bloviating did not make our Webster's Unabridged Dictionary, nor is it a word that in any way could apply to Mr. E. B. White.

The *Times* published my anti-Sheed screed, and I sent the clipping to Andy, along with a misplaced modifier newsbreak about a pianist who appeared to be named nimbly. My non-dancing dinner partner replied.

March 14, 1977
Dear Nardi:

It was good to hear from you, but I heard also from about ten thousand other people, thanks to my wild fling in the world of published letters. A man my age should know better. When will I learn anything? When oh when?

I'll try to get that pianist nimbly into the magazine, and if he lands you will reap your reward.

Thanks for leaping into the Times Book Review at my side. Anybody who uses the word "bloviating" shouldn't be allowed to review books. I wouldn't even pal around with anybody who uses the word "serendipity," which is at least in the dictionary. That relieves Horace Walpole of my company—he put it in.

And now back to hammering out a few more sentences about small matters.

Yrs. gratefully,
Andy

"Wow!" Tom said. "You're on a first name basis." But, alas, that was the last letter I ever received from my pen pal.

On October 3, 1985, *The New York Times* announced that E. B. White, "one of the nation's most precious literary resources," had died at eighty-six in his home in North Brooklin, Maine. He had Alzheimer's disease. William Shawn, the editor of the *New Yorker* who was quoted at length, said E. B. White was a great essayist and a supreme stylist who "never wrote a mean or careless sentence."

The obituary called E. B. White an agnostic. Maybe. He knew the Unitarian creed, didn't he? And he was the sensitive observer who wrote: "I am always humbled by the infinite ingenuity of the Lord, who can make a red barn cast a blue shadow."

❧ 23. "Speak What You Feel"

The hardest thing for me to write about actually rescued our family from life on the surface. After much pain, we began to grasp what King Lear had to lose his mind to learn: "Speak what we feel, not what we ought to say." We're still working on it.

One night in 1963, Tom called up the stairs, his voice urgent. "Nardi!

Get on the phone." Tommy was calling from Dartmouth. He didn't sound like himself. Talking a mile a minute, he switched from the Dartmouth student who had just drowned in the Connecticut River, to what he'd do after graduation, to his girlfriend at Skidmore, to the meaning of life. On and on he went. As I listened, my heart sank. I felt sick and sat down. Clearly something was wrong.

At last Tom interrupted. "Son, do you want us to come up there?"

"Good idea. Do that."

"I'll be glad to see you, Tommy," was all I could manage.

"Okay."

I hung up and burst into tears. Tom bounded up the stairs. We clung to each other, speechless. We both knew that our doted-on oldest child was having a breakdown. We were reeling. What should we do? If he'd broken his leg, we'd know what to do. But an emotional break? I shivered. In 1963 the word breakdown wasn't just negatively charged, it was taboo.

Neither Tom nor I realized it until later, but each of us was haunted by a childhood ghost. At Fort Leavenworth, my friend Alice had an unbalanced brother we never saw. Joe was kept upstairs, hidden like Boo Radley. I caught a glimpse of him only once, but I still remember his frightening, vacant stare. I was gripped by the fear that Tommy might end up like Joe.

Tom's older brother was his nightmare: Edward, a beautiful child who appeared normal, never talked. He was institutionalized while Tom was a toddler. Since nobody could explain it—autism was unknown—Tom's imagination ran wild. As a boy he saw *The Phantom of the Opera* and imagined that Edward looked like Lon Chaney in the movie. When his mother took him to visit Edward, he turned out to be silent, listless, handsome, and harmless. But the damage had been done—Tom's weird images stayed with him. Edward died in the institution at twenty-eight.

Sick with apprehension, Tom and I left for Hanover at dawn in our VW bug. Pinkie, our live-in life support, took over the kids. The four-hour drive took forever. What would we find when we got there? We reacted to anxiety differently—I couldn't talk; Tom couldn't stop talking. "How's he going to take our showing up? We know he gets fed up with us—he's made that clear. Remember when he handed me his An-

Marriage, Kids, and The New York Times   117

dover diploma after graduation, and vanished? He flew home in a rich friend's plane."

"Maybe he feels overpowered by his family."

"Maybe. Sometimes I feel overpowered by your family." That made me mad, but I let it go. Tom kept coming back to "How can we get him to a doctor?" The thought scared us, let alone the reality. What would the doctor say? My strange encounter with Alice's brother flashed to mind.

We went straight to Tommy's room. Empty. Clothes and books strewn around. We sat, waiting nervously. The alarm clock sounded like Big Ben. At last Tommy walked in, his face thin and gaunt. "Been on the river all night—can't find the body. We've . . ."

Tom took a deep breath and interrupted. "Son, what would you think of seeing a doctor?"

No hesitation. "Good idea."

Whew!

Tom left to make the phone call. Tommy rattled on. "Who knows what happened? He took out a kayak yesterday morning. Last night they found the boat upside down at Wilder Dam, but no body. What happened to him, that's what I want to know. They're dragging the river."

Tom returned quickly. "Doctor's name is Bob Weiss—he's the Director of Student Health. He'll see us at eleven. Do you want to get some breakfast?"

"I have to go to an English class."

Tom and I looked at each other. "Can we go with you?" I asked quickly.

He shrugged. "Why not?"

Sarah Orne Jewett's novel about Maine, *The Country of the Pointed Firs,* is forever embalmed in my mind. The heavyset, bespectacled English professor lectured on it for fifty minutes. I took notes to try to calm myself, but Tommy didn't. Tom stared into space. Totally bewildered, I felt as though I were living someone else's life.

The three of us walked in silence across the street to the Mental Health Center. Dr. Weiss—graying hair, warm smile, firm handshake—talked only to Tommy. "What's up, Tom?"

"I've been on the river all night searching for the body. I feel sort of unhinged."

"I don't wonder. How would you feel about checking into the infirmary?" Tommy shrugged.

If only the rest of this experience had been that simple. We were headed for unknown territory.

We waited while Dr. Weiss took Tommy over to the infirmary. Neither of us could speak; we were on dead center. I concentrated on the doctor's diplomas. Tom stood at the window looking out. Later he told me he couldn't get Edward out of his mind.

Dr. Weiss returned, saying in a kind voice, "He's going to be all right. Try not to worry. Can you come back early tomorrow?"

Try not to worry. Try not to breathe would have made more sense. "Can we see him?" Tom asked.

"Yes, but he may be sleeping. We gave him a shot to calm him."

Tommy was asleep. He looked so long, so thin, so vulnerable, I began to cry. As Tom hugged me tight, two tears rolled down his cheek. We both loved our firstborn beyond the telling of it.

We spent a terrible night at the Hanover Inn, unable to eat, unable to sleep, unable to talk about the feelings that swamped us. We were immobilized by fear and confusion.

The next morning Dr. Weiss said, "You did the right thing coming when you did. Your son is sick, you know that. He knows it, too. He put himself in the infirmary last week. These things sometimes happen to students when they face their future. I've found a place for him at the Adolescent Treatment Center in New York City. They only take adolescents. Can you drive him down there today?"

"Of course," Tom said.

"Tommy's not an adolescent," I protested. "He'll be twenty-one next month."

Dr. Weiss's smile was kindly. "Some people are adolescent at forty," he said.

The trip to New York was a relief. At least we were doing something. Tommy sat beside Tom and I curled up in the small back seat, exhausted. They talked constantly—about the New York Giants, new cars with fins, the Dodgers, Bobby Kennedy, desegregation—anything so long as it didn't touch what we were all afraid of. I stuck my face in a pillow and mercifully slept.

The Adolescent Treatment Center on East Eightieth Street was a stark brick building, and Dr. Barish's office looked like a cell. A calm, middle-aged man in an old tweed jacket, he was reassuring. "I've spoken with Dr. Weiss. We have cases far more serious than your son's." I looked at Tommy. Staring at his shoelaces, he seemed to be in another world. I wished I were.

"We don't believe in restraint," the doctor said. "Our patients can come and go any time. We never lock our doors."

I gasped. "Is that safe? Don't some leave and never return?"

He shook his head. "They all come back."

"Why?"

"Because they're getting help."

As we entered the dingy hall, two girls in jeans clattered past us, chasing a redheaded boy. They dashed up the stairs and a door banged. Dr. Barish smiled wanly. "Our kids are not inhibited."

Leaving Tommy in that barren institution was the hardest thing Tom and I had ever done. I sobbed and he tried to comfort me—then he stopped abruptly. "I feel so damned guilty. What did we do wrong?"

"Me, too," I wailed. "It's always the mother's fault." Fortunately that made Tom laugh. "Yes," he said. "It's all your fault," which made me laugh. In a way Tommy's breakdown was a relief. We had known there was a problem. If upset, Tommy could dominate us with angry silence. It could take days to get him to talk to you.

Our ignorance of psychology was prodigious. Children had to obey their parents—that was rule number one. If your child had problems, you never discussed it with friends. One weekend when Tommy was still at Andover, Tom drove up to talk to the elderly dean. We were frustrated by our son's rejection of us and wanted the dean's help. The dean, a minister, suggested prayer. "We tried that," Tom said dryly. "God heals all wounds" was the reply.

After leaving Tommy at the center in New York, we had to explain to the kids what had happened. It was impossible. We didn't understand it ourselves. Toby, fifteen, looking woeful, tried to comfort us. Cissa, twelve, sniffled in silence. Russell, seven, asked, "When will I see Tommy again?" We couldn't even begin to answer.

I drove up to Andover to tell Tad, now in his last year. We took a long walk in the bird sanctuary. I did all the talking. It was therapy for me but not for Tad. Although he well knew how unpredictable his brother could be, Tad grew up thinking Tommy was king.

A psychiatrist had told us to reassure our children that what happened to Tommy need not happen to them. I asked him, "How come children with the same parents turn out so differently?"

"They don't have the same parents," he said. "By the time each child was born, you and Tom were different people."

Toby, who was in Bronxville High School, seemed hardest hit. One Saturday he got on the train and went in to see Tommy. They spent the afternoon walking around the city. We thought that was a good idea, until Toby wrote about his brother's crisis for the school literary magazine. I told Toby he should not publish it. What would people think? In those thankfully long-gone days, emotional illness had to be hidden. It was a disgrace.

"He's your son," Toby said, "but he's my brother and I have a right to express my feelings about what he's going through, what we're all going through." I opened my mouth to object. "That's what writers do, Mom. You know that."

That did it. Despite our objections and those from the kindly beloved principal, Dr. Misner, Toby published his powerful piece about visiting Tommy at the treatment center. It is hard now, when people are so open about emotional illness, to realize how extraordinary that was. When I read Toby's piece I died a thousand deaths. Tom took it in stride. I never knew how others reacted. Nobody ever mentioned it to me.

Fortunately, *The New York Times* was way ahead of its time. Their insurance covered mental illness long before others. If they hadn't, our finances would have collapsed.

Tom's parents accepted the situation gracefully. I dreaded telling my family. To my surprise, Mother, who thought we were all perfect, took it best. "Tommy is going to be all right," she said with such conviction that I believed her, almost. Julia had a diagnosis: "Tommy never got over Tad's birth." Red and Fred, so like Daddy in this respect, said they were sorry, and that was that.

One person—and only one—our friend Dorothy Bainbridge, said the right thing. She must have been around this track herself. "When this is over you will be thankful it happened. Everything will be so much better."

I couldn't imagine it ever being over, much less better.

The treatment center required parents to go into therapy. We were ashamed and eager at the same time. We had more than we could handle by ourselves. The trouble was that I had no clue what Tom was telling his therapist and vice versa. Over many cocktails—we thought booze was balm—we discussed our sessions. Even those highly selective, alcohol-fueled talks started us communicating on a better level.

I had never grasped what the sudden death of Tom's mother when he was fourteen—and his father's refusal to speak about it—had done to him. And he didn't understand my mother's influence on me. All mothers in those days were in mortal fear lest their daughters get pregnant out of wedlock. That and my mother's Southern overemphasis on family had been hard for Tom to accept.

Tom was not impressed with his therapist, told him so, and got another who was much better. I liked mine, appropriately named Mrs. Wisch. Therapy helped us both, slowly. One day I told Mrs. Wisch, "I think we made a mistake sleeping in twin beds. We inherited them."

"Well," she said, "why don't you get a double bed?" Tom almost fell over when he came home and found, in place of two beds, a brand new queen-sized bed. "What the hell is going on here?"

Family reactions to the double bed varied.

Russell: "It looks like a trampoline."

Cissa: "Why didn't you get one with a canopy?"

Toby: "Who's in charge of the electric blanket controls?"

Tad: "Good for cold weather, not hot."

Tommy (when he came home, sense of humor intact): "Ladies and gentlemen, start your engines."

Tom: "I never had it so good."

Me: "Why didn't I do it sooner?"

Family communication was beginning to improve.

Dr. Barish had told us, "Don't be surprised if Tom does not want to live at home. The last thing these kids want to do is deal with parents."

Of course we went to see him on a regular basis; it was impossible to stay away. One rainy night Tom was slated to take Tommy out to dinner.

It was November 22, 1963. Tom was working at the *Times* when President Kennedy was shot. As soon as he could, he called us. Like everybody else, we were devastated. "I'll see you after I have dinner with Tommy—that's more important than ever."

When he got home he was still stunned by Tommy's reaction to the assassination. "I feel I don't know him anymore. The murder of Jack Kennedy didn't seem to affect him. It was as if he were sealed off from everything."

"That's just what he is," Mrs. Wisch told me later. "Sealed off is a perfect description. When you can't handle turbulent emotion, you shut down your feelings."

The first time Tommy came home he brought along a bottle of thorazine, the aspirin for emotional problems in those days. It was a stilted evening and everyone was relieved when he left, Tommy most of all.

Luckily, we owned a funky railroad boarding house on Long Island that we had converted into Duck Out, our beach house. Amagansett was unstylish then. Its "suburb," Springs, was a cheap retreat for poor artists like Pollock and De Kooning. Tommy moved to Duck Out with Ben, his new red setter puppy. The two of them lived alone for three months, walking the deserted Amagansett beach and collecting firewood.

The solitude seemed to do wonders for Tommy. But when Tom drove out to see him one weekend, the dam burst. Tommy exploded in rage at his father, detailing the wrongs he had suffered, real and imagined. Thank God it was Tom, not me. He was able to do what I never could have done: he just took it. But he never forgot the power of that anger.

Soon after that, Tommy began to get better. In July he went off to Harvard Summer School to make up his lost credits. Ben stayed with us. We were relieved that Tommy wanted to return to Dartmouth and we were all crazy about his gangling, playful puppy.

One hot afternoon Tom and I went sailing with our nautical friends Helen and Ernest Gordon. We got home, took one look at Tad and Russell, and knew that something terrible had happened. Tad could barely tell us. "Ben ran across the street and a car hit him. Russell and I dug his grave and buried him in the backyard."

"How could you?" Tom said. "That ground is baked solid."

"We didn't know what else to do."

"Wasn't easy," Russell piped up.

We were all in shock. Tom said, "I hate to call Tommy. He and Ben were so close." He came back from the phone shaking his head. "All he said was 'too bad,' as though Ben had stepped on a piece of glass. He was detached, just like with the assassination." He stopped. "I guess we've got a long way to go."

In the end we all went the distance together. The following June Tommy got his Dartmouth degree. On Commencement Day we couldn't hold back the tears when the voice boomed out: "Thomas Baird Campion, Junior." We were so proud of him.

Eventually, Tommy emerged from his emotional crisis. The fall after graduation he went off to Ireland and got a master's degree in Yeats at University College Dublin. Then he got a law degree at the University of Colorado and practiced law. He married Lynn Hillyard and they had two wonderful daughters, Ashley and Berit. Eventually he got a Ph.D. and taught English at Colorado. It wasn't all smooth sailing, but he came through. To us it is a triumphant story.

Dorothy Bainbridge was right. After the breakdown, things did get better for our family. It wasn't easy, but lessons learned the hard way can change your life.

We're still struggling to "speak what we feel, not what we ought to say."

24. What? Me Cook for Craig Claiborne?

Tom came home from work one night and announced, "I've invited Craig Claiborne to dinner."

"And I'm dining at the White House."

"I'm not kidding."

"Craig Claiborne? You want me to cook a meal for the food critic to end all food critics? You must be kidding. What are you doing, trying to teach me humility?"

He didn't laugh. "I work with Craig at the *Times* and I like him. I invited him to our house for dinner, period."

"No way," I said flatly. "I never promised to obey you, remember? *No-body* asks Craig Claiborne to dinner."

"That's what he said. Craig is a comfortable old shoe from Sunflower, Mississippi. He hates pretense. Just have a regular dinner—meatloaf and mashed potatoes will do. I'm sure he won't expect much."

Against my better judgment, I agreed to cook a meal for Craig Claiborne.

How many friends do you invite to dine with a living legend? Tom said, "I think eight is the right number. Remember Craig's article that said if you want good conversation, seat ten people at a table for eight, eight at a table for six, and so on."

With "I'm sure he won't expect much" ringing in my ears, I decided to serve only surefire, never-fail dishes, as gourmet-ish as possible. Oysters for openers. You can't miss with plump fresh oysters on the half shell, lemon wedges, and seafood sauce jazzed up with Tabasco and horseradish.

"Craig doesn't drink cocktails," Tom said. "We should have wine with the oysters."

"Ye gods. What wine goes with oysters?" I asked.

"Chablis."

"How do you know?"

"It just sounds right." We were both flying blind.

No cocktails, no hors d'oeuvres. Good. I'm a flop at itsy-bitsy munchies.

If your guest of honor is Southern, there is one entree devoutly to be hoped for—Smithfield ham. My mother had sent us one for Christmas and, luckily, Tom is an expert carver. Southerners require their Smithfield ham sliced paper thin. I cooked the ham several days ahead and made my famous hot mustard to go with it (make a paste with dry mustard and water and let it sit.)

Tom said, "Smithfield ham calls for brandied peaches."

"Too expensive. This is running into money."

He loved a challenge. "Okay, I'll make 'em myself." I told him how the Godfreys did it, omitting the burial. He drained a can of peach halves, stuck in some cloves, put them in a mason jar and filled it with brandy.

"What wine goes with Smithfield ham?" I asked.

"Beaujolais," Tom said, "probably. And lots of it. That salty ham would make a camel thirsty."

The only thing I felt comfortable about was the bread. My mother's oatmeal bread is a never-fail no-brainer. Heated and served with sweet butter at room temperature (Tom: "Only Eskimos like cold butter"), homemade bread will cover a multitude of sins—or feed a multitude of sinners.

For a vegetable? Tom had the answer to that, too. Wherever we lived, he planted a vegetable garden. "We'll have fresh peas from my garden. Drop them in boiling water for two minutes. Remember what Truman Capote wrote: 'The rich eat unborn vegetables.'"

The salad would be a separate course, accompanied by Brie—soft, not runny—and thin Norwegian flatbread. Watercress, bibb lettuce, and endive, mixed at the table with an olive oil and lemon dressing my father had perfected in his "salad days" at the University of Michigan.

Tom said, "We can't have anything rich for dessert. Craig watches his weight." We hit on Grapefruit Red Reeder, named for my brother who invented it. Cut half a grapefruit into sections and replace the juice with green creme de menthe. Decorate with a fresh strawberry and mint leaves. We'd cap the dinner with espresso and small squares of Great-Grandma Sutherland's Scottish shortbread.

As our menu evolved, my elevator-stomach subsided—slightly. Our hard-to-ruin recipes gave me a wee sense of security. I might be able to manage dinner for Craig Claiborne after all. I decided to wear my long black velvet skirt and play Hostess. Host Tom wore his father's velvet smoking jacket. "I feel like we're in a play," he said.

Simplicity was the watchword, but we did add one complicated, smasheroo dish. I discovered I could get a great cook named Mrs. Evelyn Tuck to help on the night of the party. ("Craig Claiborne? You bet I can come!") Mrs. Tuck and I decided that for a dash of glamour we'd serve individual cheese soufflés with the Smithfield ham. Tom went out and bought eight white china ramekins. By now we were past caring about cost.

Mrs. Tuck is the Queen of Soufflés but she had never done individual ones, so the night before the dinner she came to our house and practiced. Russell, age ten, ate three and said, "Not bad."

The night of The Party arrived. I was more or less a wreck, but Husband was as cool as Grapefruit Red Reeder. Craig Claiborne turned out to be a gentle man with courtly manners, a Southern drawl, thinning white hair, and a blue-eyed twinkle. He was relaxed, so I relaxed—a little.

Daffodils and yellow candles made our dinner table look festive. Russell and his friend Jimmy, in white shirts and bow ties, made classy waiters. Conversation and laughter flowed with the wine. Craig asked about the brandied peaches. "Imported," Tom said.

Tom proposed a toast: "To the one and only Craig Claiborne and to your Average Eater." Craig responded with a toast: "To dining at home with friends instead of dining out with pencil and paper."

The meal took almost four hours. Eating slowly and laughing a lot seemed to enhance the flavors. Were the wines all right? All I know is we had no problem with leftovers. I was beginning to feel proud of myself.

The individual cheese soufflés wowed even Craig Claiborne. After dinner, the Dean of Diners said, "Tom, I'd like to meet your cook." Craig peered over his half glasses at Mrs. Tuck and congratulated her on those eight breathtaking apparitions.

Her reply restored my humility. "Oh, Mr. Claiborne," she burbled, "I'm glad you thought the soufflés were all right. They were much better when I made them last night for our practice party." I could have beaned her.

Craig thanked me for not having a rich dessert—a food critic's waistline is in constant peril. "I enjoyed coming to your house," he said. Then he added wistfully, "Nobody ever asks me to dinner."

Why? I wondered. There's nothing to it.

❦ 25. Searching for Robert Louis Stevenson

Tom kidded me about being a grave-hopper, but it was his idea to visit Yeats's grave in Ireland. ("Cast a cold eye, on life, on death. Horseman, pass by.") And he masterminded our most spectacular pilgrimage, a visit to the grave of Robert Louis Stevenson in Western Samoa.

We were flying to Tonga in 1968 to visit Toby's Harvard buddy, Sione Toupounia, when Tom got the idea. When we were in Pago Pago, the capital of what was then American Samoa, he booked us for a short flight in a flimsy plane to Apia, the capital of Western Samoa, simply because his boyhood hero lies buried there.

Apia, 2,200 miles from Honolulu, was a small town with smooth beaches and potholed streets. We stayed at Aggie Grey's Hotel, the quintessential South Seas inn decorated with grass mats, seashells, and primitive carvings. Aggie herself, who was the model for Bloody Mary in *South Pacific,* greeted us in the dining room with a hug. Her Samoan headwaiter seated us with a chatty New Zealand couple who had never heard of Robert Louis Stevenson. "That's a bit much, coming all this way to go to some chap's grave."

After fresh flounder poached in lemon and lots of kava, the slightly narcotic Polynesian national drink, Tom delivered a lecture on R. L. S., from *Treasure Island* to *The Strange Case of Dr. Jekyll and Mr. Hyde.* I said, "I could never remember which was the bad guy."

"Why do you think he was called Hyde? Not to worry—they're really one person, his good side and his evil side."

"You just lost me, matey," said the New Zealander, pouring another gin.

At five A.M. we rolled out of bed, breakfasted on papaya dipped in lime juice, tea, and toast, and set out on our quest. Tom said Stevenson rode his horse Jack all over the island looking for his final resting place. He finally selected the top of Mount Vaea. It's a daunting five-hundred-foot climb to get up there, but our spirits were soaring—when we started.

The foot trail went steadily upward through lush green foliage. As we climbed it got hot, hotter, hottest. When the rains came we were already soaked. Tom called over his shoulder, "Rain feels good."

"Not to me." The tropical shower passed, the sun came out, and we started to steam. "I made a poor choice of shoes," I said. He didn't seem to hear me. We mushed upward. "I made a poor choice of legs," I said.

Tom stopped. "Do you want to go back?"

I knew he had his heart set on getting to that grave. "We've come this far," I said, attempting a smile, "let's push on."

"No place to go but up," he laughed. "Remember what R. L. S. said, 'To miss the joy is to miss all.'"

I missed the joy. Tom didn't. He never did.

Our path began to dwindle—then it vanished. The humidity was stifling and mosquitoes were whining when we lost our way. "I've no idea where we are," Tom said.

I was panting. "I'm ready to quit."

Out of nowhere four nearly naked urchins suddenly appeared, chirping, "Stevenson's grave? Stevenson's grave?" Guiding lost pilgrims to the grave was a big source of family income.

"How much to the top?"

"Dolla American."

"Sold."

Two boys pulled my hands and one pushed my back. It was the longest fifty yards I've ever experienced. Tom gave each guide two dollars, which made them squeal.

At long last we walked out on the summit, as flat as a table top. Spread out far below on every side was the breathtaking blue of the South Pacific. In front of us stood the cement tomb of Robert Louis Stevenson, decorated with carvings of Samoan hibiscus and Scottish thistle. We sat down on a bench.

In a husky voice Tom recited from memory the verse "graved" on the tomb:

> Under the wide and starry sky,
> Dig the grave and let me lie.
> Glad did I live, and gladly die,
>   And I lay me down with a will . . .
>
> This be the verse you grave for me;
> Here he lies where he longed to be;
> Home is the sailor, home from the sea,
>   And the hunter home from the hill.

"Look at this," Tom said. He read aloud a plaque on the bench: "'Presented by the Stevenson Society of Edinburgh, Scotland.'" I knew there used to be a Stevenson Society—my mother belonged to it. Now you can't even find his grave." We sipped hot water from our canteens, gazing out at the ocean. "This is the best water I ever tasted," Tom said. We sat in silence, holding hands.

"R. L. S. died with his boots on," Tom told me. "His wife wrote that he was chatting gaily, stirring oil and lime into his special mayonnaise. Suddenly he put his long thin hands to his head. 'What's that? Oh, what a pain! Do I look strange?' 'No,' she lied. He fell down, unconscious from a stroke. A few hours later he was dead—at age forty-four." Tom hesitated, then continued. "They called him Tusitala—Teller of Tales. He was beloved by the Samoans. In the tropics a twenty-four-hour burial was mandatory, but how to get his body to the top of Mt. Vaea? Scores of young Samoans arrived with axes and knives and chopped all night to make the trail. As they worked, Stevenson's bodyservant Sosimo recited Catholic prayers for the dead.

"The next day strong Samoan pallbearers led the ascent, carrying shoulder-high, the pitifully light coffin. They were followed by nineteen white people and sixty Samoans. Some people dropped out, but not Stevenson's intrepid Scottish mother in her black silk dress and bonnet."

Tom paused, deep in thought.

"The better the communication," Mrs. Wisch had told me, "the better the marriage." Slowly we learned that the harder it is to talk about something, the more necessary it is to talk. Talking came easily to both of us, deep communication did not. I pushed myself to the avoidable topic. "Tell me more about your mother's death."

Tom said nothing. My usual urge is to fill in every conversational crevice. For once, I kept my mouth shut. Thank heaven. In a low voice he finally said, "It was the worst day of my life. Christmas 1930."

"Do you want to talk about it?"

"No. Yes, I do. I was fourteen and had just finished my first term at Andover. I could hardly wait to get back to Columbus for Christmas. I was eager to see my mother. She and I had a lot in common—we were both afraid of my father. We loved Pop, but he could wither you with his sarcasm. On Christmas Eve Mother wasn't feeling well but she and Gram were wrapping gifts when I went to bed.

"I slept in the same room with Frank, who was nine. Early Christmas morning Pop woke us. I'd never seen him look so white. He sat down on Frank's bed. 'Boys,' his voice sounded thick, 'Mom has left us.' That's all he said. That's all he ever said. There was no explanation. Later we learned she died of a cerebral hemorrhage. We never saw her body. We never got to say good-bye. She just vanished.

"I don't remember her funeral. All I recall is the train trip to Youngstown, Ohio, where we buried her in the Johnson family plot. I wasn't even convinced her body was in that coffin. It was all so unreal.

"Going back on the train, people talked about everything but Mom. I wanted to cry out 'Stop it! Mom is dead.' I went back to Andover in a daze." His voice broke. I waited.

"If only Pop had been like your mother, Nardi. She introduced you to death. She wanted you to understand that death is part of life."

We sat in silence. Finally he said, "My mother fell in love with R. L. S. in 1908, when she was at Smith. Her favorite quote was 'Wealth is only useful for two things: a yacht and a string quartet.' She indoctrinated me when I was little, reading *A Child's Garden of Verses*—'O, how I love to go up in a swing / Up in the air so blue' and 'I have a little shadow / that goes in and out with me.' Later we had fun reading aloud *Treasure Island* and *Kidnapped*. How I loved those books."

"I wish I'd known your mother, Tom."

"You and she would have loved each other. You had more in common than just me." He paused. "Stevenson was a mother's boy, you know. She coddled him so much he had to run away from her. But Margaret Stevenson, a widow, could not live without her only child. She even left Scotland by sailing ship and went to live with Louis and his wife in the South Pacific."

Tom put his arm around me. "Most men marry their mothers, in a way."

"You didn't marry your mother, did you?"

He kissed me. "No, you're my girl, my only girl. Forever."

"Here Beginneth a New Life"— Amherst, Massachusetts

By 1970, Tom was the director of production of the *New York Times*. It was a big job but not the biggest. Long on energy, long on ambition, he wanted to be a vice-president. A man who worked for him got that job. Tom was crushed. We were all crushed. Tom was not only the smartest man we knew, he was the best. If he lacked anything (some thought not), it was aggressiveness. By nature he identified with the underdog.

His boss, Punch Sulzberger, told him he would have a good job at the *Times* forever, but that wasn't Tom's style. "The hell with them," he said. "I'm going to change careers. I always wanted to be in education anyway." That gave me a stab. He would have been a gifted professor, but his father said teaching did not pay—and what Pop said went. Via Harvard Business School, Tom had lots of choices. He picked vice-chancellor of the University of Massachusetts in Amherst.

The day we moved from Bronxville to Amherst I hit bottom. Saying good-bye to my friends and to the house I had loved made me feel as though my moorings had been ripped loose. Growing up as an army brat, all I wanted was to belong somewhere, and for twenty-two years I had. My sense of belonging was kaput. We didn't know anybody in Amherst. How could I ever belong there?

Russell went into Amherst High School without a hitch. It helped that he landed on a basketball team that won the Massachusetts state championship. Tom and I never missed a game, which was a challenge.

The other kids were off on their own. Tommy was going to University of Colorado Law School and skiing daily. Tad was teaching at a windowless grade school in Harlem and taking organic chemistry on the side to get into medical school. Toby and Anita were in cold Chicago (her Mexican blood froze) while he finished his fourth year at the National Chiropractic College. Cissa was in Baltimore, taking Russian literature, religion, and music at Goucher College while organizing Vietnam War protests.

By rights the move should have been harder for Tom, but it wasn't. The hundred-percenter threw himself into his new career. The lostness, the aloneness of moving to a strange place suffocated me. "Myself am Hell," Satan says at the end of *Paradise Lost*. "Right," I said. "Myself am Hell." But I didn't know what to do about it.

We moved into a rented apartment on the Amherst campus. Tom kept calling it "our new home" (it wasn't new and it wasn't home). I was so steeped in self-pity I almost ignored the letter from my friend Betty Smith. She and I had counseled each other endlessly but I was beyond counseling. Her help was one more thing I had to do without.

But something prompted me to re-read it.

I sank down on the carpet and read. Tom had said I was in danger of becoming entombed in a "sarcophagus of self." The phrase burned in my mind.

The simplicity of Betty's advice took my breath away. She said that one time when she had an attack of "me-sickness," she invented six rules to live by. They still helped her, and she thought they might help me, too.

EVERY DAY I WILL DO:
1. Something for someone else.
2. Something for myself.
3. Something I don't want to do.
4. A physical exercise.
5. A mental exercise.
6. An original prayer that starts with counting my blessings.

Betty said she limited herself to six rules because she felt that number to be "manageable." I was not surprised she had trouble with number six. She had left the Episcopal Church—too much ritual. "I can't concentrate in church," she wrote. "I find myself appraising the hats, but sitting in solitude on a rock by the brook, I can pray. I count my blessings, always beginning with my family, without whom I would be lost." I could identify with that. Eventually, she became a Quaker.

When I put down Betty's letter, tears were in my eyes. Oh, how I missed her. That night I showed the letter to Tom. "Maybe it wasn't just chance she wrote when she did," he said. "Betty has sent you a gift. Why don't you give her six rules a shot?"

I ignored him, and continued coasting downhill.

One day I lay on the bed, staring at the ceiling. I thought about what Tom had said. Should I try Betty's formula? I had nothing to lose. I could continue as a lump of misery, or I could test those rules by doing something for someone else. I could, for instance, phone my ninety-year-old neighbor, who was ill and lived by herself. Tom's phrase echoed in my head: if I ever hoped to escape from "the sarcophagus of self," I'd better start now.

That insight did it. I would not allow myself to be buried by ego. I got up and dialed Miss Phillips. She invited me for tea.

It was a start. Miss Phillips was delighted to have someone listen to her. As she rattled on in that musty parlor, my mind wandered. I faked interest in the details of her illness. Then I heard her say something that snapped me to attention.

"Sometimes," said Miss Phillips, "the thing you dread doing is the very thing you should do, just so you can stop thinking about it."

I walked home turning over her sentence in my mind. Miss Phillips had cast a new light on Betty's third rule. *Do something I don't want to do.*

Since our move, my never tidy desk had become a disaster area. Tom called it Mt. Pleasant Cemetery. I made up my mind to get the mess in order. I bought a file cabinet and colored folders, and every paper on my desk went into a file or into the trash.

Two hours later I put down a new green blotter and a small philodendron plant. I beamed. I had done something I did not want to do and I felt good. Tom was stunned. "Who says you can't move a cemetery?"

Physical exercise wasn't quite so successful. I signed up for a jazzercise class and hated it. Fortunately, the teacher danced so hard she detached her retina and cancelled the class. I switched to jogging, until it dawned on me that I hated every jog.

"What's wrong with walking?" Tom asked. He offered to join me each morning before breakfast. We found walking to be wonderfully conducive to communication. Sometimes evening walks even replaced cocktails. We felt healthier than we had in years.

"I'll bet you'll ace Betty's 'do something for yourself' rule." Tom said. He was kidding, but not much.

"I'm more interested in her bath therapy." She had written: "A bath should be the ultimate place of relaxation. Gather mint, lemon verbena, and lavender. Steep the dried leaves in boiling water and strain into the tub. Lie in the bath and do not think while soaking."

Miss Phillips, still chattering away, happily supplied me with herbs from her garden. I put the herbal mix into the tub, turned on the warm water, stretched out, and let the tensions of the day melt away. Sensational.

Tom noted the new me. As we walked in the woods he remarked, "I like it when you're relaxed."

"Better enjoy it," I grumped, taking his compliment the wrong way. "It won't last." But I did ask Tom to add herbs to his garden, and I made bath sachets for Christmas. Doing something for myself had turned into doing something for someone else.

The mental exercise was even better than the bath—well, almost. I audited an Emily Dickinson course at UMass. The professor loved Emily Dickinson and soon I did too. I read all 1,176 poems and was enthralled. I also discovered a new motto: "I dwell in Possibility."

Our teacher was big on memorizing, which turned out to be the best mental exercise of all. I began with "I'm Nobody! Who are you?" and progressed to Tom's favorite, "Because I could not stop for Death, He kindly stopped for me." He had started memorizing poems for Emory Basford, his great English teacher at Andover. "The good thing about keeping poems in your head," Tom said, "is that you can pull them out and enjoy them anywhere."

Across the miles, Betty had reached out and helped me. Her prayer rule was the most helpful. Tom and I found composing a prayer difficult but valuable, especially if two people are able to do it together. We tried to make up a short prayer everyday, always including thanksgivings (that was the easy part).

Can life be lived by a formula? All I know is that instead of wallowing in self-pity, I finally began to escape that sarcophagus of self.

Emily showed me the way: "It is easy to work when the soul is at play."

❦ 27. Mother Leads the Way

On July 4, 1952, my mother, age seventy-three, ran away and got married. She had been a widow for ten years, living alone at her home, Reederhaven, in Phoebus, Virginia. On that day her devoted suitor, Clifford Whitehouse, known as C.E., four years younger (she liked that), stunned her by announcing "Narcissa, today I'm driving you to Elizabeth City, North Carolina, and we are going to get married."

She gasped, "Oh, C.E., you can't mean that."

He meant it. He suspected, correctly, that they would run into opposition. Elopement was the way to go. The next day she wired her children and all hell broke loose. Children of any age seem to resent another man taking their father's place, and my siblings ran true to form. Eloping at seventy-three? Unheard of.

I thought it was romantic. My brothers didn't say much; my sister Julia said a lot. Tom was on Mama's side. He sent her a telegram. "This is the greatest Independence Day since 1776. Hip, Hip, Hooray from all Campions."

Mother rode out the storm, saying "I refuse to be chicken-pecked."

One of her friends asked, "How did you dare elope at your age?"

"At my age," she replied, "how did I dare not to?"

The seventy-three-year-old bride had some adjustments to make. Unwrapping wedding gifts, she held up an iced tea glass and exclaimed, "That's queer! This glass has 'W' on it." There was a silence. The groom said in a small voice, "Our name is Whitehouse." He had to remind her of that more than once. Fortunately, they both thought it was funny.

She and C.E. had ten happy years. Suddenly he had a stroke and died.

At his funeral she told me, "I have only one regret about eloping with C.E. I was so excited when he carried me off, I forgot my hat and gloves."

Once when she came to see us, we landed on the Jack Paar show.

In 1961 I was on the Paar Show, ostensibly because Little, Brown published my "Patrick Henry." Actually, I was there because Randy Paar, Jack's adored only child, had a crush on our son Toby. Jack introduced me condescendingly, "And now a mother . . ." Clearly, my son was the important one. "Is Toby a writer, too?"

"Oh, yes, he puts out a neighborhood newspaper. One item was 'Mr. Smith is 90. He just had an operation. It was for phosphate.'"

Jack exploded with laughter. When I told him my mother eloped at 73, he stared with his trademark long pause, then said: "Can you come back next week and bring your mother?"

And I did.

My mother grew old the way she lived—full speed ahead. When she was ninety, she told Tom, "I've had bad news. The *Times* says soon there will be one million people over a hundred."

"Don't worry, Mama," he said. "Your fourteen-carat sense of humor will save you."

"I may go on and on," she laughed. "Very few people die after ninety."

Her full name by then was Narcissa Pillow Martin Reeder Whitehouse. She said she didn't need to embroider pillows, she was one. "Laughter is what makes old age bearable," my mother said. She was a world-class laugher. A world-class laugher is easily identified: someone who can laugh at themselves (like Tom).

But as Leonard Woolf titled the last volume in his autobiography, it was "Downhill All the Way." First the widow Whitehouse made an apartment in Reederhaven and rented out the rest of the house. Then she had to sell the house and move to the Chamberlain Hotel, where she could be waited on. Then she needed more care and had to move in with Julia and Charlie in Boston. Mother was ninety-two when Julia telephoned me in Amherst. "My heart is acting up again. It's time for you to take Mother now. We've had her for two years."

Mother's nightmare was coming true. She had often said, "I pray I will never have to live with my children."

My spirits sank. I adored my mother, but living with us? I couldn't face it. It wasn't that Mother was difficult, but she needed nursing. Tom had his hands full as vice-chancellor at UMass. And we were absorbed in building our dream house in an apple orchard. (Tom christened it Iduna for the Greek goddess of apples.)

I was overcome with guilt by my reluctance to add my own mother to our busy life.

I'm still shocked by my selfishness. St. Thomas, of course, didn't see it my way. On that golden September day when we drove to the Summeralls to get her, he said. "I don't understand you. I am happy to have Mama live with us." I didn't try to explain it.

I should have known my mother had her own plan. Driving back to Amherst she announced, "It's time for me to go into a nursing home."

Fred had always said, "If Mother ever has to go into a nursing home, that will be the end of her." We both protested. Tom meant it when he said, "Mama, we want you to live with us."

"No," she said. "The time has come." She was adamant. She was going to put herself in a nursing home.

One of the worst days of my life was the day I drove my mother to the nursing home. If it was her worst day, you'd never have known. Dressed up in her purple hat, mink scarf, and white gloves, she sailed in with all flags flying. She announced, "I can't tell you how delighted I am to be in this lovely place." The jaws of the receptionist and nurses dropped. I am sure that was a first.

She had to take the required physical exam. Fortunately, the doctor had charm, which for Mother was more important than degrees. "He's really handsome!" she said. The doctor also charmed me when he called up. "I just want to tell you that your mother is one of the most outstanding and amazing ladies I've ever met."

I wrote Julia, Red, and Fred. "Our mother is made of strong stuff. She can cope. If we ever forget the example she has given us of how to face illness and old age, we will be disgraced."

Long ago she had made up her mind that she'd never be a burden to her children. She had nursed her own mother through a lengthy terminal illness, and she was determined to spare her children that heart-breaking obligation. Going through her papers after her death, I found this statement, which she had had notarized:

> While I am of sound mind, I want to state my earnest request that if I ever need "keeping" I wish to be put in a Nursing Home, even if I object at that time. I do not wish my beloved and wonderful children criticized for carrying out my sincere wishes.

Once settled into the nursing home, she made new friends and soon knew the name of every nurse. I recalled her hairdresser telling me, "Your mother never saw a stranger."

Like most old people, she began to repeat; unlike most old people, she never complained. She may have forgotten Coué's mantra, "Every day and every way, I'm getting better and better," but it had become part of her. She said over and over, "My, I am lucky to be in this nursing home." I knew she was protesting too much, but she sure was protesting in the right direction.

And, as always, laughter helped. One afternoon I found her chuckling to herself. "It's those old men in the wheelchairs," she whispered. "They can't remember to zip up their pants."

Red frequently made the five-hundred-mile round trip from his home in Garrison, New York, to see Mother. By then, conversation was nil, so he always brought his favorite book, *Huckleberry Finn,* to read to her. I don't think she heard it.

The Bible was her favorite book. Over the years, she quoted a passage in the fifth chapter of St. Paul's letters to the Romans, King James version, of course. Now I was reading it to her daily. It helped me, too. "We rejoice in our sufferings knowing suffering leads to endurance. Endurance leads to character. Character leads to patience. Patience leads to hope. And hope does not disappoint, because God's love has been poured into us through the Holy Spirit."

My mother lived to be ninety-four. "Too old," she said, begging the doctor to help her out of this world (he would not). It broke my heart to see her weaken until she could not get out of bed. I didn't want her to see my tears. Tom, who was as upset as I was, tried to comfort me. "Mama keeps her smile—she is finishing in style." That made me cry harder. My mother showed us how to die. And how to live, too.

Example is not the best way to teach. It is the only way to teach.

We buried Mother in St. John's Cemetery in Howerton next to C. E. She had failed to persuade the War Department that she should be placed next to Daddy in Arlington (no remarrieds allowed).

Julia carried the ashes—and at the gate her pacemaker set off the alarm. Great excitement. St. John's had dug Mother's grave in the wrong place. She would have loved all the confusion.

⚘ 28. Left at the Gas Station

New England was deep in mud season and it was mud season in my soul. No matter what relationships you have in life, you only have one mother. To lose her is to lose part of yourself.

Tom and I were wallowing in a slough of despond, when we got a call from old friends in Florida. "How about coming down for a visit?" We jumped at the chance. Tom took time off from UMass, and I got a substitute at the Dickinson Homestead where I was a guide. We headed for sunshine.

We flew to balmy West Palm Beach, rented a bargain car, and set out for Hobe Sound where the Auers lived. "We expect you for dinner," they had said. We had to be prompt. Dinner is an event in Hobe Sound, retreat of elegant retirees.

As Tom drove north from the airport, I climbed into the back seat for a quick nap. Later, when I woke up, we were parked in a gas station. I looked out and saw him talking on an outdoor phone. I knew he was calling for directions. (We get lost a lot.)

I climbed out and went into the gas station to the bathroom, a normal thing to do. I saw Tom and assumed he saw me. Who said "Never assume anything—*assume* makes an *ass* out of *u* and *me?*"

When I came out he wasn't in the phone booth. I looked around—no car. He must be getting gas, I thought. I walked around the building to the gas pumps. No little blue car. Glory, glory, how peculiar. But maybe it wasn't blue. Maybe it was gray or greenish blue. Who remembers the color of a rental car?

I took a survey of the gas station, sticking my head inside every automobile regardless of its color and getting some indignant stares. I could not find him. He's gone. *Gone!* Husband had driven off and left Little Woman in a gas station in the middle of Nowhere, Florida.

What to do? Tom must have thought I was still asleep in the back seat. He would miss me and come right back. I would just go inside and wait. But will he remember which gas station? Florida is full of gas stations and he just came in to phone. I started to laugh and couldn't stop. Laughing is okay if you laugh with someone. If you're laughing alone, people assume—there's that word again—you're bonkers. The brassy blonde behind the cash register stared suspiciously. "Can I help you?"

I opened my mouth, but I just couldn't say it. I do not have what it takes to say, "My husband has driven off and left me." I smiled weakly and mumbled, "I'm waiting for someone to pick me up."

"Oh?" she said, very strong on the question mark. She was wearing an orange t-shirt, braless, tight jeans, high heels. Her hair matched her shirt and her purple eye shadow matched her fingernails. Her stare told me I was from another planet.

I stopped laughing and cast around for something to do. Luckily, I took my purse into the ladies room. I fished out coins, got a can of diet soda out of the machine, and sat down on the only available chair. Dragon Lady sat at the cash register exuding bad vibes.

I sipped my drink and waited. And waited. And waited. My faith in Old Reliable never wavered. Like Emily, "I dwell in Possibility." He would come back.

D. L., speaking slowly, as if to a backward child, said, "You are *sure* someone is coming to get you?"

"Oh, yes. He'll be here soon."

I was beginning to feel a little queasy. Time stopped. Nothing to read except maps, so I just sat. I thought about the cold, wet New England spring and tried enjoying Florida's sunny warmth. Nothing. On to a second can of soda. I sipped and watched the red sun sliding slowly past green palm trees and dropping below the blue horizon. Florida is full of primary colors. But I was stuck in a gas station. I didn't even know where I was. Was this some kind of Kafka trial? All I wanted was to escape.

It grew dark—still no husband to the rescue. Maybe he didn't miss me. I *had* to do something. I dug out a dime and went outside to telephone our friends in Hobe Sound. I had no idea whether I was making a long-distance or short-distance call, so I used my credit card. Bernie answered, and I began to laugh, somewhat hysterically. "Bernie, you're not going to believe this. Tom has driven off and left me in a gas station."

A long pause. Then Bernie said, "You're right. I don't believe you."

I smothered my hysteria and tried to describe my plight. He was unmoved. "I can smell a practical joke miles off," he said. "You're putting me on."

"No! This is no joke. I am stranded in a damned filling station and—"

He interrupted. "It isn't even a good practical joke. Getting left behind in a gas station is an old joke. You've thought up a cliché."

"Bernie!" I yelled desperately, "you've got to believe me. This is real. I have been *left*."

"Where?"

"Er-er-er . . . Oh, ye gods, nowhere. I don't know where I am. Wait a minute." I ran inside and shouted, "Where are we?"

Dragon Lady left the drawer of the cash register open to walk over to me. She put her face close to mine. "You got a problem, ma'am?"

I slowed down. "Could you please tell me the address of your gas station?"

"Corner of Vine and Ocean Boulevard."

Back to the phone. "I'm at a Mobil station on the corner of Vine and Ocean Boulevard."

"What town?"

"Oh, hell. Wait." I ran back into the station.

D. L. closed her purple eyelids and shook her head. "You again."

I hesitated. I didn't want to sound more stupid than absolutely necessary. "Are we north of Palm Beach?"

"Yes."

I tried again. "Are we near Lake Worth?"

"No. Isn't that too goddamn bad?"

I had to say it flat out. "What town *is* this?"

Silence. She hesitates a long time. She does think I'm a mental case. Pausing between each word, she intones, "This—is—Riviera—Beach—lady—and—that—highway—out—there—is—I-95. *Get it?*"

I ran back to the phone. By then Bernie was laughing hard. He also believed me. "I'll rescue you, but if Tom realizes he's left you and comes back, keep him there until I come. Otherwise we'll be chasing him up and down I-95 all night."

"He won't know I'm missing until he gets to Hobe Sound. Then he'll say, 'Wake up, honey, we're here.' When he looks around, he'll get a ghastly shock. He'll probably have a heart attack."

Bernie said it would take him forty-five minutes to get to Riviera Beach. Rather than risking another encounter with the D. L., I strolled up and down outside, watching the grass grow.

At last Bernie's sleek station wagon pulled up and I hopped in. He did not seem as overjoyed to see me as I was to see him. His opening remark: "You sure played hell with the cocktail hour." The cocktail hour is to Hobe Sound as Mass is to the Vatican, only it lasts longer. "Shouldn't you tell somebody in the gas station where you're going, in case Tom comes back?"

I thought about it. "No-o-o. I think she'd rather not know."

All the way home Bernie worried about what Tom was doing. He was sure he had no clue which gas station he left me in. After all, he just made a phone call. He was sure Tom was driving up and down the interstate, stopping at every gas station and saying, "Did I leave my wife here?" My feelings were mixed: half exasperation, half anxiety.

I still dwelled in Possibility. "Tom is very smart. When we get to your house, his car will be there."

Bernie's car crunched down their gravel driveway. Empty. Our rental car was nowhere to be seen. Carol came out looking worried. "Tom hasn't come and he hasn't even called. I can't imagine what has happened to him."

Bernie turned to me. "I thought you said he was smart."

"Well," I said lamely, "he used to be smart."

Bernie looked at his watch. "It's after nine. Maybe we should call the police."

Carol collapsed with laughter. She could fake it no longer. She and Tom thought it would be funny to fool us by hiding the rented car behind the garage.

My dear husband walked coolly out of the house, martini in hand. He was laughing, too, but he looked a bit sheepish.

"When I got here," he said, "I switched off the engine and then I had this funny feeling. You know how you can tell when you're alone? I didn't have to turn around and look. I knew you weren't there." He put an arm around me. I began to feel better.

"And you didn't even have a heart attack?"

"Nope," he gave me a big hug. "You can't have a heart attack when you're laughing."

After the Kids Leave, the Fun Starts

❧ 29. Grandchildren Are the Real Payoff

"Change is the name of the game," Tom said cheerfully.

"It doesn't have to be," I protested. "We can stay right here at Iduna, playing tennis and eating apples until our teeth fall out." Tom had just added a tennis court to our dream house in the apple orchard. How could we possibly leave Amherst and move to Hanover, New Hampshire?

Tom was fed to the teeth with being a vice-chancellor of a huge state university. He hated all the political shenanigans, within and without. I, however, was blissful. Incredibly, I had composed Emily Dickinson's first obit for *The New York Times*. Harrison Salisbury, who originated the op-ed idea, devoted half the page to "A Delayed Obituary." Encouraged beyond reason, I was now writing full speed ahead. "I don't want to move again," I said.

Tom answered slowly. "For Dartmouth College to invite me to create a parents fund is a vote of confidence. I'm going to accept."

"I'm not leaving Iduna." My voice rose. "You commute—I'm not going."

"All right then, I'll come back every weekend. It's only two hours."

We tried commuting. Not good. Then Bernie Auer, visiting from Hobe Sound, looked me in the eye and said, "What every marriage requires is T.C."

"True Confessions?"

"I'm serious, Nardi. A successful marriage requires Total Commitment. Stop grousing and move to Hanover."

Of course Bernie was right. We sold Iduna, *avec* tennis court and apple orchard, and rented a tiny house in Hanover I called Le Petit Dump.

Eventually, I had to eat my words. I wouldn't have returned to Amherst for anything; I loved Hanover. Russell was a junior at Dartmouth. Tom called to ask how he felt about his parents moving to town. There was a long silence—too long. Then he said, "I don't think it would be too bad." It was fun. We saw Russell and his buddies whenever they were hungry or wanted to wash their cars.

After we moved into our roomy new house on Wren Lane, we relaxed and enjoyed our so-called empty nest. The kids were all chugging along. Tom and Lynn were in Ketchum, Idaho, where he was prosecuting attorney. Tad and Anne were living in Brookline—he was the chief of geriatrics at Mass General. Toby and Anita were still in Chicago, running a chiropractic clinic and a yoga center. Cissa was farming in Vienna, Maine, with her significant other, Bill Bagley, on ninety acres, no electricity, in an elegant, handmade house. They ran an herb business and belonged to the Red House Circus, a highbrow group of professional medieval musicians.

In December of 1983, Tom and I spent Christmas with Tad and his family in Boston. "Grandchildren are the real payoff," he said. And he meant it. By then we had six grandchildren: Ashley and Berit in Idaho, Peter and Ned in Massachusetts, and Iris and Manolo in Chicago.

Harrowed by the holiday season I snapped, "I wouldn't go that far." Our grandchildren rule the roost and they never go to bed.

Christmas was joyous and hectic, as usual. The day after, seven-year-old Peter looked at his pile of presents and said, "I don't have anything to do."

"How about coming back to Hanover for some skiing?" Gapa Tom asked, ignoring my glare. I was already thinking peace and quiet.

"Do you have any snow?"

"There's always snow in New Hampshire," Tom said. He was enjoying—really enjoying—his third career as a fundraiser at Dartmouth.

Peter jumped up and down. "Can I go, Dad? Can I, can I?"

"Well-l-l," said Tad, "you've never stayed away from home . . ."

Peter didn't even hear his father. He was rummaging in the closet, dragging out his skis, poles, and ski boots, making a wild clatter. He pulled on his racing helmet and goggles and was ready to zoom down a slope. Peter was six but he had nine-year-old ideas. He was the apple of

Tom's eye because the older grandkids were a continent away and Peter's brother was too young to play games.

Peter kissed his parents and baby Ned good-bye and away we went. The drive from Boston to Hanover, New Hampshire, takes two and a half hours. It seemed like four hours. Tom and Peter were having a high old time. "Let's play Favorites," Tom suggested. "Name your favorite things."

Peter took a deep breath. "My favorite teams are the Red Sox, the Patriots, and the Celtics. My favorite song is "The Star Spangled Banner." My favorite food is chunky peanut butter. My favorite word is awesome."

"*Awesome?*" asked Gapa Tom.

"That's what the sportscasters say." Peter lowered his voice. "This team is awesome."

"Why 'The Star-Spangled Banner'?"

"Because they play it before all games, except football. Why don't they play 'The Star-Spangled Banner' before football, Gapa Tom?"

"They do play it, but the networks think viewers would rather watch commercials."

"Don't be a cynic," I muttered.

"Cynic?" he winked at Peter. "Is that where we wash dishes, the kitchen cynic?"

Peter laughed. He always laughed at Gapa Tom's jokes, whether he understood them or not. He peered out the window. "No snow," he said.

"Let's sing something," Tom suggested.

"'O say can you see,'" Peter sang with gusto, "'by the dawn's early light . . .'" We sang "The Star-Spangled Banner" again and yet again. "'By the rocket's red glare'?" said Peter. "They didn't have rockets in those days, did they?"

"Not rocket ships," said Gapa Tom, "but believe me, in the War of 1812 when that song was written, they fired rockets at each other."

As we drove into our garage I said, "We sang 'The Star-Spangled Banner' thirteen times."

"It grows on you," said Tom.

"Not me."

Peter went straight to bed, but at five A.M. he charged down the hall and jumped into our bed. He snuggled under the covers and kept on snuggling. "There's an eggbeater in this bed," laughed Tom.

Peter's presence wasn't conducive to sleep, but we didn't complain.

We didn't want him to get homesick. After half an hour of churning he said, "Would you mind if I went back to my own bed now?"

"Would we mind?" whispered Tom. "Is the Pope a Catholic?"

We had planned to spend the week skiing. Peter, who seemed to have unlimited energy, was ready to roll. There was just one little problem—the ground was unseasonably brown. What to do? Tom said, "We will not stoop to the TV babysitter. In the country we make our own fun." Then he went off to work.

I decided I'd teach Peter to help around the house. You're never too young to learn that, and it would take up a lot of his time and, I hoped, free some of mine. I drew up a Chore Chart and said that if he got daily checks in every box, at the end of the week he would win a prize.

"What are chores?" he asked.

"Jobs you do every morning."

"Why?"

"In a family, everybody has to help."

"Why?"

"Because there's lots to do to keep a household going."

"Why?"

"Why not?" I snapped.

The first day Peter folded the laundry enthusiastically and emptied the dishwasher rapidly, breaking only one glass. But his interest soon flagged. I tried to make a game of it, singing my favorite song from *Ruddigore,* "'Duty, duty must be done / That fact applies to everyone,'" but the game didn't catch on.

Tom called to cheer me on. "I wish I were there to play with Peter." I tried to sound cheery, "We do too, Tom." I had to trot around with my helper, emptying wastebaskets, taking out garbage, bringing in logs, spraying house plants. The last chore was a mistake. Never give a seven-year-old a sprayer full of water. I had to trail him with a bath towel. Daily chores proved time consuming, all right—for Grandma.

The second day Tom said (as he left), "Try art." Peter and I drew with crayons, made things with construction paper, and painted with finger paints. (You can forget finger paints.) Neither of us was artsy-craftsy. "I haven't got anything to do," muttered Peter.

"I'll show you how to make a silhouette," I said, reaching back into my own childhood. We tacked white paper on the wall and with a flash-

light I cast the shadow of his profile on it. He had to sit still, no small
feat, while I traced the outline with a felt pen. Then he cut it out in black
paper and pasted it on a white background. Presto—Peter's silhouette!

"Awesome," he said. "Now what do we do?"

That night his grandfather got out the Christmas toys Peter had
brought with him. Tom opened the first one and ran into those dread
words, *some assembly required.* He slammed the lid shut. "Why don't you
play outside tomorrow?"

Peter and I played with his street-hockey set in the driveway until the
puck vanished into the bushes. As he observed wistfully, "The puck is
the most important part."

That night when Peter was asleep Tom made up a treasure hunt,
using pictures instead of words for clues. It took him three hours to lay
out the treasure hunt. It took Peter fifteen minutes to run through it. I
called Tom to complain. "Try Parcheesi," he suggested. Parcheesi *is* a
time consumer. But you can spend only so many hours counting those
little colored spaces before you go bonkers. So we tried *Charlie and the
Chocolate Factory,* a good book, but reading aloud made me drowsy.

Not Peter. "Don't you have any video games?" he asked.

"How do you play video games?" I asked.

"Oh, wow," he said.

On the Fourth Day of Peter, Tom tried to lift my sagging spirits by
remarking at dinner, "The weatherman says it may snow tomorrow."
Peter dashed out of the room and came back wearing his racing helmet,
which he kept on all during the meal. He was raring to go, but no more
than I. I was getting desperate.

Tom kept trying to boost my morale. "There's nothing wrong with
you a snowstorm couldn't cure," he laughed. Unfortunately, there was no
"cure" in sight. Not that day . . . nor the next . . . nor the next. "I guess
snow is over," Peter said sadly, gazing out the window.

That evening we made a major mistake. We called Peter's parents and
let him talk to them. Never, never allow a visiting child to call home. We
were stricken when tears started rolling down his cheeks. Tom rose to
the crisis. "Want to go to Ben 'n' Jerry's, Peter?" Crisis cured.

Seeing that the way to a grandson's heart was through his stomach, I
took to cooking—and eating—with Peter. He stood on a stool, swathed

in a big white apron, and did the mixing while I read aloud the directions on the box. Our carrot cake was a howling, messy success. With total attention from the designated *sous chef* (me), Peter went on to make chocolate chip cookies and fudge. My emergency post-holiday diet collapsed. Gapa Tom suggested we write a book called *Peter and the Calorie Factory.*

I telephoned a young neighbor to ask how she and her kids were surviving the endless snowless days. "Skating on the pond," she said.

Ice skating—the very thing! Tom offered to take us to the indoor rink. "The ice is smoother," he said.

"Ex!" Peter said. He meant excellent; he was big on abbreviations. "I love to skate."

Tom invested in a pair of ice skates for Peter and a Dartmouth hockey jersey with "Peter" lettered across the back. "How steady are you on ice, Peter?" Tom asked. "We want to hand you back to your parents in one piece."

"No problem," Peter said.

Tom skated like a pro, but Peter and I with our spaghetti ankles must have been a sight. Peter didn't exactly skate; he bent way over and walked fast, pumping his shoulders up and down. When he fell, which was every few minutes, he didn't have far to go. When I fell, it was a long way down. Tom quoted Mark Twain. "You two would make a cow laugh."

The skating was risky but fun and we made a valuable discovery. After an afternoon of ice skating, a steaming hot bath, and a big dinner, must sleep follow, as the night the day. Peter was sound asleep before seven and I was nodding. "I can remember when you were still awake at eight P.M.," Tom laughed.

"That was B.P.," I murmured drowsily. "Before Peter."

At long last, Peter's parents and baby Ned pulled into our driveway. Ned with his apple cheeks and wide smile looked like a Christmas tree decoration. Peter smothered them with kisses.

After his family came Peter never said, "What'll I do now?" I've never seen such a cooperative little boy. He waited on his mother and followed his father like a puppy.

The weekend went well. It was not until they were getting ready to leave Sunday afternoon that the big crisis occurred. Peter's father started the engine to get the car warmed up. Gapa Tom and I went out to wave good-bye, thinking about the nice drink we'd have by the nice fire when we were alone in the nice, quiet house. Suddenly, Peter's mom cried out, "Peter has locked all the car doors and the keys are inside the car! We can't get in!"

"Where's your extra set?" asked Tad.

"In my purse," Anne replied. "Locked in the car."

Awesome—and getting awesomer.

"Peter," said his father, speaking slowly and pausing between every word, "why—did—you—do—that?"

"It was just a little joke," he said in a small voice.

"What is it you want, Peter," scolded his mother, "attention?"

His face lit up. "Yes. I want attention."

The situation deteriorated rapidly. I whisked the two boys into the house, away from the bad language. We stood at the window and watched Tom lead the mad ballet round and round the humming automobile. Peter, for once, had nothing to say.

Tom came in for a screwdriver. With it, he pried the car window down half an inch. He tried to unlock the doors with a coat hanger. No good. He tried fishing for the keys with his fishing rod. The rod broke.

"Perilous," said Peter, calling on his "Star-Spangled Banner" vocabulary.

One hour later the car was still throbbing, still consuming gas, and the ballet dancers were still circling. Finally, Gapa Tom marched in, mouth set, opened the hardware drawer and took out the hammer. Peter's eyes rolled heavenward. SMASH! Problem solved.

"Wow," said Peter, like his grandfather an optimist. "Isn't it lucky there was a *small* window they could break."

When the car pulled out of the driveway, we breathed a sigh of relief. Tom said, "Grandchildren are still the real payoff, but God knew what He was doing when He gave kids to the young. Let's have a hot buttered rum." We had several.

The next day we telephoned Peter. "We miss you," Tom said. "We don't have anyone to go ice skating with."

"I wish you were here, Peter," I said.

"Me also." I thought he sounded a little teary. Then he added, "Could we make this short? I'm watching some Germans holding a girl in an empty shack in World War II."

We hung up. I peered out the window. "Tom!" I cried, "It's snowing." "Ex!" he said.

P.S. Naturally, I wrote up Peter's visit. I got a lot of letters, mostly from overworked grandmothers, but one indignant woman stunned me: "At the doctor's, I picked up *Family Circle* and read the article you wrote about your grandson's visit. I did not enjoy it. I have grandchildren who are a great pleasure to me. They love me and I love them and I just feel sorry for someone like you who does not appreciate grandchildren."

I forwarded her letter to Peter, saying "I guess I owe you an apology." He wrote back, enclosing a letter for "the lady that said I don't like the way you take care of Peter."

In August 2002, when Amy Thomas and Peter were married in Vermont, friends and relatives at the rehearsal dinner heaped praise on the tall scholar, by then a Stegner Fellow teaching poetry at Stanford. Finally I stood up. "You all think just because he's a poet, Peter's gentle. Well, I've got news for you. Peter Campion is an attack kid." I read aloud the letter he had written twenty-four years ago. (Like Gertrude Stein he didn't do punctuation.)

Dear lady are you waiting for brain surgery because if you arent I recommend it I dont want to say any more mean things to you so get well soon from brain surgery I dont know if I should say my grandmother is the best or the worst because you are probably thinking the opposite!!!!!! from your arch enemy PETER CAMPION.

When they were honeymooning in Paris, Peter sent me a blissful e-mail. He signed it: "Your Arch Supporter."

❧ 30. My Husband the Car Thief

Tom filled a lot of roles, and well, but the one he loved best was grandfather. Unfortunately, Tommy's girls were inaccessible. They grew up in Ketchum, Idaho. They didn't think they lived in the boonies, but they did. When you go that far to visit, you do not stay a short time.

Playing games with Ashley, twelve, and Berit, ten, was fun, but eventually even dedicated grandparents need time off.

After a heavy snowfall, we arranged an escape to Tommy and Lynn's cabin at Spruce Creek, two hours north. Tom rented a car for our Pooh-like "expotition."

"All set," said the man at Budget Rent-A-Car, "take the little yellow job in the lot. Keys are in it."

We knew right off that something was wrong with the car. Tom said, "Can you believe it? He gave us a car that's almost out of gas."

"What is that ice chest doing in the back seat?" I asked.

"How do I know? Maybe Idaho people only rent cars to go hunting and fishing."

Heading north, he drove the little yellow job and I rode with Lynn. She was going to show us the ins and outs of cabin living. The little yellow job stopped twice. The second time we went back to see what was the matter. He was shoving our skis into the car. Tom had a patient nature, but not with mechanical failures. His short fuse was growing shorter. "I asked for a ski rack but this is a piece of junk. The whole damned rig is coming off."

Near Spruce Creek we parked in what the English call a lay-by. Lynn assured us it would be safe to leave the rented wreck there overnight. With our backpacks in place, we set out on skis for the cabin, about a mile through the woods. Leading us across the snowfields and into the pines, Lynn said, "The beauty part of our hidden retreat is that it's completely isolated."

The cabin stood on a hill. The sinking sun cast a pink glow on tall pines and snowy peaks. It looked like Switzerland. Lynn showed us the battery-operated electricity, the outhouse, the down sleeping bag for two, the all-important wood supply. Then she skied off and left us alone. And I mean alone.

For an hour we explored the glittering silence on skis, with no clue what dark suspicion our tracks on virgin snow might raise. Back at our hideaway, we lit the candles and melted snow to wash and cook with. Then we warmed ourselves with a roaring fire, sherry, a garlicky steak, a bottle of Bordeaux, laughter.

And so to bed in the loft. More than slightly tipsy, we snuggled into our double sleeping bag, listening to the whistling wind and groaning trees. Tom sighed, "Peace. It's wonderful."

BANG! BANG! Someone was pounding on the door. BANG! BANG! BANG! BANG!

We sat upright, gasping. Loud banging on the door in the middle of the night would scare anyone. Alone in the woods, miles from anywhere, it is congealing. My spine felt like an icicle. Tom was breathing heavily. "Omigod," he gasped. He's at his best in emergencies.

BANG! BANG! BANG! "Open up!"

Disappearing down the ladder in his long underwear and knee socks, he looked vulnerable. All I could think of was Capote's *In Cold Blood* and the slaughter of the Clutter family on that farm in Kansas.

BANG! BANG! BANG! "Open this door or we'll knock it down." The voice was rough.

"One of the best things about the cabin," Lynn had said, "is there is no phone." Eventually, someone would find our bodies, of course.

BANG! BANG! BANG! BANG!

Tom: "Who is it?"

"The sheriff. Let us in RIGHT NOW, or we'll break down the door."

Peering down the ladder I called in a stage whisper, "Murderers always say they're sheriffs."

Tom unbolted the door. I held my breath. In walked two men, one very tall, one very short. They looked like Mutt and Jeff. The short one was wearing a fur cap with ear flaps and a sheriff's badge.

"How the hell did you get in here, mister?"

"We skied in."

"We know that. We followed your tracks, for God's sake. I mean how did you come?"

"We came in a car."

"Car? Where is the car?"

"Parked out by the road."

"There's no car out there. No car anywhere. No car at all."

"Impossible! I left it in the turn off. It's a little yellow Subaru."

"Oh, you did, did you? And where did you get your little yellow Subaru?"

"At Budget Rent-A-Car in Ketchum. I rented it."

"Where's the proof? Let's see some papers."

"Of course I can prove it." Husband picked up his parka and pulled out a rumpled slip of paper. "See?"

"What's the license number?"

The short fuse ignited. "How the hell do I know the license? I only rented it yesterday."

"Can you identify the man who rented it to you?"

"Sure. Why?"

"You've got a stolen car, mister, that's why."

"Stolen? That's a stolen car? Who stole it?"

"*You* did."

"Me? Me? Listen, I didn't steal that car, Sheriff, I rented it. IT'S A RENTED CAR!" Now Tom was the one shouting.

"Oh yeah? You took the car all right. We know that. You're under arrest. The owner of that car works in Sam's Sport Shop. He looked out the window and saw you climb into his car and drive off with it."

"If that's so, why didn't he stop me?"

"He said he thought you must be one of his friends. He leaves the keys in it so they can use it. Then his girl called up and told him she saw a strange guy filling his car with gas. She knew you didn't have any business with that car. And what are you doing in this cabin? Hiding out?"

"It belongs to my son. We came up here for a little rest."

"For a rest? In this weather? Who made all those tracks up the mountain? Did you rifle some of the other cabins? How many are in your gang anyway? What's your son's name, mister?"

"Tom Campion. He lives in town. This is his cabin."

"Tom Campion?" The sheriff's jaw dropped. "The prosecuting attorney?"

"Right."

"Jesus." The sheriff took off his fur hat and rubbed his bald head.

For a long time he didn't speak. Then he said, "I'll be dogged. Who would believe that the prosecutor's father steals cars? Wait a minute." He took a radio phone off his belt and dialed. "That you, Tom?"

"Yeah." Even over the squawk box he sounded groggy.

"You asleep, Tom?"

"Not any more. What's up?"

The sheriff talked fast. "Now don't worry. Everything's going to be okay. You're not going to believe this, Tom, but there's a fellow here who stole a car. He says he's your old man."

"My father did WHAT?"

"Well, this stooge claims he's your father. He took another guy's car, a yellow Subaru. We caught him red-handed, hiding out in your cabin. Nothing to worry about, just relax."

"I was relaxed—until you called."

Suddenly Tom started to laugh. He grabbed the phone and said, between guffaws, "Tombo! This is Dad. I know what happened. When I asked for a car the fellow said, 'Take the little yellow job.' There weren't many cars in the lot, so I didn't pay attention to the make. I'm not big on cars, you know? There must have been two yellow cars out there with keys in them, and I got into the wrong one." He paused. "Sorry we woke you up, son."

Tombo was laughing, too.

The sheriff looked dumbfounded. He took back the phone. "I guess it was all a mistake," he muttered. "Sorry, Tom."

"My pleasure," said Tom.

"Nice place you got up here, fella," the sheriff added lamely, and hung up.

Tom grinned at the sheriff and the sheriff began to laugh. His tall silent partner laughed. We all laughed, hard. The sheriff wiped his eyes. "We put you on statewide alarm."

"What happened to the car?" I asked. "Why isn't it parked where we left it?"

The sheriff started laughing again. "Someone spotted it and called the owner. He was spitting fire when he got hold of me. He came all the way up here to get it because he had lots of food in the ice chest. He told me to bring along a bodyguard because, judging by all those ski tracks, there was a gang of thieves up here. You'd better give me his other set of keys."

Tom handed them over. "Tell the owner I said people who leave keys in a car are asking for it."

Next morning we had to hitchhike back to Ketchum. We were in the real boonies now. We walked an hour, skis heavy on our shoulders, before we saw a car. "Why are you walking?" the driver asked, stopping to pick us up.

Tom smiled enigmatically. "We got tired of skiing."

He was still seething with indignation when he confronted the rental man. "I'll be damned if I'll pay one red cent for that wreck of a car."

"Mister," the rental guy said, "you don't owe me a penny. I should pay you for the best laugh I've had in years."

❊ 31. What Is Really Worth While?

At Julia's funeral I sat holding Tom's hand in the stained-glass silence of All Saints Episcopal Church in Belmont, Massachusetts, thinking about my big sister. Wiping away tears, I recalled my irrational resentment of her. Julia, thirteen years older than I, was the matriarch of the family. Tom and the kids adored her. She treated our children like adults but me like a child. "Julia is so damn bossy," I complained to Tom.

He always took her part. "Maybe you need bossing." (Who, me?) "But I don't think that's the problem. What you suffer from is sibling rivalry."

"Like you and Frank?" I shot back. Unlike my mother's family, Tom's had sibling rivalry.

"Touché," he said. Growing up, Tom and his brother, five years younger, were not close. Frank was Pop's favorite, Tom his mother's, a sad but not unusual situation that pits one child against the other. Then Frank, addicted to cigarettes, got throat cancer. Over the next ten years— Frank died in 1989—they developed a golden bond.

I was seventy when my sister died in 1987, and still avoiding the eternal question: What is worth while? Julia seemed to know the answer in her bones.

My sister was everything I wasn't: unselfish, adored, centered. I grew up green with envy of her, but I was shattered by her death. She had had three heart attacks and two open-heart surgeries. With those warnings, why was I so undone?

I can't forget the sermon that Reverend Anne Fowler later preached about her. "Julia was energized by her desire for justice. Charm and wit never completely camouflaged her indomitable will. And yet she never took herself too seriously." Perfect.

When we buried Julia, I dissolved into a pool of guilt and regret. I realized that her bossiness was her way of expressing fierce love of her family. Why didn't I know this when she was alive?

As we sang "A Mighty Fortress Is Our God" I had a vivid flashback. She and Charlie Summerall were married in 1926. The next year I, the ten-year-old sister, took an overnight steamboat from Fort Monroe, Virginia to visit them at Fort Hoyle, Maryland. In those days, children could travel alone.

One night, in their tiny newlyweds' apartment, I glanced into their bedroom and caught Julia in the act.

Wearing a long lavender nightgown, her brown braid hanging down her back, she was kneeling by their double bed saying her prayers. "What a strange thing for a grown woman to do," I thought. "Now I lay me down to sleep is for little kids."

Later, when I was a know-it-all Wellesley student, she and I began our long-running debate about the meaning of life. No small thoughts for the Reeder sisters. Julia's faith was rock solid; my "philosophy" was all questions. "Belief in immortality," my sister told me firmly, "is the only way you can make sense of the universe. Without it everything is meaningless."

"You're just talking religion."

Exasperated, she asked, "What do you think is worth while, Narcissa?"

"I can't answer that."

"I'll put it another way. What is your purpose?"

Time out while I thought about that. "To enjoy myself. This is the only life I have."

She stared at me. "The purpose of your life is not you, Narcissa."

"You're too damned certain," I said lamely.

She grew old as she lived, undaunted. After Charlie died, she became even more hardheaded. In her eighties she turned the wrong way and totaled her car. Fred bought her a new one and one week later she was back at the wheel.

We worried about her living alone in the old Victorian house in Belmont, but she didn't. "I can't leave my view of the Boston skyline" was her reason for refusing to budge. We were right.

One night when she was closing the windows, the sash broke and a window crashed down. Both her hands were trapped between the heavy window and the sill. There was nothing she could do. Julia calmly hooked a leg around a chair and dragged it so she could sit down. There she remained all night, trapped. *Nine hours* later a neighbor found her, slightly disoriented but intact. When her hands were released she said, "I knew help would come."

Unbelievable.

I asked her what she thought about during that long night. "Our ancestors. In the early days they endured real hardship. And Mother losing little Nat. And Charlie commanding an artillery battery at Kasserine Pass. But mostly God." Julia's faith never failed her.

Looking back, I recalled a fact I'd long forgotten. Julia was five years old when little Nat suddenly died. In those darkest days, only one thing kept the family going—our mother's deep faith.

Emily Dickinson: "By a departing light / We see acuter, quite . . ." Death is a great teacher, but my sister did not need awareness of death to make her kind to others, or define what is important. Apparently I did—the jolt of losing her somehow refocused me.

On the day of her funeral, sitting in the candlelight of All Saints, I recalled her unshakable faith. I thought about the ring of conviction in Dr. Harry Emerson Fosdick's voice when, trying to bolster my wavering faith, he spoke of his belief in God. I asked him to write out what he said, which he did.

"I believe there is mind behind the universe," Dr. Fosdick wrote, "purpose running through it, ultimate meaning in it, and destiny ahead of it. Affirmation of God is, at the very least, the affirmation of these four factors. And denial of God is the denial of all four, leaving the universe mindless, purposeless, ultimately meaningless."

Suddenly the truth struck me. I was not jealous of Julia's long chestnut hair, her merry laugh, her many friends. What I coveted was that unshakable faith.

"The best thing for being sad," Merlyn had advised young Arthur, "is to learn something."

Tom, as always full of empathy, understood my *crise,* but he had to return to work. Grieving, I once again repaired to the library at Wellesley. I browsed through the stacks, searching for solace. As if by magic, the title on a small book caught my eye: *What Is Worth While?* It was a slender volume redolent of another era, bound in white vellum with gold lettering and decorated with purple violets.

I sat down to examine it, thinking about Julia. Who dared call a book *What Is Worth While?* No name on the cover. Inside I discovered the author was Anna Robertson Brown.

Tucked between the pages I found a yellowing *New York Times* obituary dated March 1, 1948. I scanned it eagerly. On her death, the *Times* saluted Anna Robertson Brown, Wellesley College, B.A. 1883, M.A. 1888, as the first woman to earn a Ph.D. at the University of Pennsylvania and one of the first "female" Phi Beta Kappas.

Anna's life was a student's dream. At sixteen you write a thesis for a Wellesley philosophy course and call it *What Is Worth While?* Ten years later, Thomas Y. Crowell decides to publish it. Your little book sells four hundred thousand copies, is translated into Arabic and Japanese, goes into seventy-five editions, and stays in print sixty-two years. Wow.

I settled into a purple armchair that overlooked the ice blue fountain splashing on Longfellow Pond. Why would such a modest little book go into seventy-five editions? What did Anna consider worth while one hundred years ago? Was she a woman of faith like Julia, or full of questions like me? Could this have any relevance to my dilemma? Could the sentimental past speak to the hard-boiled present? What *is* worth while, anyway?

Anna's opening sentences are riveting: "Only one life to live! We all want to do our best with it. We all want to make the most of it. How can we best get hold of it? How can we accomplish the most with the energies and powers at our command?" I gasped. This woman is writing for me. I read the little book straight through and my spirits began to lift.

Like my sister, Anna was grounded in faith. She makes one key assumption: there is more to life than meets the eye. If you believe this life is the be-all-end-all, then *What Is Worth While?* is not for you. Anna be-gins: "Life is large. We cannot possibly grasp the whole of it." Then she asks, "What is vital? What is essential? What may we profitably let go?"

Reaching for the stars, she answers: "We may let go all things which we cannot carry into the eternal life."

Using this as her golden yardstick, she measures her values and es-tablishes rules. If we don't want to "cumber our lives," Dr. Brown (she always used her academic title) has four recommendations:

1. We may drop pretense.
2. We may drop worry.
3. We may let go of discontent.
4. We may let go of self-seeking.

I put down the little book and gazed out at the slender shaft of the fountain. Anna Robertson Brown and Julia Reeder Summerall. They never met, of course, but on this day they met in my mind. For both of them faith was as natural as breath. In their heart of hearts, they knew life is eternal.

People like Anna and Julia can accept dying as a natural progression because they believe life has meaning. Anna had written, "Sharp sorrow is given us that, having felt, suffered, wept, we may be able to under-stand, love, bless."

After my mother died, I couldn't stop crying. Julia put her arms around me. "I want to tell you what Mother told me when we buried little Nat. I was only five but she spoke as though I were grown. 'Always remember this,' she told me. 'Faith comes through pain.'"

At Julia's service the priest had said the ancient English prayer, "Life is eternal, and love is immortal, and death is only a horizon—and a horizon is only the limit of our sight."

Such unquestioning faith was not going to happen to me.

But mulling over the faith-filled lives led by my sister and Anna, I began to feel less fragmented, more centered. Anna Robertson Brown, Wellesley Class of 1883, was calling to me across a century, telling me to ponder "What Is Worth While?" She was telling me to focus on things unseen. She was telling me to let go of everything I cannot carry into the eternal life.

Eternal life?

"Yes!" my sister Julia was calling to me. "Ahead the doors are open!"

❧ 32. New York on $1,000

T he great pitcher Satchel Paige lived to be eighty or ninety; he didn't
know which: "Our midwife died and all the books burned up."
When he died, Tom cut out his prescription for longevity and put it on
the fridge.

OLD SATCH'S SIX RULES FOR KEEPING YOUNG
1. Avoid fried foods which anger the blood.
2. If your stomach disputes you, lie down and pacify it with cool
   thoughts.
3. Keep the juices flowing by jangling around gently as you move.
4. (Tom's favorite) Go lightly on the vices, such as carrying on in society. The social ramble ain't restful.
5. Avoid running at all times.
6. Don't look back. Something may be gaining on you.

In our Grandma Moses town we didn't have to worry about the social ramble. Hanover was a three-stoplight village without private clubs,
country or otherwise. Things were so laid back in the eighties the hot
political issue was, should parking meters go from twenty-five to fifty
cents an hour?

Tom and I loved the easy living; but once in a great while we wanted
to carry on in society. For our wedding anniversary, our kids gave us two
nights at the Carlyle Hotel. It zapped us when we drew out our spending money. New York on $10 was long ago and far away.

Eager for the social ramble, I boarded the train to New York in White
River Junction, Vermont, at midnight. Tom was already in the city on
Dartmouth business. Stars were bright and the locomotive was blowing
clouds of steam. It was a scene out of *Anna Karenina*. Struggling to my
berth, I peered over the shoulder of the indifferent porter. Unlike the

snappy uniformed porters of my youth, he wore a white shirt and sleeve-less red sweater. He was reading *I and Thou* by Martin Buber.

Tom met me in bustling Penn Station. He still liked to tease me about being a Virginia hayseed. He called out, "Hey, hick!" and twenty New Yorkers turned around, thinking he meant them.

E. B. White told me at the Gills' long-ago party that "People will pay good money for clearly written accounts of other people's disasters." Tom and I have disasters the way some people have freckles. Our anniversary trip to New York was no exception.

He whisked me off to a French patisserie on Madison Avenue for a sophisticated breakfast: just-squeezed orange juice, flaky golden *crois-sant* with sweet butter and raspberry jam, hot foamy *cafe au lait*. Tom winced at the bill. "Remember when two dinners *avec vin* were $4.75?"

It turned out we were both hicks. New York was too much for us, and I'm not just talking money. The first afternoon I had a written appointment to interview film writer Garson Kanin for a *Reader's Digest* article. I went to 200 East Fifty-seventh Street, where the doorman said: "You want Mr. Kanin, the writer fellow? He moved out. Hasn't lived here for years." I raced to the telephone. Garson Kanin was unlisted. What to do? My appointment was for three; it was now ten of.

I grabbed a cab to the hotel, ran back to our room and found Mr. Kanin's letter. His address was 200 *West* Fifty-seventh Street. Weird. A helpful cabby zipped me across town at hair-raising speed. I arrived at Kanin's office, panting, only fifteen minutes late. His smiling secretary said, "Mr. Kanin is still at lunch. He should be back soon."

Tom fared no better. He had an appointment at 55 East Fifty-second Street but could not find any building with that number. He phoned the Allegheny Corporation and the secretary said, "We're at Park and Madison. You can't miss it." But he did—and had to call back. She said: "You again? Do you want me to come down there and lead you up?" It turned out that the number 55 was *etched* on glass doors, impossible for aging eyes to see in sunlight.

To recover, we spent the afternoon at a movie. It cost six times what we paid in 1950 to see *The Lady's Not for Burning* on stage. We picked *My Dinner with Andre* because Wallace Shawn is the son of our friends Cecille and Bill Shawn. It's a dialogue between a Yuppie (Wallace Shawn) and a Consciousness Raiser (Andre Gregory). Brilliant, but unsettling.

Wally said, "It's that moment of contact with another person. That's what scares us." Right. Especially in Manhattan.

The next day, while Tom was buttering up Dartmouth donors, I headed to New Jersey to visit a friend. Nothing in the entire state of New Hampshire is as big as the mind-boggling Port Authority Bus Terminal. Maybe Mount Washington. I picked out daffodils and blue iris from a flower vendor to take to my hostess in Princeton. The vendor said, "How long outta water?"

"About three hours."

"No good. No can sell 'em to you."

"What do you mean, you can't sell them to me?"

"They stop drawing water, never start again. Daisies O.K. You can have daisies."

"I don't want daisies. I want daffs and iris."

"O.K., then get something to put water in."

"Where am I going to find a vase in this mausoleum?"

"Looka around. Looka around."

I looked around. I located a trash barrel and fished out a big styrofoam cup. Vendor beamed, poured water into cup, put flowers in water, and wrapped it up. As I left, I heard him saying, "How long outta water?" I sat for hours on the bus, holding the damned cup of flowers. My hostess gasped, "How clever of you to think of a way to keep them fresh!"

On my return the cheerful cab driver said, "Lady, how much did you pay this morning to go from your hotel to the bus station?"

"Why in the world do you want to know?"

"Because I forgot to turn on the Goddamned meter, that's why." We had a good laugh, negotiated a fee, and parted chums.

Back in the hotel room I found a shattered husband slumped in a chair, staring into space. He had lost his wallet. Not stolen. Must have "lost" it in a taxi. No idea what cab company. Everything gone—cash, driver's license, credit cards. He had to hike twenty blocks in the rain to the hotel. Head hurt, feet ached. What to do? "I need a stiff drink," he said. "Oh, I forgot, no money." He decided to take a hot bath.

He called from the tub, "Einstein said there are only two ways to live—as though nothing is a miracle, or as though everything is a miracle." Silence. I expected him to say he believed in miracles. Instead he moaned, "I feel sick at my stomach."

"Don't forget Satchel Paige's advice. If your stomach disputes you, lie down and pacify it with cool thoughts."

He was stretched out on the bed when the phone rang. "Hullo," he mumbled. Suddenly he sat up straight. "My God!"

A man at a midtown branch of Citibank had the wallet. Some fellow walked in, put it down, and vanished. Clerk found T. Campion's name and address in the wallet, got our New Hampshire phone number from information, found out from our dog-and-cat sitter where we were staying, and was so happy to reach us. What are the odds on that happening?

Pulling on his clothes, Tom yelled, "Lend me a twenty for a cab. Hurry! It's almost closing time." The door banged and he was gone.

But he could not find a taxi—it was rush hour. He ran through the rain until he finally snatched a waiting cab, nearly knocking over two old ladies. "Sorry, this is an emergency." The taxi driver provided another hair-raising ride. New York cabbies enjoy a challenge.

Citibank was locked up tight. Tom went to the back door and knocked. Good Samaritan Clerk appeared and handed over the wallet. The cash was gone but the credit cards were still there. Whew! He talked Good Samaritan into cashing a check, slipped him a reward, and got the name of his boss. Later he wrote a glowing letter of thanks and praise. Tom was always big on follow-up.

We fell in love with the Big Apple all over again.

That night we picked a seafood restaurant on Broadway for R. and R. We ordered the shrimp hors d'oeuvre. Our plates appeared with shredded lettuce and one shrimp. Tom complained. Waiter said: "Shrimp can be singular or plural."

We had tickets for *Othello*, the play, not the opera. When Iago said "Who steals my purse steals trash," Tom nudged me and grinned. After the theater we went to an oyster bar. Oysters were three dollars *each*. Who wants to know what each oyster costs? Weary, I looked to see how late it was. Ye gods! My watch was gone. Impossible. How could I have lost the beautiful watch Tom gave me on our twenty-fifth anniversary? He was as upset as I was.

We ran all the way back to the Winter Garden. The theater was dark and Janitor was locking the front doors. Tom gasped, "Please, can we look for my wife's watch? We were sitting in the fourth row." I shuddered, visualizing heels crunching my watch. Janitor was kind but shook his head sadly. "Lights are off, sir, and I don't have no flashlight. Try the stage door."

We raced halfway around the block to the stage door on Seventh Avenue, pushed a bell, and held our breath. A handsome blond man, one of the actors, stuck his head out the door. "What do you want?"

"Can we come in to look for a lost watch?"

"What kind of watch?" he asked suspiciously.

"A small gold Seiko."

"We have it. Somebody found it and just turned it in." He closed the door. We stood there a long time. Maybe he was kidding. Ten minutes later he returned and handed Tom a brown envelope. Inside was my watch, unharmed. Tom fished in his wallet for yet another reward but the man had disappeared.

"What a weekend," Tom said. "You and I shouldn't be allowed out alone."

"Maybe we should hire a keeper."

We couldn't stop laughing. By now New York was our Big Two-Hearted City. We learned the hard way that the Big Apple has a core of gold.

"Ole Satch said it all," said Tom, steering me into yet another cab. "The social ramble ain't restful."

❉ 33. Lost in the Moscow Metro

Our love affair with winter peaked during a huge blizzard. All New England was snowed under. As Tom was leaving Boston Mayor Sargent announced on the radio: "No automobiles are permitted to enter or leave Boston until further notice."

Back in Hanover I waited nervously by the radio—this was B.C., before cell phones—knowing full well that Tom the Undauntable would head for home no matter what. He did not switch plans easily. As I fidgeted, winds howled, pine trees twisted like tops, snow pounded the windows. Eventually, Tom stamped in looking like the Abominable

Snowman. "I had to leave the car on Route 120 and wade through huge drifts." I hugged him, ice and all.

Snowed-in-dom was delicious: blazing logs, steaming tea with rum, cinnamon toast. The phone didn't ring and television didn't intrude— all cables were down. We curled up by the fire as cozy as cats.

The golden glow of the kerosene lamp gave enough light and suddenly there was time to read aloud. Tom began with Snow-Bound. He shared Whittier's delight in being shut in from all the world without. "Blow high, blow low, / not all its snow could quench our hearth-fire's ruddy glow."

After the oil burned out, we sat in darkness enjoying the firelight, the quiet, the swirling snow at the windows, and each other. Emily D. had it right in her shortest poem: "Winter under cultivation / Is as arable as spring."

A few years later, New Hampshire had an "open winter." Longing to ski, Tom found an inexpensive cross-country ski trip in Russia run by the Citizens Exchange Council, a non-profit dedicated to hands-across-the-sea. Our friends couldn't believe it. "You're going to Soviet Russia in January? You must be out of your tree." We nodded happily.

Three days before we were to leave I, the cross-country ski nut, slipped on the ice. Snap! There goes my right wrist. Driving me to the emergency room, Tom was more upset than I, but I was glum. "There goes our one and only trip to Russia," I said. No reply came from the born optimist.

The cast on my arm was daunting. I couldn't tie my shoes or put up my long hair. As a lady's maid, Tom got A's in shoelaces and flunked hairdressing.

We were going to cancel the trip, but our orthopedist, also a skier, said, "Go ahead. Your cast will hold your bones in place just as well over there as over here." I cut a slit in the sleeve of an old parka to push the cast through, found a heavy sock to use in place of a glove, and we were off.

We were crazy about Russia. It snowed every day we were there— light, fluffy snow. "I think I've died and gone to heaven," Tom said. We skied on flat, well-groomed trails in Kalinin, Olgino, Leningrad, and on the campus of Moscow University. It was surprisingly easy for me to use one pole and swing the arm-in-the-cast. I did fall a couple of times, but it was like collapsing on a down quilt.

However, you *can* get too much of a good thing.

One Moscow morning we awoke to twenty-two degrees below zero. Skiing in Gorky Park, or anywhere else, was o-u-t. Tom grinned. "Isn't that lucky? Now we can explore the city."

We thought we liked winter but walking through the sub-zero city almost did us in. Our guidebook had said "Public transportation in Moscow is cheap and efficient and a good way to get out and meet So-viets on one's own."

After a long caviar and blini lunch at the venerable Hotel Metropole on Red Square, Tom and I thought we were fortified with enough vodka to do anything. We weren't. We only knew three words in Russian: "hello" (*privyeht*), "thank you" (*spasibo*) and the name of our metro stop (*Ler-montovskaya*), but we weren't worried. Our Intourist guide, Nellie, had told us, "*Da*, go by yourselves. No problem. All Russians study English in school." Nellie was a full-time propagandist. "We have no poverty in Russia," she said flatly.

Our first mistake was stopping by the Gum Department Store to buy batteries for my tiny tape recorder. Since I couldn't write, I talked into it all the time. I hoped they'd take me for a spy but only one Soviet offi-cial, a guard in the Folklore Museum, questioned my electronic diary.

Shopping at Gum's was a challenge, but I had married a man who liked challenges. First he had to find out which alcove in a beehive of al-coves sold batteries. Then he had to find out the cost of the batteries. Then he had to find out where to pay for them. Then he had to stand in line to fork over the rubles. (Soviet clerks were not allowed to handle money.) Then he had to take the slip showing he had paid back to the electronics cubby hole. *Then* he got the batteries. He enjoyed it. "What they have a lot of in Russia is Process."

All unsuspecting, we headed for the famouts Moscow metro. As the Russian proverb says, "It is better to see once than hear a hundred times." I still can't get over it. The Russians lagged miles behind us in automobiles, highways, and supermarkets, but their subway superiority was staggering.

It was almost five o'clock. Rush hour in any city of seven million people is frantic, but in Moscow it is frightening. Everybody rides the metro. The lucky few who own cars seldom use them; gas is out of sight. The station entrance was jammed by a huge, strangely silent crowd. The moody Muscovites in heavy overcoats and fur hats dusted with snow were straight from central casting.

We inched forward in a human iceberg. Russians push discreetly— shoving was bad form in the U.S.S.R. They were as eager to get home as we were, but they knew the way. I was thankful for my broken wrist. To protect it, I had to hold the cast above my head like a periscope. Other- wise, Tom would have lost me in the crush.

We oozed along with the crowd toward a turnstile. Watching others, Tom cleverly put twenty kopecks into a machine, got change, and took us through the gate. The Moscow metro is cheap. You can ride all day for five kopecks (six cents). First hurdle surmounted.

Then the excitement really began. Because the metro was built six hun- dred feet below the Moscow River—an astonishing feat of engineering— the escalators descend at a sharp angle with death-defying speed. An at- tendant stands at the bottom to whisk away any stumbler. One fall would create an epic pile-up.

We zoomed down to track level. Then we looked around—and gasped in astonishment. Nothing in the bleak city above had prepared us for this wonderland of marble columns, vaulted ceilings, glittering mosaics, statues, and crystal chandeliers. The benches were upholstered in rich leather cushions. The marble floors were gleamingly clean.

It's as though instead of cathedrals, the Soviets worshipped in sub- ways. Not too farfetched when you consider what the communists did to Leningrad's beautiful Kazan Cathedral. That hallowed space where czars were crowned, with its lofty arches and green malachite pillars, was desecrated. The communists converted it into "The Museum of Athe- ism." When the Soviet Union collapsed, the Orthodox church immedi- ately reclaimed Kazan Cathedral. We wished we could have been there for the celebration.

The Metro is kept at sixty-eight degrees, deliciously warm to Mus- covites. The elegant subway, built sixty-five years ago by the rigidly aus- tere Stalin, piqued our curiosity. Why were the spartan Soviets so lavish in decoration and carefree in spending? Was it to give their citizens hope for the future? To enrich their drab lives? To impress visitors? It does that, all right. And just *how* is a subway kept in such pristine condition? Who knows?

When we stopped gawking, we felt stampeded. Which was the right train? We asked dozens of people if they spoke English. They said *nyet* or just turned and walked away. Maybe they were afraid to get involved with Americans. Or perhaps they did not know what we were saying. "A good way to get out and meet people"? Forget it. We were lost, and all of the signs were literally Greek to us. (The mysterious Cyrillic alphabet used by the Russians was named for a ninth-century Greek who converted Slavic into a written language.) We learned what it is like to be illiterate. Terrifying.

"Are you scared?" Tom asked.

"No," I tried to smile. "You always get where you're going."

At that moment, he spotted a word in English. A sign over a wall phone actually said INFORMATION. Hooray! He picked up the receiver and got a stream of Russian. He asked if anyone spoke English. The voice said, "Sprechen sie Deutsch?" He repeated, "Do you speak English?" The voice said "*Nyet*" and hung up.

Panic was setting in as the crowd surged around us. People to whom we said "*Lermontovskaya?*" gave us blank stares. We just *thought* we could pronounce it. What to do? We looked around frantically. I felt my temples start to throb. Out of the crowd stepped a little man in a gray karakul hat. He approached us with a reassuring smile. He must have sensed our fear.

Tom smiled back, held out his pocket map, and pointed to our stop. The Russian spoke no English but his kind twinkle spoke volumes. He studied the map for a moment. Using pantomime, he motioned us to go up one flight, walk left—now he was walking with his fingers—and descend two flights to our train. We all grinned and shook hands. I could have hugged him.

Zipping up and down on those escalators, we held on for dear life. Young lovers on the fast moving stairs were oblivious to all around them. Later we learned that the temperature-controlled stations offer the young "privacy" they can't find in their crowded apartments. Older people go there, too, to take ice and snow-free walks. The metro may be cozy to them but Tom and I were longing for the log-fire security of our own home.

We jostled onto a platform, but was it the right one? We were beginning to panic again. Things happen fast in the Moscow metro. Trains roll in, silently, and a flashing sign tells you how many *seconds* until the next one comes. You don't have time to consider.

Was this the track we wanted? We looked around frantically. And there was the little man in the karakul hat. He smiled and waved. He had followed us to make sure we got on the right train. As we pushed into the car, he raised both fists, thumbs up, and gave us a big wink. I blew him a kiss. At least we had one friend in the Soviet Union.

It was snowing hard when we stepped out of the metro. Tom gasped, "Can you believe it?" He pointed to a snowblown sign: Lermontovskaya. I felt like Clara in the *Nutcracker* snow scene, throwing her head back to catch the drifting flakes. As relief surged through us, he squeezed my hand. Then the Indomitable Snowman paid me a compliment I still treasure. "You're a good woman to get lost with," he said.

❊ 34. Landing in Ann Landers

One morning, the "Compleate Angler," also the "compleate" newspaper nut, exclaimed, "Holy cow! Listen to this." We were enjoying freshly ground coffee and sticky rolls on our Wren Lane terrace. Yellow forsythia and daffodils were glowing in the pale sunshine and Tom had just quoted, as he did every spring, Robert Frost: "Nature's first green is gold."

"Listen to what?"

"Ann Landers's column."

I laughed. "You're into Ann Landers?"

"You will be, too. In fact, you are in it, though not by name. Listen: 'Dear Readers, For at least the past five years, various versions of "Senior Citizens" have crossed my desk. Dozens of people have claimed authorship. I have no idea who wrote the first one, but if I had to bet my life, I'd go with the Vassar graduate who read her composition at a class reunion.' Then she goes on to quote your 'We Were before Pantyhose, Credit Cards, Penicillin' article, the one that's usually by Anonymous, the one I told you to copyright, but you didn't."

"I'll be damned" was all I could say.

Tom suggested that, like the rest of America, I should write a letter to Ann Landers. Not the usual no-name, no-address request for advice, but a signed letter to protest her calling my piece "Senior Citizens" and suggesting I was a Vassar woman, of all things.

"Protest is right," I said. "I'm not a senior citizen yet, except when I go to the movies. And I'd hate to be a Vassarite; it sounds like underwear."

So I wrote my "Dear Ann" letter. I thanked her for saying out loud that many people have claimed authorship of "We Were before Pantyhose." I quoted Tom, "All work and no plagiarism makes a dull essay," and ended by alluding to a talk I was giving at my fiftieth reunion at Wellesley called "Fifty Years of Sex."

Tom took to reading "Dear Ann" aloud at breakfast. He relished her one-liners, such as, "Dear Jealous in Joliet. Mind your own business. Thanks for writing."

Sometimes Ann gave him pause. "Today she says: 'Never yell at each other unless the house is on fire. Thanks for writing.' Have I ever yelled at you?"

"Come to think of it, no. Have I ever yelled at you?"

He chuckled. "Don't ask."

One day he said, "Ann gets away with murder. Is anything taboo? Now she is endorsing mutual masturbation for everyone from teenagers to the elderly. She calls it 'a safe and realistic alternative.' What would Wellesley's Dr. DeKruif say to that?"

"She'd faint dead away."

A few months later Tom exclaimed, "Listen to this—Ann answered your letter. 'Dear Nardi, A thousand mea culpas—one for every low life who stole your brainchild. Send me a copy of your essay on Fifty Years of Sex. I'll print it and beat all those thieves to the punch. Thanks for writing.'"

"Fame at last!" I cried, innocently.

Appearing in Ann Landers's column by name is a one-way ticket to bedlam. Tom's childhood buddy called from Plattsburgh, New York, with congratulations. Tom said, "Funny Wayne should get excited over a couple of sentences in advice to the lovelorn." The air seeped out of my ballooning ego.

I heard from people I thought were dead. My quavery kindergarten teacher in Honolulu sounded as though she were calling from Beyond. My high school science teacher wrote from Panama: "Now that you've hit the Big Time, I know you will want to contribute to your school's alumni fund." (I want to, but not very much.) A jeweler called from Bronxville. He said tersely: "We have been trying to locate you. You owe us $13.40."

A woman Tom used to date telephoned from Sydney to ask how to get a letter published in Ann Landers's column. She said she had written to Ann five times, without success. Would he mind putting in a word for her? "You two know Ann, of course, don't you?" He said no, we didn't. "It must be an inside job," his old girl said. "Your wife's letter wasn't that good."

A stranger called from Tacoma, Washington, to ask if I would mind calling her collect to read all of "Senior Citizens" to her over the telephone. She didn't care how much the call cost. She planned to give my talk the next day at her high school reunion. That struck Tom as funny. "Maybe plagiarism by phone is okay." He revived his aphorism, "All work and no plagiarism makes a dull speech."

Friends in Dallas sent a testy postcard. How come we had time to write to Ann Landers but couldn't find time to answer their Christmas letter? (How do you answer four Xeroxed pages that begin, "Joe fell down the stairs and broke his nose and four ribs, but he's still cheery, and so is Mabel in her automated wheelchair"?)

Tom's favorite was the letter our granddaughter Iris wrote. "Dear Grandma, My teacher read your letter to Ann Landers to our class and said that it shows you don't have to be young to do things."

A cousin called who has not spoken to me since I inherited the portrait of Great Grandma she thought should come to her. She just wanted me to know she was still mad. I told my cousin I had not pinched the portrait and she was my great-grandmother, too. She snapped, "Just because you're in Ann Landers's column, you think you're so great," and hung up.

Our five children were strewn from Boston to L.A. Every one of them read Ann Landers and reached for the phone.

The kids did not exude enthusiasm for Mom's big breakthrough. Comments ranged from "It's pretty unnerving to find your mother in an advice-to-the-lovelorn column" to "What do you *mean* your next topic will be Fifty Years of Sex? *Really*, Mom." Tom said, "I thought those highly educated kids read intellectual stuff, which shows how much a parent knows."

When you're in "Ask Ann Landers," you do things Ann's way, but I hated her calling "We Were Before . . ." my creation. I would never refer to my writing efforts as "creations." In my life, I have achieved only five creations, and I have to credit Husband with an assist on each of those.

Our Ann Landers communion with dear ones far and wide was fun, sort of. But had I known my letter was going to raise such a hullabaloo, I might have relaxed and let that busy writer Anonymous take credit for my stuff. However, Tom pointed to a real plus. "When it comes to establishing authorship, a U.S. copyright is a weak whistle compared to Ann's clarion call to millions of readers."

He thought it was nice that Ann Landers had turned America into a global village. Because of her, in those pre-internet days, people miles apart could chat as cozily as folks around a pot-bellied stove in the general store. "Ann fulfills a need deep in all of us," Tom said, "the urge to air our problems—and to enjoy the misery of others."

Fifty Years of Sex

❈ 35. Fifty Years of Sex

I never did send Ann Landers my Wellesley speech. It was long and her column was short. However, it did appear in *The New York Times Magazine.* A few years later, on our fiftieth anniversary, another part was published on the op-ed page in the *Times.* Editors compose titles, not authors. This was the only time an editor ever used my title. But it wasn't even my title. Tom thought up "Fifty Years of Sex."

To our surprise, Russell landed us on the front page of the same edition. We exploded with laughter when we read the tiny ad at the bottom of the page. "Happy Anniversary to Mom and Dad from their five kids."

One of Tom's maxims was, "If you want money, ask for advice. If you want advice, ask for money." But if I asked him for advice, I got advice—and it was good. When I was invited to speak at my fiftieth reunion, I asked Tom what to talk about.

He instantly replied, "The Sexual Revolution." Cissa, Wellesley Class of 1982, seconded him and supplied her generation's point of view.

Tom picked a hot topic. *The New York Times Magazine* actually censored it. Editor Jim Greenfield said, "The word vagina has never appeared in the *Times* and never will." (Fifteen years later the *Times* printed this sentence: "Madonna, the sexibitionist, masturbated on stage and simulated oral sex with a bottle of soda.")

Tom, who loved to tease me, said, "'Fifty Years of Sex' suggests you've led a more colorful life than you have. There's a big difference between fifty years of experience and having the same experience fifty times."

When the Boston Harvard Club asked me to give the talk, they refused the title. Tom came up with "The Fertility Dance." David Mc-

Cord, Harvard's witty wordsmith, said that at our age we should call it "The Futility Dance," or even "The Sterility Dance," and quoted Malcolm Muggeridge: "Sex is a funny thing and the older I get, the funnier it gets."

Here is the talk that Tom and Cissa and I cooked up.

I think that the primordial drive for reproduction is as powerful as nuclear fission. Generations of reformers have tried to suppress it, always without success.

For our generation, sex was a mystery and people wanted it that way. They used to put marble fig leaves on nude male statues. Simone de Beauvoir said her devoutly Catholic mother told her never to look at herself when she was naked. "I was obliged," de Beauvoir writes in her memoir, "to change my underwear without uncovering myself."

My own mother said that when she was eighteen she told her mother "I see Annie Miller is expecting" and got squelched for making a risqué remark. Pregnancy had to be hidden. It was proof positive you had slept with a man. By the time I was eighteen, you could mention pregnancy, but if an unmarried girl got pregnant, she had a shotgun wedding or vanished.

It was all so mysterious. We didn't know anything. One friend asked her mother, "Where does the baby come out?" The mother, blushing, replied, "Can't you just *imagine* that?"

In *One Writer's Beginnings* Eudora Welty says that time after time she asked where babies come from, and her mother would answer, "The mother and the father both have to *want* the baby, Eudora . . ." Then there would always be a welcome interruption—welcome to mother, not daughter. "The fact is," Eudora writes, "she never did tell me. I doubt that any child I knew ever was told by her mother any more than I was about babies."

If we knew the correct word for anything, which is doubtful, we could not utter it. Today, a five-year-old's vocabulary is better than ours was in college. When my classmate Martha Sneath spilled hot coffee in her lap, her little granddaughter lisped, "Gwanny, did you burn your wagina?"

Now, not only husbands but whole families show up in the birthing room. All of the mystery has vanished, even whether it will be a boy or a girl. Tom said, "We enjoyed the mystery, didn't we?"

Garrison Keillor, years younger than we are, describes his birth control instruction at Lake Woebegone: "Every spring we all trooped to the Catholic church to hear Father Emil, the priest at Our Lady of Perpetual Responsibility, give his annual sermon on birth control. Father Emil's message was simple but direct. 'If you didn't want to go to Minneapolis, why did you get on the train?'" Keillor is the one who said: "Sex is good, but not as good as fresh sweet corn."

"Marriage itself was sexy," wrote Michael Arlen, Harvard '52. "Imagine sharing your bed with a female every night!"

Tom told me that at Harvard, birth control was considered a trade school subject—no "how-to" stuff in those hallowed halls. Even the faculty was fuzzy. A government professor made Cambridge history by announcing at a dinner party, "My wife and I have five children, each the result of a different method of contraception."

For his Harvard reunion book, Robert Benchley sent in a snapshot of himself with his two sons. Beneath it he wrote: "My wife and I tried sex twice and it worked both times."

Were we better than our parents when it came to telling our own children about sex? No. I grew up inhibited, and when our children were young my vocabulary, at least, was still inhibited.

Tom and I both taught Sunday School, and I discovered that sixth-grade girls were still innocent. Giving a test on the Ten Commandments, I asked what does "adultery" mean? One girl wrote: "Adultery is the sin of saying you are older than you really are." The class wiseacre wrote: "Hester Prynne got an A for adultery. Now she'd get a C+."

All of us were bumping along as best we could, sexwise—then came the sixties. Television became the nation's sex instructor, and the pill promoted experimentation. The sixties changed everything.

Winds of change swept all campuses. The New Age dawned at Wellesley—where men had never been allowed above the first floor—the morning a reuning alumna, Class of 1919, tottered into a dorm bathroom and ran smack into a young man. Flustered but polite, she said graciously, "It's a—a—a nice day."

"I wouldn't know," he growled. "I haven't been out yet." Soon after that, the college decided reunion classes would return to campus after the students had graduated. Years later the same lady (and lady is the right word) told me, "I don't mind the sexual revolution. I'm just sorry I missed it."

I was shocked by the advice I heard Margaret Mead give to Dartmouth students. She stood on the lecture platform in her flowing cape, grasping her South Sea Island staff, and thundered, "For heaven's sake, live with a person before you get married. If you want to have children, for heaven's sake get married. If your marriage doesn't work, for heaven's sake get out of it."

I was even more shocked by the letter we got from our Dartmouth sophomore, Tombo, who had a summer job in Norway. "Over here," he wrote gleefully, "parents put the visiting boyfriend right in the same bedroom with his girl."

A few years later, Tom and I faced the same decision. Should we put a son or daughter in the room with their significant other? Many other parents agonized over this question. We demurred until we were stung by the comment, "You know we live together—how hypocritical can you be?" Tom told me, "Our kids are uninhibiting us."

In fifty years our generation went from a sex-oppressed society, to a sex-obsessed society, to a sex-drenched society. It is refreshing when someone suggests that the whole subject may be overblown. In *The Thanatos Syndrome*, Walker Percy describes two Southern doctors drinking together. One asks, "What are the two most overrated things in the world?" In unison, they then chant: "Sexual intercourse and Johns Hopkins University."

John Cleese, in one of the Monty Python movies, gave us a glimpse of where we may be headed. A naked Cleese and his naked wife are giving a sex demonstration before a class of adolescents. Suddenly, Cleese explodes in anger. Instead of watching the copulating couple, the students are sneaking peeks at copies of Virgil hidden in their laps.

It's impossible to keep up with the changing mores. A recent *New York Times* quoted a female college student: "A year ago, I wouldn't be caught dead with a condom, but now it's like an American Express card—you can't leave home without it." When I was in college I didn't know the word condom, and I thought oral sex meant talking a good game.

Now the threat of AIDS has colleges handing out Safer Sex Kits and the U.S. Health Service issuing 107 million pamphlets on the disease. I am thankful for that, but one sentence in the pamphlet shook me: "Dating does not mean the same thing as having sex." No one had to tell us that.

Am I getting too familiar with the word condom? The slogan for National Condom Week is, "Slip a condom into your Valentine." I overheard a student say, "I hate Valentine's Days. That's the day my high school boyfriend told me he was bisexual. I had to look it up in the dictionary." When I was in college, bisexual wasn't in the dictionary.

Sexual ambiguity, newly surfaced, is not new. The ur-couple, Adam and Eve, couldn't have suffered from gender confusion if they had wanted to, but every generation after them has. Consider Shakespeare. His transvestite heroines, Rosalind and Portia, impersonated men so well other women fell in love with them. Since young men played women's parts, that meant Shakespeare had men acting as women pretending to be men making love to men pretending to be women. Talk about gender confusion.

Today's press is full of it. A woman in California writes Ann Landers because her husband has had a sex change. Should the children go on calling him Daddy? If they call him Mommy, what should they call her?

As Saul Bellow wrote in *A Theft*, "By now nobody can draw the line between the natural and the unnatural in sex." Nor in nature. Some inventive biologists inserted a gene from a lighting bug into a green plant— and the plant lit up. They are planning to clone this fluorescent monster, called, perhaps, *Lightningbugia*.

When Tom and I started our family, there was only one way to have a baby. Now there are seven and counting. One is called "host uterus," meaning a fertilized egg is implanted in a rented uterus. Host and hostess are Emily Post words. What would Mrs. Post say about the etiquette of the host uterus?

Fifty years out of college, our generation is well tested. We have gone from premarital chastity to Posslq's (the Census Bureau's official term for persons of opposite sex sharing living quarters); from selecting a mate to selecting what sex we want to be; from *American Girl* magazine to *Screw* magazine; from the unmentionable topic, homosexuality, to Gay Rights; from campus curfews to free condoms in the library; from "It Happened One Night" to a movie called "Sammy and Rosie Get Laid."

Could B. F. Skinner be right, "The object of life is to gratify yourself without getting arrested"?

How does a sexagenarian sort it all out? Surely it was a mistake for the wellspring of life to be unmentionable, or mentioned only in "dirty" jokes. Our generation has been rendered shockproof by the repetition of four-letter words and the proliferation of sexually explicit shows. But I take it as a sign of health that today anything can be and *is* discussed.

Enlightenment took a long time. I don't think we'll ever return to the "morality" I grew up with. You can't pour champagne back in the bottle. But gradual discovery just might be more exciting than being born knowing all about sex. As one still seeking enlightenment, I'm happy to discover that although people age, emotions do not. After umpteen years, that young blade from Harvard still delights me.

Only one thing is clear. Whether sexual liberation or Puritan repression is in the ascendancy, reproduction's beat will pound on, as powerful as nuclear fission. Some say we may be nearing the end of the present swing. If we swing back, will it be to hearts and flowers and tangos on a darkened dance floor? Will the young discover that a little mystery, a little longing, can be enticing?

We survivors in our anecdotage just want to know one thing: *What Is Next?*

❦ 36. There's No Such Thing As a Twenty-Five-Cent Cat

Our two best possessions cost twenty-five cents apiece. I bought our golden retriever, Buttercup, as a birthday present for Tom. He unwrapped the big box and the tiny puppy hopped into his lap. It was love at first sight. Tom named Buttercup after the fat girl in *Pinafore* who loved everybody.

On Mother's Day, Tom handed me his fur-lined glove. Peeking out was Hamlet, a yellow tabby cat. Who could have guessed Hamlet, prince of Denmark, would grow up to be the King Kong of cats? He never saw a mouse he couldn't catch.

The dog and the cat were inseparable. Hamlet used to nap on top of Buttercup. Stretched out, the snoozing marmalade cat and the relaxed golden looked like Dr. Doolittle's two-headed pushmi-pullyu. Tom called them the Odd Couple.

Buttercup retrieved full time. On our doorstep she deposited children's hats, stuffed toys, milk cartons, a *pair* of mittens, and objects unidentifiable. I didn't discover the bag with the painter's lunch until after the poor fellow went home, presumably hungry.

One peaceful spring afternoon as Tom and I were having tea, wild barking shattered the quiet. Rushing out, we found Hamlet lying motionless on the grass and Buttercup standing over him. "Hamlet's dead," I thought, "and Buttercup's keening."

Tom picked up the body and Buttercup subsided into whines. The cat, limp not stiff, was still breathing. "We've got to take him to the vet!"

"How? Car's in the shop."

"Call a taxi. Quick!"

"A taxi?" We lived in New Hampshire. Our veterinarian was across the bridge in Vermont.

"Hurry!"

Wrapped in a warm blanket, Hamlet revived slightly during the cab ride. But he collapsed when the receptionist placed him on the linoleum. "You'll have to leave him overnight," she said. "The doctor's left for the day. We'll call you. Don't worry, he'll live 'til tomorrow." She eyed us closely. "Senior citizens get a ten-percent discount."

To ease our minds and pocketbooks, we walked home. It took forever. As we trudged along I muttered, "This thing is going to run into money."

"How can you think of money at a time like this?" Several answers came to mind, but clearly Tom wanted support, not sass.

At breakfast Buttercup was droopy. She put her head in Tom's lap and rolled her eyes. "She wants Hamlet," I said.

"Me, too," he said, rubbing her head. The four of us had so happily filled the empty nest.

This was our worst pet crisis since Buttercup came to the door five years ago with a baby skunk in her mouth. Our horror was total. Tom coaxed open Buttercup's jaw and the little skunk waddled away unharmed. We later discovered that baby skunks can't spray.

That afternoon Tom called the receptionist. "This is Hamlet's—er—father. Is he alive—or what?" I held my breath, hoping it wasn't "or what."

"He's alive, but gravely ill."

"May I speak to the doctor?"

"He's with a patient."

"With a patient?" I echoed. "Vets who think like that must be costly."

After supper the vet himself called. "Your cat was hit by something," he said, "or maybe somebody kicked him. I can't imagine how he got home." We knew; Tom patted his heroine, the full-time retriever.

I could hear the doctor's voice squawking, "I gave Hamlet a tetanus shot. We're waiting for the x-rays. I'll call you tomorrow." He hung up.

"*X-rays?*" I gasped. "How much does it cost to x-ray a cat?"

"How the hell do I know?" Tom growled. "When a person is sick, you don't ask such a question."

"This isn't a person. This is a twenty-five-cent cat."

He glared at me. "There is no such thing as a twenty-five-cent cat."

The discussion continued in bed. I said I couldn't imagine what hit the cat and he said a lot I cared and I said I loved Hamlet but we weren't rich and Hamlet's father said he didn't give a damn how much it cost, just so Hamlet got better and I said nature has always been a pretty good doctor, and reasonable, too. And then we stopped talking and slept back-to-back.

In the morning, conversation was nil. At the clinic, the doctor greeted us formally. He displayed Hamlet's x-rays on a screen. "I recommend an orthopedic surgeon," he said. "He could operate and insert a metal clamp to hold your cat's broken bones together."

"*Orthopedic surgeon?*" Even the last of the big spenders was rocked. "Is that necessary?"

The animal physician looked pained. "It's up to you." I opened my mouth but nothing came out. The doctor shrugged. "You can take your cat home if you want, and try to nurse him back to health."

Tom nodded. "Maybe we should."

The vet dismissed us crisply. "Hamlet can't go outside for five or six weeks. I'll give you two kinds of pills. The antibiotic is very important."

We drove home in silence. Hamlet, curled up in my lap, was motionless. "I imagine those pills are solid gold," I said.

"He *gave* them to us."

"I bet."

When Tom carried in Hamlet, Buttercup's hind end did a hula. We fixed up a convalescent corner in the kitchen with Hamlet's basket and freshly laundered blankie. For three days he just slept. On the fourth day Tom let out a yell. "My God! Hamlet's gone!"

Inexplicably, our pitiful sick cat had vanished. Frantic, we searched the house. We looked behind every chair, under every bed, in every closet. Nothing. Then my spouse turned on me. "You let him out."

"I did not."

"Then where is he?"

I'm not known for my patience. "Maybe he died and went to heaven." Suddenly I felt I needed air. I marched to the closet and put on my hat and coat. I tried to put on my fur-lined boot—and there was Hamlet hidden inside. He cocked a sleepy eye at me and yawned. Tom and I fell into each other's arms. Our laughter was almost hysterical. "Our lost child is found!" I exclaimed. "Alleluia!" he crowed. "Praise the Lord!"

With the Odd Couple reunited, we were beginning to put the feline fiasco behind us when an envelope arrived with the vet's name in the corner. The senior citizen discount didn't make a dent. The astronomical bill included all pills and "nursing care." This time both of us were staggered. Rather grandly I said, "I'm not going to say I told you so."

"What's the difference between saying 'I'm not going to say I told you so' and saying it?" Tom pulled out his checkbook. "This is only the beginning, you know. Our animals aren't getting any younger. There should be Blue Cross/Blue Shield for pets."

The years rolled by and Buttercup turned thirteen. One morning Tom went down to let her out. I was making Sunday morning coffee when he came into the kitchen looking shocked. "Buttercup is dead," he said. "I went to let her out and saw her tail lying still." He choked up. Words were useless. We just stood silently hugging each other.

"Come downstairs and see her," Tom said. I recoiled. I recalled my mother's words, "Never forget that death is part of life," but I was afraid of death and Tom knew it.

"You'll be glad you did," he said gently. "Remember what Bob Coles said."

We once heard Dr. Robert Coles tell medical students that as soon as his mother died, he rushed out of the room. An older nurse stopped him. "Don't leave," she said. "Go back and experience your mother's death."

I took a deep breath and followed Tom down the stairs. Buttercup was lying half out of her bed, stretched out, utterly still. We patted her. She did not feel cold. I was glad Tom had urged me to share the experience. "I think of death as a friend," he said.

I shivered. "I wish I could."

"She always made me feel so good," he whispered.

Later, we sat silently by the wood stove. What should we do with her body? Tom said, "I'll go call the vet." I was resting my forehead on the palm of my hand when he returned. "The vet says to bring Buttercup in. He'll dispose of the body. Or we can get her cremated and bury her ashes." Neither of us spoke. Tom broke the silence. "I'd like to bury Buttercup right here in our yard."

I nodded. "But of course."

There ought to be a ritual to help people mourn the death of a beloved pet. Rituals are healing. Tom and I made up our ritual as we went along.

First we called two Dartmouth students to help us. Jonathan Good, a medievalist, who would one day get his doctorate in Medieval history, dug the grave. Mary Kate Schroeder, who would one day become an Episcopal priest, performed the service. They both loved Buttercup. Tom selected a spot near the apple tree Cissa gave us. Jonathan dug the grave deep and about five feet long. When he stood in it, the blue clay came to his waist.

Our solemn procession moved slowly through the golden autumn sunlight. First came Mary Kate with her prayer book; then Jonathan with Buttercup's body in the wheelbarrow, a homemade bouquet of yellow chrysanthemums resting on her; then Tom and I, supporting each other arm in arm.

We sang "Now the day is over / Night is drawing nigh." Mary Kate read Tom's favorite prayer from the *Book of Common Prayer:* "Oh Lord, support us all the day long, until the shadows lengthen, and the evening comes, and the busy world is hushed, and the fever of life is over, and our work is done . . ."

After Jonathan filled in the grave, we placed the chrysanthemums on the soft dirt and walked slowly, silently, back to the house, wiping our eyes. "Tears are healing, too," Tom said. He raised his glass of cider. "Here's to Buttercup who loved everybody."

One friend was appalled when we told her. "You used the Episcopal burial service for your *dog?*" she gasped. "Isn't that sacrilegious?"

Tom, who seldom snapped, snapped. "Not if you believe God is love."

After Buttercup's death, Hamlet fell into a deep decline. One day, he simply disappeared. Tom shook his head sadly. "Cats know. They do that when it's time to die." We searched the house, the neighborhood, even my boots, but never found the body. It was awful. Tom said, "Let's hope the Odd Couple are together in heaven." He was silent.

His voice broke. "Life is letting go."

❦ 37. Is a Harvard Man Smarter Than a Chicken?

One morning Tom put down his newspaper and exclaimed, "I don't believe it. The *Times* is running an obituary for a chicken. Listen. 'The chicken in Chinatown that played tic-tac-toe with customers is dead.' That has to be a first."

"That must be your chicken," I exclaimed.

"Of course. I feel like I've lost a friend."

The obit said Samuel Palmer, owner of the Tic-Tac-Toe Chicken, claimed he paid more than one thousand dollars for his trained performer but lost money on it. He said people came to his arcade because they read about the chicken in the guidebooks. "The trouble is," Palmer complained, "the tourists didn't play enough games to make my famous fowl pay."

If Palmer failed to get his bait back, it's not Tom's fault. He gave the late bird his all.

One Sunday he happened to be watching Charles Kuralt's show when Calvin Trillin was pitted against the wily bird in a game of tic-tac-toe. "CHICKEN WINS" kept lighting up. My husband, Harvard '38, MBA '40, muttered, "Any fool can beat a chicken."

Later, in a movie called *Falling in Love* we saw Meryl Streep and Robert De Niro gamble with the same chicken. The chicken got the best of them, too.

Tom Campion brooded over that chicken. He swore he could beat "Gallina." (He never got over his Harvard Latin.) I bet him fifty dollars he couldn't—not small change then.

Tom wrote Calvin Trillin at the *New Yorker* for the chicken's address. He replied by postcard: "Go to the low-numbered end of Mott Street and ask any kid." So we headed for New York City, our Mecca.

We had no clue when the chicken started to gamble, but Saturday noon seemed a good bet.

Our cab driver was from Afghanistan. In those days, Afghanistan was just a place that made beautiful rugs. The cabby spoke five languages, had fought the Russians for eight years, and had been to (the real) Mecca, but he had never heard of Mott Street.

"It's in Chinatown," Tom explained. "We're going to play a game with the Tic-Tac-Toe Chicken."

"Oh," said the Afghan, "*Mought Strit!* You're going to play a game with a chicken? Nobody in America has time to play games, not even the chickens." In Chinatown we told Hajii we hoped to see him again. He shrugged. "I drive five A.M. to five P.M. After five, city is a jungle."

Looking for the famous bird was a wild chicken chase. The children Tom asked were stunned, their mothers alarmed. One kid said, "You, like, soft in the head, man?"

Tom marched into the Unisex Hair Parlor. "Where's the famous Tic-Tac-Toe Chicken?" A woman plaiting a man's black pigtail said: "Arcade—two doors down."

Over the door at 8 Mott Street was the sign:

CHINATOWN FAIR
WORLD FAMOUS
DANCING AND TIC-TAC-TOE CHICKENS
OPEN 10:00 A.M. TO 2:00 A.M.

Tom rubbed his hands together. "Watch out, chicken, here I come."

The Tic-Tac-Toe Chicken squatted inside a glass box, a fat white hen with a limp red crown. Her sign read: LARGE BAG OF FORTUNE COOKIES

IF YOU BEAT THE CHICKEN. 75 CENTS PLEASE. SHE'S NOT CHICKEN, ARE YOU? Next to her cage was a glass tic-tac-toe grid, with instructions: *Birdbrain will take first turn with "O". For each of your turns you have 9 seconds. Press the button on the square of your choice.*

Tom put in three quarters. The grid lit up. Chicken continued pecking grain. We waited. Chicken finished meal, strutted to small box on wall labeled *Thinkin' Booth*. She stuck her head into the box and pecked. An "O" lit up on the tic-tac-toe board. Tom pushed a square and an "X" appeared. Two turns later, Chicken cleverly put "O" where she could get three in a row, two different ways. He played and the sign flashed: CHICKEN WINS.

Tom put in more money. This time the chicken took the middle square. Three moves and CHICKEN WINS. He fed in quarters. The chicken kept winning. I said, "Gallina's skill may be gender-related. I don't see any roosters playing tic-tac-toe." Not funny.

Harvard man refused to quit. He got more quarters, played more games. And then it happened. A new sign lights up: CHICKEN TIED. "Eureka!" Tom crowed. "I did it!" Grinning, he counted out five ten-dollar bills and handed them to me. "Worth every cent," he said. "I gave that old bird a run for the money. Let's go back to the hotel. I'm ready for a drink."

Mott Street was gridlocked, but no taxis. On the next street we finally grabbed one. Unbelievably, it was the taxi driven by our friend Hajii. He said he'd been all over town since he'd let us out two hours ago. I said, "What are the odds on getting the same driver twice in New York City?"

"One in thirty thousand," said Hajii. "That's how many cabs."

The Competitor, still glowing, said, "Thirty thousand to one—about the same odds as beating a chicken at tic-tac-toe."

Russell and Missy, in New York on business, were waiting at the hotel to take us to dinner and the theater. Tom couldn't wait to tell them. "Guess what! I tied the Tic-Tac-Toe Chicken!"

"You tied her?" Russell rolled his eyes. "Well, congratulations."

"Listen, boy, I may have lost the bet with Mom but a tie isn't half bad. The damned bird gets to go first every time. And she plays all day, too."

Russell patted Tom on the shoulder and shook his hand. "Harvard wasn't wasted on you, Pop. Congratulations."

Requiescat in pace, Gallina.

✻ 38. We Quit Drinking

After Tom retired from Dartmouth in 1990, he became depressed. Retirement does that to people. I said, "Remember what Dr. Fosdick said. 'Retirement is a great shock to a man.' You need to talk to somebody."

A few days later Tom said, "I called a psychiatrist in Norwich. But he's a couples' therapist. I said I'd bring my wife."

As we had learned with Tommy's breakdown, everybody needs a therapist. New insight: all marriages need a therapist. We were still talking to Dr. Bob Simon in 2000 when Tom died. Communication *is* the name of the game.

Bob used to query us about driving and drinking. After a while, we began to hear him.

One New Year's Eve, we overdid the champagne, as usual. I said, as I have before in umpteen years of marriage, "I think I should drive."

Tom answered, as he has before, "You drank more champagne than I did. I will drive." He drove, and not too well.

In times past that little contretemps would have led to an argument and, once we reached home, an angry, silent nightcap. My husband was a prince among men, but he was not above a battle. Nor am I. Abetted by a little, sometimes a lot, of alcohol we knew how to fight to the finish. Fortunately, we also knew how to kiss and make up.

This time it was different. We drove home in angry silence. But when we got there, instead of pouring a drink Tom lit the wood stove and said, "Sit down. There's something I have to talk to you about. First, I'll make some coffee."

Sipping the black coffee, he started on a high plane. "You know what William Blake said, don't you?"

"No, Mr. Bartlett's Quotations, I don't know what William Blake said."

"Blake said, 'You never know what is enough unless you know what is more than enough.' I know what's more than enough. Period."

"Enough what?" I asked, hoping he didn't mean me.

"Enough alcohol, that's what. I mean for a lifetime. I'm sick and tired of waking up with headaches and sleeping through shows and spending a lot of money to mess up my body and my memory. Worse, I am scared of the way we drink and drive." Dramatic pause. "I want to quit drinking."

"*For good?*"

"For good and all. I'm talking forever."

"Whoa. I don't know about that. Who wants to be the only ones at a party not drinking?"

"Just give it a try. You can get used to anything."

"You don't even have cocktail parties if you don't drink."

"One up for me," he said. "I hate cocktail parties."

"You've certainly made that clear. When I show up alone, your friends say, 'Too bad you're married to such a jerk.'" I made that up.

Angry silence. "Don't get mean."

I faked empathy. "I know why you're worried. It's those alcoholics in your family."

He bristled. "There are alcoholics in every family. You've got 'em, too."

"Mine are cousins. Cousins don't count."

"You never did know how to count straight."

"Touché."

Angrier silence.

"Maybe we ought to ding this conversation." I got up and poured myself a slug of vodka. Raising the glass, I said, "Here's to better times."

"How can it ever get better if you keep sopping up booze?"

"I'm not the only one. Suppose we do quit, how can you toast without drinking?" Now I was hitting him where it hurt. Tom enjoyed composing funny toasts. People like to do what they're good at.

"Sparkling cider," he said with a shrug. More silence, thoughtful, not angry. "I know you don't agree. But think. We could improve the quality of our life a thousand times over." He had me there.

Friendly silence.

I got up slowly, walked over to the potted palm and poured my vodka into the dirt. I turned around and just looked at him. Those brown eyes were swimming. He came over and gave me a long kiss. Neither of us spoke. He said, "God help us." And he wasn't kidding.

"Think about Emily Dickinson," I said. "We'll dwell in Possibility." He poured two glasses of buttermilk to celebrate.

And so we made the Big Decision, just like that. We had given up drinking before, of course. Frequently for Lent, but never successfully. In 1991 we gave it up for life.

Two questions had tipped the scales for Tom. Dr. Simon, our indispensable therapist, asked us: "If you could not last the forty days of Lent without a drink, who is in control?"

"Our son the doctor" and "our son the chiropractor" both asked, at different times, "Do you know alcohol kills brain cells?" They didn't have to spell it out. We knew we had reached the stage where we did not have brain cells to spare.

Tom and I quit drinking, cold turkey. I don't think either of us could have done it alone. Our togetherness instantly increased. That sounds far-fetched. It isn't. We also found it much easier to quit for good than to stop for forty days. Once we turned our back on liquor, it lost its lure.

"What we need," Tom said correctly, "is a fresh set of habits." Every night, just as we used to do, we enjoyed a cocktail and hors d'oeuvres together by the fire, or on the terrace in summer, but now it was tonic with lime—and clearheaded backgammon after dinner.

Tom and I had grown up in the booze generation. In Winston Churchill's phrase, we took more out of alcohol than alcohol took out of us. When we were married no one was surprised that one of Tom's groomsmen got soused, hit his head on the toilet, and missed the ceremony. That's what happened at weddings. In those days too much to drink was barely enough.

My sister, eleven years older than I, grew up in the roaring twenties. Our mother knew how to get her to go against the flow. "If you want to stand out in the crowd," she told Julia, "be the only girl who doesn't drink." Julia bought it and became the belle of Honolulu. (She would have been anyway.) In later years she managed to serve drinks to her guests, but without enthusiasm. Julia's way of offering a second cocktail was, "Do you want more alcohol?"

Did giving up drinking improve the quality of our life? No. The truth is we acquired a new set of problems. Tom claimed I overstated them; I claimed I understated them. "You have never in your life been guilty of an understatement," he laughed.

Dry as bones, we were beset by strange difficulties. Take, for example, the first time we gave a post-cold-turkey party. While plying our guests with scotch, vodka, and wine, we sipped soda water. By ten o'clock, the guests got sleepy and went home. All wound up, we jabbered on for hours. So much good repartée, and no one to enjoy it. We called Russell in Chicago. He gasped, "Has something happened? What's wrong? Why are you calling at this hour?" We said we just wanted to chat. He mumbled, "*Chat?* In the middle of the night? You've had one too many. Call tomorrow after you sober up."

In our drinking days I used to fall asleep as soon as I hit the pillow (or before)—and wake up around four A.M. Knowing I'd never get back to sleep, I'd put on a headset and listen to books on tape. Night after night a woman with an exquisite English voice used to read *Pride and Prejudice* to me. Mark Twain said the only way he could read *Pride and Prejudice* was on a salary, but I ate it up. Those delicious nocturnal sessions with Jane Austen were lost forever. Like bears, we both slept straight through the night. How boring.

Mornings were different, too. Instead of starting as slowly as cold maple syrup, we woke up raring to go. No more lolling in bed, icing aching heads. No more zesty alka seltzer. We had energy to burn. If we didn't jump out of bed and start incinerating calories, the energy just piled up.

Which brings us to the weight problem. Soon after we stopped drinking I lost five pounds; Tom lost seven. (He must have drunk more.) Just when I was about to buy a new pair of slacks, my tight ones turned into a sleek fit. Soon our clothes began to bag. Tedious trips to tailor and dressmaker loomed ahead. Being forced to buy new clothes was more fun.

Another downer was not needing to diet any more. I liked bouncing from the Scarsdale Diet to the Atkins Diet to the Bananas and Skim Milk Diet and back again. Tom's favorite used to be the Drinking Man's Diet. A diet makes you feel strong while you are on it and is cause for rejoicing when you quit. But what is the point of dieting if you can lose five pounds without even trying? As Robert Frost said of unrhymed poetry, it's like playing tennis with the net down.

Problems, lots of weird problems. Take our time-tested talent for procrastination. Procrastination was out. If we had to do something, we did it right away—and that just led to more time. People stopped asking us to drop by for a drink, and that led to *more* free time. We no longer spent hours on the ritual of preparing hors d'oeuvres and selecting wines. We zipped in and out of cocktail parties. Or, to Tom's delight, we didn't even get invited. Having more time suddenly appear in your life was weird.

Just as we adjusted to not being able to remember, memory raised its ugly head. A refreshed memory may be the weirdest problem of all. We didn't say, as we used to, "Who *is* that woman who claims we met her at a cocktail party?" We didn't stop in the middle of a story because we had forgotten what we were saying. We could remember what people said at parties, ourselves included. This was not popular. Most cocktail talk isn't worth remembering, of course. One of our drinking friends said, "I only drink to make other people seem interesting." Oh, to recapture that first fine careless rapture when memory was sloshed.

Another problem was the kids. They used to call a lot to check on us. Tom took up my mother's term "chicken-pecked." After we quit drinking, the kids quit worrying. We didn't miss their bossing, but we did miss the calls.

Then there was the money problem. It piled up. Compared to scotch and brandy, tonic and non-alcoholic beer are practically free. Our credit card company was worried. Was there some reason our restaurant charges have dropped so sharply? Our insurance company was threatening to lower our rates. People who drive and don't drink don't have so many accidents. Who needs lower insurance rates? Worst of all, statistics show that non-drinkers live longer. It looked like this mess would just go on and on.

Like President George W. Bush, we once drank too much and now we don't drink at all. Who said, "If you think you can do something, you're probably right"?

We tried not to crow about our new life, but when Dr. Simon smiled at us and said, "Good for you," Tom looked into my eyes, and winked. Afterward he said, "I feel as though we both just won the Nobel Prize."

I was feeling sentimental. "I couldn't have done it alone," I said, getting out a handkerchief.

Tom put his arm around me. "It's love what does it," he said. "Not love for alcohol, thank God, love for each other. Love is the golden key that unlocks Possibility."

⚘ 39. Nobody Wants to Interview Hillary

Hillary and Bill Clinton came to New Hampshire to campaign for Bill's nomination in 1992. The Gennifer Flowers story had just broken and Bill's chances looked dim. Hillary was to speak at Dartmouth and I asked my editor at the *Valley News* if I could interview her. "Why not?" Anne Adams shrugged. "Nobody else is interested. Just be sure you ask about Gennifer."

That made Tom laugh out loud, "I have a picture of Nardi Campion, Girl Reporter, digging into that hot potato."

He made me mad. "Okay, Know-It-All, just you wait."

"I've a twenty that says you'll never do it. Want to bet?" I shook my head—and hoped he was wrong.

Professor Larry Radway and his Wellesley wife, Pat, invited us for morning coffee with the Clintons. I couldn't go, so grandson Peter, then a Dartmouth freshman, accompanied Gapa Tom. They came home dazzled by Bill's charisma and brain power. "You'll have a lot of fun interviewing Hillary," Tom chuckled. "She never opened her mouth." I wasn't worried; if nothing else, we always had Wellesley.

I was dazzled by Hillary. She spoke for an hour, sans notes, fielding questions expertly, always focused on "what my husband plans to do." Afterward I had an hour alone with her in a small office. She talked easily about the issues, but we also laughed a lot and gossiped about Wellesley. She graduated in 1969, thirty-one years after I did, but we both loved our college. I was still avoiding the hot topic when her press secretary, Lisa Caputo, opened the door. "You've time for two more questions." I said, "How do you handle competitive feelings when both husband and wife are talented and ambitious?"

Hillary looked surprised. "I've done lots of interviews, but nobody ever asked me that. I've had to deal with a sense of competition and I think Bill has, too. It's not easy but we have the same priorities: our daughter and our relationship." She rose to go.

Now or never, ask about husband's womanizing. (Is a woman ever accused of manizing?) Girl Reporter took a deep breath, "How about the story that just hit the fan?"

Her blue eyes looked straight into mine. "My husband and I know everything about each other. Our marriage is solid, full of love and friendship. We're committed to our future together."

As soon as I got home Tom said, "Was it hard getting her to talk?"

"Hard to stop her. Too bad I didn't take the bet." I sat down at my Mac and tapped out the column. Tom, who edited everything I wrote, said, "Isn't your opener a bit overboard?"

"Understatement," I said firmly.

I still stand by my opener. On January 25, 1992, my column began: *I have found my candidate for president of the United States: a successful lawyer and experienced administrator, age forty-four, who is highly educated, articulate, dedicated to helping the underdog, and has a sense of humor. Her name is Hillary Rodham Clinton.*

Some of my Republican friends stopped speaking to me.

After Bill won the nomination I did a piece on Hillary for *Wellesley* magazine, interviewing her by phone. A year later I landed the interview everybody wanted—a chat with the new First Lady in her White House office.

At the White House entrance, I stared through the iron gates and felt as I did on the first day of kindergarten. "What in the world am I doing here?"

I had written Hillary to ask if I could do "Wellesley Woman's First Year in the White House" but got no answer. After many phone calls, her press secretary said yes. And here I was.

I told a guard with a pistol on his hip that I had an appointment with Mrs. Clinton at three. He said: "Photo I.D., please."

I fumbled for my driver's license, glad we lived in New Hampshire; no pictures on Vermont licenses. The guard studied picture and studied me. He consulted his computer. "You're not in the system."

I gulped. "Call Lisa Caputo." If only I had brought something in writing. He disappeared. I wait. He returned. "We're putting you in the system." It was two-thirty. Would I be in the system by three? Why hadn't I allowed more time? Getting past Saint Peter should be a breeze after the gate to the White House. The guard disappeared, returned, smiled. "You're in the system." He examined my bags and had me walk through a metal detector. He hung a visitor badge around my neck and swung open the magic gate. "Okay, ma'am."

I was bewildered. "Where do I go?"

"Press office is on the lower level."

All alone, I hurried up the curving drive. People were staring through the iron spikes. I said to myself, "They think I know where I'm going."

It was a golden autumn afternoon. Yellow sunlight slanted across the emerald lawn and struck the large marble fountain, ringed by red and white chrysanthemums. Above the house where Lincoln lived, the American flag flapped slowly. Stationed about the lawn are six television rigs covered with canvas, each waiting for a different commentator to spout news in front of that all-important backdrop. I felt like Dorothy in the Land of Oz.

I entered the briefing room with the presidential seal behind the lectern. Half the size it looks on TV, the room was strewn with coffee cups and papers. No people.

Hesitantly, I entered a tiny press office where three women younger than my granddaughters were typing and talking on the phone. One rang up Lisa Caputo and told me, "Someone will come for you in ten minutes." *Whew!* It was five of three. I looked around; no chairs. "You can sit behind that desk."

Lisa appeared and took me to the tiny outer office. It was twenty past three, but who cared? I was where I was supposed to be. Through the wall, I heard Hillary's hearty laugh and then a man's. My stomach churned. What was I going to ask her? My mind was a perfect blank.

The door opened and out walked our neighbor, "America's Family Doctor," former surgeon general C. Everett Koop. Tom attributed Chick Koop's success to his affidavit face. I said it was the beard plus remembering everybody's name. "Why hello, Nardi," he chuckled. "Hanover Old Home Week at the White House."

Hillary welcomed me with a warm smile, her blue eyes shining. She was the first First Lady to have her own office in the West Wing. It was tiny and feminine, with a soft blue carpet, a satin-striped couch, and an American flag next to her desk. Three poster-sized pictures hung on the wall: one of Bill laughing, one of Bill pensive, and one of Bill and Chelsea, heads together, giggling.

Next to a large photograph of Eleanor Roosevelt is one of six women. "Out of one hundred senators," she said, "we have only six women. But we're going to have more." She pointed to an impressionist painting of men in top hats and ladies in long dresses on a seaside porch. "That's Campobello. When I heard it was the Roosevelts', I moved it in here. Blanche Cook's biography of Eleanor has made her live so vividly in my mind. The more I learn about Mrs. Roosevelt, the more admiring I am."

"Speaking of role models," I ventured, "our granddaughter Iris in California says kids fight over who gets to be Hillary in the Hillary game."

"Oh my gosh!" she laughed. "That's sort of overwhelming."

Things have changed since our first interview. Then, dressed in her all-purpose blue wool suit, she sipped a can of soda with her feet propped on a chair. It was "Hillary" and "Bill," and the White House seemed as remote as Mars. At this interview, in short black skirt, black stockings, high heels, and gold-buttoned red jacket, she looked executive. We sipped tea and spoke of "The President." What had not changed was Hillary. She was the same in the White House or on the campaign trail. Except her haircut; it was better.

This time Lisa Caputo stayed with us, taking notes, and I had been given just twenty minutes. I switched on my tape recorder and asked about her first impression of Wellesley. "I had never been East," recalls Hillary Diane Rodham Clinton. "Wellesley was beautiful but I felt lost and everyone was so smart. I called my parents in Chicago. 'I want to come home.' My father said, 'You come right ahead.' My mother said, 'Oh no, you don't. You stay right there and bloom where you're planted.'"

"Are you blooming where you're planted?"

"I feel like it," Hillary said. "I love the opportunity to meet people. I've learned so much about the way Washington works, for good and for ill." She laughed. "It's like a continuing education course, all the time."

As my time ran out Hillary switched to her big topic, health care. I asked if there was a way to simplify the plan so people like me could understand it?

I touched a nerve. She jumped up and handed me a new paperback, *Health Security*. "This book simplifies it and explains what people will pay." Hillary could talk all day on health care. I quickly switched to values—what shaped hers?

"My father. He was a tough-minded pragmatist. He could always ask the question that put things in perspective."

She was silent. I knew her father had died the previous April. "Death is a great reminder, with a capital R, of what's really important." (I could identify with that.) "The time in the hospital when my father was dying was clearly among the most important times in my life. Our whole family, including Bill, was together physically and together in spirit. Even in the midst of pain, it was joyous and fulfilling for all of us."

"Hugh Rodham was a Republican, right?"

"I'll say—and so was I. At Wellesley I rang doorbells for Goldwater. All that changed when I met Bill at Yale. My father liked Bill in spite of his being in the wrong party. He would come down to Arkansas and stay with us and gradually he began to work for Bill, telling him, 'You are not only married to my daughter, you've got good sense.'"

Hillary said her faith shaped her as well. "I'm a Methodist and Bill is a Baptist, so when Chelsea was thirteen we let her choose. She decided to become a Methodist. Chelsea and I go to the Foundry United Methodist Church on Sixteenth Street."

I say I admire the way they keep Chelsea's life private—it must be hard. She nods. "Children deserve to have their own childhood and to become whomever God meant them to be."

What does she do for down time? "Oh, take long walks. We drive somewhere and get out and walk. I go on bike rides. I watch a lot of videos and use the White House movie theater. As you know, I read a lot—just finished James Carroll's thriller *Madonna Red* that you sent me. It'd make a good movie."

Lisa Caputo: "Time for one more question."

One more? By dumb luck I picked something Hillary wanted to talk about: "How did the president manage to give his speech on health care to Congress, when the wrong speech appeared on his teleprompter?"

Hillary's eyes lit up. "Oh, it was incredible. Watching from the balcony, I thought things weren't right. When Bill started, I knew for sure something was wrong. But once he got his rhythm I relaxed. It was a fine speech, delivered beautifully.

"Later he told me what happened. His previous speech had never been erased. When they called up the president's speech, instead of the one just entered, they got the old one. But, you know, he kept his concentration and kept going.

"I've always said about my husband, he's not only the smartest person I have ever met, he is the best in an emergency. When the pressure is on, Bill Clinton has the ability to do whatever needs to be done. I've always known that about him. This was just one more example—for the whole world to see."

"Why did the media ignore such a big story?" I asked.

Hillary laughed. "My husband makes a lot of things that are hard look easy."

"Time," says Lisa.

When I climbed into the taxi, I felt limp. The driver glanced at me and said, "What were you doing in the White House?"

"Interviewing the First Lady."

"Are you still working?" he exclaimed.

As we headed toward the airport, the setting sun cast a golden glow on the Washington Monument. I settled back to think about Wellesley's First Lady. It seemed to me Hillary Rodham Clinton is all of a piece. She has no side; she is who she is, take her or leave her.

And she's still my candidate for president.

The Beginning of the End

❧ 40. White House to Cancer Ward

At the bottom of the deep blue invitation with silver lettering it said: *R.S.V.P. giving date of birth and social security number. Present this non-transferable card with a photo I.D. at gate.*

Our invitation to a Christmas reception at the White House set off a small explosion. Tom put his foot down. "Too much money, too much hassle, too many people. We won't get near the Clintons."

"So what if we don't see them? We'll be guests at the White House. When will we ever get another chance?"

"Look, hon, this is no time for you to travel. We don't even know the date of your surgery."

He had me there. We were living in suspense. Two weeks earlier my doctor had found cancer cells in my uterus and ordered a hysterectomy. As if on cue, the phone rang. I hung up and turned to Tom. "The operation is two days after Christmas. Nurse said, 'Do whatever you feel like doing.' I feel like going to the White House."

We compromised. That is, he agreed to go. I bought a new hat—gold cloth trimmed with a band of fake fur that made me look like one of the Wise Men—and we were off to see the King and Queen. We hoped.

The paper said the Clintons hold two Christmas receptions per night from December 4 to December 23. Sometimes there are six hundred guests—or more. We were lucky—only four hundred invited to the press party. How do they stand it? I mean literally, they never sit.

After guards checked us in, we walked past big blow-up murals of Hillary, Chelsea, and Bill. Tom: "Take a good look. That's as close as you'll come." We were greeted by young men and women in dress uniforms of the army, navy, marines, and air force. They were handsome beyond belief. Each smiled and said, "Welcome to the White House."

A marine officer, stunning in her floor-length blue skirt and red brass-buttoned jacket, was playing "Deck the Halls" on a gold harp. A spicy fragrance of evergreens floated in the air. One of the thirty White House Christmas trees—undecorated—sparkled with tiny white lights.

We walked up a staircase into the white marble grand foyer, whose tall doors led out to the pillared portico we see on TV. No decorations or trees in the grand foyer, to prevent people jams. A naval officer in gold braid was playing "Silent Night" on a piano with golden eagles for legs. The foyer was dominated by a gold-framed, brooding, full-length portrait of JFK. We walked straight ahead into the oval Blue Room and admired another of the thirty trees, an eighteen-foot blue spruce, gorgeously decorated.

We strolled through rooms filled with people, looking for the Clintons, ogling as we went. "Yes, ma'am," says a white-coated waiter, "this is the State dining room—140 people, 10 to a table." We picked up gold-rimmed plates, silver forks (sterling), and napkins (paper). We helped ourselves to jumbo shrimp, wafer-thin sandwiches, and—a first for us—baby lamb chops served as a dainty finger food. The shrimp soon vanished and the waiter growled, "The press eats everything except the wallpaper."

We were offered non-alcoholic punch, white wine, or the famous White House eggnog. For three weeks every December a small white refrigerator truck sits next to the White House. It holds hundreds of gallons of White House eggnog that will be served to thousands of guests. Not for sissies. We took one swig and switched to punch. "It's a good thing we quit drinking," Tom said. "This could flatten you."

We strolled back to the East Room. There were fireplaces everywhere with mantelpieces decorated by miniature scenes from *The Nutcracker,* the ballet Chelsea was dancing in that Christmas. Here we found whipped-cream desserts, hot coffee, flutes of champagne for all. But our hosts, no. Tom chuckled. "I told you we wouldn't see them."

I ignored him. "What is this huge room for?" I asked a marine.

"Abigail Adams used it for drying her laundry," he replied. "Now it's for after-dinner dancing."

How come we were moving in these lofty circles? Hillary and I had become correspondents after our initial meeting. I looked for things that would make her laugh, such as the cartoon of two dowagers leaving a cemetery in a limousine, one remarking, "Charles was battered by market swings, but it was Hillary that finished him off." Later when she flew to New Hampshire to campaign for Democrats she had someone call me. I went to the airport to see her and became an Important Democrat.

As we sipped club soda, the band swung into "Santa Claus Is Coming to Town." Suddenly a handsome corporal announced, "Get in line for your picture."

I said, "They're going to give us a picture of the Clintons?"

The woman next to me laughed. "Now everyone gets their picture taken with the Clintons. We call it grip and grin." I gripped Tom's arm and he grinned.

In the marble foyer people jammed around the stairway. Tom counted, "Only seventy-five ahead of us." We waited. A man in a tuxedo announced: "The president is running late." Woman in sequins: "So what else is new?" I peered down the line and couldn't believe it. There was Robert Novak—big stomach, red vest, mussed gray hair—waiting to have his picture taken with Bill Clinton, the man he always bashed on TV. Talk about the power of the presidency.

We would have approximately ten seconds to grip and grin. What to say? We stepped into the brilliantly lit Diplomatic Reception Room— and there they were, resplendent in full evening dress, he so tall and, next to him, she so petite. Hillary, handsome in a red and gold plaid jacket, black velvet headband, and velvet skirt, looked young and full of zip. Both appeared fresh and rested in the midst of a jolly Christmas season of ten thousand handshakes.

A soldier checked the pronunciation of our names and passed the word to the man at the mike, who announced in ringing tones, "Thomas Baird Campion and Nardi Reeder Campion." We felt like somebody.

We had time for one sentence with the leader of the free world.

Tom to President: "They're still talking about your commencement speech at Dartmouth."

Yours Truly to President: "You were at your absolute best on *Booknotes*, chatting with Brian Lamb for an hour about your *Between Hope and History*." The President riveted each speaker with his blue eyes and laughed easily. Maybe he was saving his voice. Hillary was more chatty.

Yours Truly to HRC: "Thank you for including us in your press party."
HRC: "But of course."
YT: "I'm the only person in the White House wearing a hat."
HRC: "Wonderful!"
Tom to HRC: "Hooray for Secretary of State Madeleine Albright! Wellesley women are leading the way."
HRC: "I'll say!" Then, pointing to Yours Truly, "Three cheers for Wellesley!"

As we left, Tom turned to me with a broad smile. "What a good decision we made to fly all the way to D.C. just for a two-hour reception."

After our dizzying trip, we had a quiet Christmas. Thanks to skilled doctors and Tom's TLC, the cancer operation was successful, and I reaped an unexpected dividend.

A strong sense of your own mortality, hard to come by, is invaluable.

❀ 41. Mom and Dad Go to Medical School

"Old age recedes as you approach it," observed Tom's fishing buddy, Pat Neilson. True, but it will catch you (or vice versa). Tom got his anti-aging remedy from Shakespeare: "A light heart lives long." But you can't stay lighthearted forever. We knew we had to make serious decisions. We did the spadework (block that metaphor) and then wrote our progeny about our uncommon plans.

Dearly Beloved Children, Spouses, Ex-Spouses, Grandchildren,

We've just been to another funeral. That's what you do in your eighties, go to funerals. This one had the big black hearse and the mahogany casket on wheels. Last week it was the small ebony box containing a dear friend's ashes. There is no right way; there is only what feels right for you. Everything hurts, even as we cling to Emily Dickinson's opening line, one of the few she ended with a period: *This World is not Conclusion.*

Does it shock you to learn that your father and mother plan to bypass the undertaker and go straight to medical school? It shocked us at first, but the more we talked it over, the clearer our choice became.

It's time for straight talk about death, never easy, though it should be. We who have been transition-prone are now thinking about the Big Transition. Nobody can explain the great mysteries: Where did we come from? Why are we here? Where are we going? A lot of people will give you answers, but nobody really knows. Our faith tells us that after death we will meet again. This we believe. The transition we are writing you about is our leap into space, so to speak.

You've often heard us quote Ray Charles. "What is a soul? It's like electricity—we don't really know what it is, but it's a force that can light up a room." Yes, Ray, and when the soul departs, the room goes dark. To see someone die is to know with searing intensity that the soul has left. Gone, vanished. The human body, formerly the temple of the spirit, is now vacant. Nobody home.

Of course we all want to honor the body that was inhabited by the person we loved. That is a given. And there are many ways to do it. The Egyptians assembled riches for the dead to take with them. Some people find comfort in a dead body that looks lifelike. Some prefer the privacy of a closed casket. Some think cremation is best; others find that too rapid a transition. Each must decide what, if anything, might ease the pain of loss. For us, and we hope for you, it will be knowing that our bodies will be useful.

We talked with the director of the Anatomical Gifts Program at Dartmouth Medical School. She told us that the study of anatomy began in 1315 at the University of Bologna. Those first human dissections began a never-ending effort to understand the mysteries of the human body.

It is only slightly easier to get into the anatomy program than into the medical school. We're glad to report that we have been "accepted," as long as our bodies are delivered shortly after death. "We take about thirty-five bodies a year," the doctor told us, "but arrangements have to be made in advance. I must be able to tell my anatomy students that these people thoughtfully arranged for their bodies to be sent here for your education. They trust you—and so do I—to treat them reverently."

Cadavers are studied for about two years and then cremated. Some families request the ashes. Others have them buried in the campus cemetery, beside the granite gravestone marked "Dartmouth Medical School." We both would prefer to remain at DMS. Ashes to ashes and dust to dust.

Of course we each want a memorial service in our own Episcopal church (sans corpse), with organ music, choir, bagpipes, the works. There's nothing like a funeral for clarifying values. In addition to expressing grief, a funeral forces us to ponder what is worthwhile. So many possibilities, so little time.

Our decision to donate our bodies to the medical school won't feel comfortable to you at first. It didn't to us either. But if you think about it, is it any harder than turning them over to an undertaker? It should be easier really, considering the objective of the undertaker and the objective of the medical student.

Despite, or maybe because of, *le silence eternel de ces espaces infinis,* our faith in God runs deep. How can you not believe in God when you contemplate the delicate efficiency of the human eye, and the glorious reliability of the moon? We believe God brought us into this world and God will receive us when we depart. What is important— love—has little to do with our entrances and our exits.

> We love each of you more than you will ever know,
> Mom and Dad / Nardi and Tom / Gama and Gapa

When Tom died, it wasn't as hard to call the medical school as I had expected. I kept thinking of the words he often quoted from writer Richard Bach: "What the caterpillar calls the end of the world, the master calls a butterfly."

Two years after Tom's death, I attended a memorial service in Dartmouth's Rollins Chapel for those who had donated their bodies. I was hesitant. Could I say farewell to my darling Tom again? Of course.

Each family was asked to write—anonymously—a few sentences about their loved one. To condense Tom was a challenge.

My husband had a burning desire to help others. When he heard about DHMC's anatomical gifts program he exclaimed, "Wonderful. I can still be useful, although not here."

The last words of Sir Winston Churchill, who died in 1965 at ninety-one, were: "I'm so bored with it all." I'm thankful my husband, who had a Churchillian zest for life, never lost his curiosity.

He thought of death as a friend. At eighty-four he was ready to depart this world for the next, and he died with a smile.

The service, planned by the medical students, undid me, but I didn't care. "Tears are healing." After a student played a Chopin nocturne on the piano, Dr. John Lyons, chair of the anatomy department, began: "An especially warm welcome to the departed ones whom we celebrate today."

A young woman lit each of the twenty-seven white candles. When she intoned, "Thomas Baird Campion," I couldn't help smiling through my tears. We planned it that way. What hurts is trying to carry on without him.

✢ 42. A Retirement Home? Never!

To venture causes anxiety but not to venture is to lose oneself.
—Kierkegaard

My brother Red died in February 1998, a month after his wife Dort died of pneumonia. They had been married for sixty-three years, and were enjoying the Fairfax in Alexandria, Virginia, an army retirement home. Dort died January 26th. Bereft, Red threw away his heart medicine and died one month later, on Washington's birthday. He was ninety-five. The Military Academy gave him a hero's funeral and buried him with a twenty-one-gun salute in the West Point Cemetery. Carved on his red marble tombstone is his motto, "Never give up. Press on and on."

Sadly, Fred was not well enough to attend Red's funeral. Because of the bleeding ulcers he got when he was executive officer of the USS *Nevada* during the war, half of his stomach had been removed. Now his body was just giving out. A lifelong health nut, he had said, accurately, "If I take care of this carcass, it will take care of me." And it did, for nine decades. Then he had to give up golf, which was worse for him than his angina. He had retired to Laurel, Mississippi, where "The Admiral" with a chihuahua peering out of each pocket, became a legend. He died at 92, six months after Red. I flew alone to Mississippi for yet another funeral, weeping as I went. Now I was the last leaf on the tree.

Fred's service was held in St. John's Episcopal Church in Laurel, where his son Charles was a vestryman. He was cremated. Later Charles wrote me, "Right after Christmas I went out to the golf course with Susan and the children, just before sunrise. We placed Dad's ashes on a beautiful piney hillside near the eighth tee—and then the sun broke through the trees. I wished for you, Aunt Nardi."

I adored my siblings. I was eleven years younger than Fred, thirteen years younger than Julia, fifteen years younger than Red, and still thought of myself as the baby. "You're pretty old for a baby," Tom laughed.

"I'm younger than you are."

"Just barely."

A marriage without fights is like spaghetti without sauce. I'm glad to say my husband and I had many fights—some fierce, some funny, a few requiring mediation by a couples therapist. After therapy, we were still struggling to internalize Lear's "Speak what we feel, not what we ought to say." The controversies continued; they were just more honest.

A reporter asked Leon Trotsky, "What was the greatest surprise in your life?" He answered: "Old age." It happens so fast. One of our worst fights was over doing what Red and Dort had done cheerfully: moving to a retirement home.

Tom spoiled a blissful day of cross-country skiing on the Hanover golf course by saying, "I signed us up for Harvest Hill, the retirement home they're building in Lebanon."

I stopped in my tracks. "How dare you do such a thing without talking to me first?"

"I have talked to you, ad nauseam. What's the use? You've already made up your mind."

"You're damn right I made up my mind—and so have you."

Tom laughed. "What happens when an irresistible force meets an immovable object?"

"There's nothing funny about this," I said. "You go ahead and move. I'll come visit you on weekends."

"That's what you said when we left Amherst. Once we're at Harvest Hill, you won't have to do any more shopping, any more cooking, any more cleaning. We get three meals a day and they wash your sheets and towels. Doesn't that appeal to you?"

"Not one bit. I don't want to go to an old folks' home."

"That's what we are, old."

"Speak for yourself, Tom."

"I've got news for you. There are 69,000 people in this country who are one hundred years old or older."

He skied off and left me. That night at dinner, the conversation was frozen solid. Finally I broke the silence, "Just tell me one thing. Why are you so set on moving? How can you leave your asparagus bed?"

"Oh, my aching back."

"Not funny. Listen, Tom, we've had twenty-two years in our Wren House. It's perfect for old age: not too big, all on one floor, close to town. "When we can't drive any more we can walk to the post office. We're surrounded by friends, and," I knew this would get him, "we can't take Koko. She's too big for an apartment." Tom's golden lab/retriever had been at his side for the last eight years. How could he possibly let her go?

"You live in a dream world," he said. "If you can't drive, do you think you'll be able to walk a mile to the post office? Face it, hon, we're in our eighties. We need help now and we're going to need more. Of course it will kill me to part with Koko—but it's time to move on."

Silence.

He said, "Think about the freedom you're going to have."

"Freedom's just another word for nothin' left to lose."

"Don't quote Louis Armstrong to me. Irrelevant."

"How can I give up the things I love so much?" My voice broke. "Your mother's big cherry table, Grandma's silver punch bowl?"

"Remember what your mother said after movers smashed her cut-glass wedding gifts: 'They're only things.'"

"Movers!" I cried. "They'll smash my stuff, too."

"Think about the kids. Do you want them to remember us as *things-people?* Do you want to become a drag on them?"

"I want a place where they can come and stay."

"We've had that. I want them to remember us as adults able to look reality in the face. The reality is that at some point we are going to need nursing care. The reality is, if we don't clean out this house, the kids will have to." He hesitated. "Of course we will be giving up a lot, but we still have each other."

I reached out and took his hand. Neither of us spoke for a long time.

"Think about Alfred Nobel," Tom said.

"You're impossible. What's Alfred Nobel got to do with it?"

"One day, Nobel opened the newspaper and read his own obituary on page one. His brother had died and the paper mixed them up. But that wasn't the only shock. He would be remembered for only one thing, being the inventor of dynamite, a merchant of death."

"I still don't get it."

"How do we want to be remembered, that's the question," Tom said.

"You're stretching a point."

"I am not. Maybe that's the biggest question of all. *How do you want to be remembered?* Do you want our kids to think of us as burdens they had to look after? Remember your mother. Mama put herself in that nursing home so we wouldn't have to do it."

"Tom," I said, "you don't fight fair."

I didn't believe his story; it was too pat. I looked up Nobel. Tom had it right. Alfred Nobel did reinvent himself. He rewrote his will to create the world's most esteemed prize. Who connects him to dynamite now?

The next day, while I was working in the garden, I watched a sparrow fly out of the nest. She rose higher and higher. She did not take the nest along. Freedom at last, I thought. Out loud I said, "Question: How do we want to be remembered by our children? Answer: As parents who loved them, each one, beyond reason." Suddenly it all came clear.

That night, lying in bed like two spoons in a drawer, I said, "You win, Tom."

"Win what?"

"It's time to move on." I started to cry. He held me tight.

"You're more flexible than you know," he said. "As an army brat, you moved a lot, always leaving friends behind. But not this time—we're just moving a few miles. You know you can do that—you're as flexible as a flier."

I couldn't help laughing. "Flattery will get you everywhere. When I used to complain about always moving, Mama, who loathed packing, would say: 'It's what's inside that counts, and you can't pack that.'"

❦ 43. The Secret of Moving

In every way you can think of, moving was too much. I knew that—
but it was worse. It was nerve-crunching. Our happy home turned
into chaos central. You sort, you pack, you throw out, you throw up. You
throw out some more. I was a mess. Then I discovered The Secret.

The story begins on M-Day minus eight. Tom and I were having
scrambled eggs in our sunny kitchen corner, watching our cardinal
couple dart in and out of the pines, he so scarlet, she so drab, both so
monogamous.

Koko put her head in Tom's lap. "I'm going to miss Koko," he said,
rubbing her head. He leaned over and said, "I love you, Koko."

"And I'm going to miss Cissa." Our daughter is the Queen of Pack
and Pitch. She drove up from Boston, worked like a beaver, and headed
home. "She can do anything."

Tom and Koko walked out to their beloved garden. Which was
worse—giving up Koko or giving up the garden? Both unthinkable. I
sat down to address a stack of red postcards. When he returned with a
basket of tomatoes, he stared at me. "You're packing at last?"

"Not funny. I'm sending friends and magazines our new address."

He picked up a red card and read, "Dean Inge says, '*When our first parents were driven out of Paradise, Adam is believed to have remarked to Eve:
My dear, we live in an Age of Transition.*' Who the hell is Dean Inge?"

"No clue, he came up on our quote calendar, remember?"

We were both silent. I bent over my work. He just stood there. Then,
ever tactful, he cleared his throat. "I wonder if you could send those
cards after we move?"

"It's bad enough to move," I said, "but do you want to be stuck in that
place without any mail?" I had long since lost sight of first-things-first
but I certainly wasn't going to admit it.

"O how full of briers is this working-day world," he said.

"Shakespeare will get you nowhere." He and Koko left.

I plowed on. Poring over the red cards, I suddenly started to shiver. I
got up to fetch my cure-all, a hot cup of tea. The cup clattered on the
saucer. I dug out my old blue sweater, the warmest thing I could find.
As I passed by the study, Tom called, "I thought you threw that away
years ago."

When I sat down I wasn't shivering, I was shaking. Hard.

Suddenly Cissa walked through the door. Talk about psychic.

"I started home last night," she said, "but something made me turn around. I went back and spent another night at Betty's. Mom! Why are you shaking?"

"I don't know. It's nothing." My teeth started clicking.

"I'll get Dad."

"No! I don't want to upset him."

She placed a palm on my forehead. "I'm calling 911."

"Don't you dare."

In five minutes the ambulance arrived. All I can remember is those kind men placing me on the stretcher and Tom holding my hand. "Don't worry, honey. You're going to be all right." His expression said the opposite. The next thing I knew the emergency room nurse was saying, "Her fever is 104." A doctor leaned over me. "You got here just in time." The nurse injected a needle into my vein. "Liquid penicillin," she explained. I had an infection but none of the doctors could tell what caused it.

"Stress?" Tom suggested. "She's stressed out. Totally."

"Stress doesn't send your temperature through the roof," the nurse said.

Our own Dr. Ross appeared. He looked like the angel Gabriel to me. He examined an inflammation on my thigh. It took him two seconds to diagnose it. "Looks like erysipelas."

"Syphilis? I have syphilis? How could that be?"

Tom laughed out loud.

"No," the doctor said. "You have a staphylococcus infection in your blood. In the Middle Ages, they called erysipelas 'St. Anthony's Fire.' It is serious."

Tom gasped. "However did she get that?"

"A break in the skin will do it, if it gets infected."

I could feel my stomach churning. Who was in charge here? I knew I wasn't. My head throbbed. So many problems: sort the accumulations of a lifetime, move to a strange place, deal with a strange disease. "I don't think I can cope with St. Anthony."

Tom leaned over me. "Easy. Remember what Mama said, 'In a bad patch, close your eyes and count your blessings.'"

I put an arm over my eyes to block the emergency room's blinding light and started counting. Number 1: Tom. Obviously. Number 2: Our family. Number 3: Dartmouth Hitchcock Medical Center. Number 4: Friends. Number 5: Health. I may be down, but I'm not out. I intoned, as Mama did every time we moved to a new post, "Blessings brighten as they take their flight." (Later I discovered that she was quoting the eighteenth-century poet Edward Young.) Number 6, Number 6, Number . . . I drifted off.

I awoke in a hospital room. Sea-green walls, all else dead white. Make that pure white. I discovered I had a roommate. Gaunt and gray, she looked older than Time. She said, "Do you think I should go to the hospital?"

I thought about that. "No," I said, "you're better off where you are."

Tom, Cissa, and "daughter-in-love" Peggy, Tad's wife who is a skilled nurse, appeared. "Sweetie," he said, "you scared us to death. How do you feel now?"

"Like a train wreck."

"The doctor says a few more hours and you would have gone to intensive care. Penicillin saved you."

Blessing number six comes to me. "Thank God for Alexander Fleming." The British doctor—a poor farmer's son—who in the twenties turned mold into penicillin. Sir Alexander was knighted and won the Nobel Prize for medicine. He should have gotten two.

My roommate piped up. "Do you think I should go to the hospital?"

"Why not?" Tom said. Then he told me the bad news. "They have to keep you here five days for intravenous penicillin."

"Impossible. We're moving. I have to go home. I have to organize, pitch, and pack. What about all those books? I have to mark stuff to go to the thrift shop. Send the kids their old letters and pictures. Do they want their kindergarten drawings? I have to sort family photographs. I have to mail those postcards. I have to . . ."

"Mom," Cissa rubbed my hand, "relax." Peggy said, "You're already looking better." Tom said, "We'll take care of everything."

And they did.

While I vegetated, family rallied around. Each day Tom gave me a report. The first day it was that three of our sons were coming from three different time zones to help. Later he said, "Russell moved your office. It would have been easier to move a graveyard."

Then: "Toby tackled the closets. It would have been easier to clean the Augean stables."

Then: "Tad transferred your stuff into the furniture we're taking." I thought to myself, does a mother really want her son going through her bureau drawers? Tommy, stuck in Idaho, called daily to give me support: "Remember what Granny used to say, 'They are only *things*.'" The next time he quoted Red, "Remember what Unk said, 'Never quit: press on and on.'"

Maybe we should have had more kids.

Others rallied round, too. To plan the move, our friend John Kelly cut out templates of our furniture to scale. Betty Smith, our decorator, placed them on the apartment blueprint. (A place for everything and everything in its place.) Leyla, the Dartmouth student who had been my all-important writing assistant for three years, set up the computer in my new office. (How come college kids can ace computers but can't iron or drive stickshift?) Our dear friend and helper, Tina White, excavated fridge and freezer. (Unlike me, she can throw out anything.) The tag-sale lady went around pasting on prices.

Then Tom told me about Dana Pippin, the "rent-a-hand" man Betty found in the classifieds. Dana is a Paul Bunyan who can replace a whole chandelier in a trice or heft boxes of books as if they were feathers. Hours before the house closing, he and three others had to conduct Operation Trash Removal.

Tom couldn't help laughing as he described the desperate process. At first the pile of stuff looked impossible. Then Dana whipped out his cell phone and ten minutes later an enormous dumpster appeared. They all, including our cleaning whiz Janice Campbell, stood at the windows and threw things down into the dumpster. He said it was hilarious and unnerving to watch our stuff fly from the windows. Maybe that's where my straw hat went.

Everybody agreed on who was the hero. "You should see Cissa go," Tom said. "I thank the Lord for more reasons than one that 'something' made her turn back."

"It's worth filling up the house with sons to get a daughter," I added.

A clear thinker with boundless energy, Cissa knows how to organize. In Robert Frost's words, "It's what you do with things that counts." I recently discovered one box she labeled "Stuff On Floor Around Mom's Desk." On a bigger box she wrote: "To Be Opened Later In Life."

Meanwhile, back at DHMC, I was lying in fresh sheets, sipping ginger ale and reading *The New York Times*. No sweat.

At last the day came when Tom could take me to our new digs. As he was wheelchairing me out of the hospital room my roommate asked, "Do you think I should go to the hospital?"

"By all means," I said. "It's the place to be. Especially if you're moving."

Tom drove me straight to Harvest Hill. I wobbled into the living room/dining room, stood still, and gasped. It looked just like home. Only better. No packing mess. No piles of postcards. No chaos. A place for everything and everything in its place. Clothes hanging in the closet, pictures on the wall, toothbrushes in the racks, bed made up and ready to get into.

Betty, the interior designer, says your retirement home should look as much as possible like your previous home. She had selected just the right pieces of furniture, not too many, only the ones we couldn't do without. The mahogany dining room set Tom's parents bought in 1910, the yellow love seat, the blue and white wing chair, the pine coffee table, the Eskimo otter carving, the crystal egg. The blue and white lamps were lit and the china candlesticks held yellow candles.

"The only thing missing is Koko," Tom sighed.

I nodded. His eyes filled. "But she's found a happy home with Dr. McCann," he added hastily.

I sat down and looked around. I felt like Sara Crewe in one of my favorite childhood books, *The Little Princess*. When her shabby garret room was magically transformed by her unknown benefactor, the Indian gentleman, she wept. Like Sara, I went around the room touching the furniture to be sure I wasn't dreaming. I wept too. How could I be so lucky?

Oh yes, The Secret. If you have to move, try to contract a serious disease. Get sick enough and your family and friends will take over. And be sure to have a daughter.

I smiled at Tom. "You know what, if I came to a fork with one sign saying 'To Harvest Hill' and the other 'To Wren Lane,' I'd take the one to Harvest Hill. I'm glad to be here." I never thought I'd say that. "I'm glad to be at Harvest Hill. Thank you, Tom."

"I told you," Tom said, kissing me. "You'll love Harvest Hill."

"I love you," I said.

❦ 44. Good-Bye for Now

Unable are the loved to die.
—Emily Dickinson

Soon after we moved into our new old apartment, Tom's bright spirit seemed to dim. He had to be helped a lot, and he hated it. "I'm weary of considerations," he said, quoting Frost.

That night after supper I said, "Do you want to play backgammon?"

"Not tonight." He sighed. "I just want to go to bed." My dear husband was so weak he had to sit on the seat of his walker while I pulled it.

He patted my hand. "I am a very foolish fond old man."

"Not foolish, Lear, just fond."

"Yes," he said.

It took him a long time to undress, even with my help. "Do you want me to read to you?" I asked. He did. "What would you like?"

"*Charlotte's Web.*"

I chose the chapter called "The Last Day." The dying spider says she feels peaceful. "After all, what's a life, anyway? We're born, we live a little while, we die." Before I finished, he was asleep. I slept, or tried to, next to him. I was aware of heavy breathing. He awoke at two. "What is it in *Macbeth* about McDuff's leaving life?"

"'Nothing in his life became him like the leaving of it.'"

"Yes," he said. "But no *of.*" We enjoyed one-upping each other. He pointed to our wedding picture near the bed. "That's where it all began," he said.

He slept again, the breathing labored. I said, "Tom?" He did not stir. I lay there thinking about our fifty-nine-and-a-half years together, the ups and downs, the rough and the smooth. When I told a friend at the Harvest Hill Retirement Community that we'd been married sixty-nine years, Tom laughed. "Fifty-nine, it just seems like sixty-nine."

I thought about when we were both seniors in college and he was driving Joe Kennedy's car. I fell for his good looks and giddy ways. He had looked so handsome in that loud, green plaid Scottish suit. He still had those brown eyes that lit up with laughter.

Tom did not move. I think he was unconscious. My heart was in my throat but I did not call for help. About five A.M. he stopped breathing; I still didn't call anyone. I knew what he wanted. To both of us death was a friend. Too weak to dress himself, unable to walk alone, unsure of memory, he was more than ready, as they say in India, to "drop his body." He had left "no resuscitation" instructions. Could I just let him go? I could.

His death certificate said he died of "arteriosclerotic cardiovascular disease," but I know better. He died of not being able to take care of himself.

I felt numb. I tried to focus on my mother's words: "Faith comes through pain." I sat there patting him, watching the gray creep into that sweet face. Running through my head were the five words Lear cries over the body of his beloved daughter Cordelia. *Never. Never. Never. Never. Never.*

We gave Tom a hero's funeral. (He was a hero for humanity.) Eighteen of us, Campions all, children, grandchildren, spouses, marched into St. Thomas Church behind a bagpiper playing "Amazing Grace." Grady, eleven, led us, holding high an enlarged picture of a relaxed, smiling Tom. That's what Tom had, amazing grace.

Four of the children spoke. The youngest, a charter member of Weeper's Anonymous, put his feelings into the program, as did I. Russell wrote: "Pop's ire had such a soft edge on it you hardly knew he was angry. This must have been a result of his inner peace that in retrospect is obvious."

Cissa spoke first. "This isn't the first time that Tom has left Nardi." She read "Left at the Gas Station."

Tommy said Tom was a mystery wrapped in an enigma. "My father was a Harvard MBA who was not interested in making money."

Toby said, "Dad taught us by example not to be afraid of strong women."

Tad said, "I saw Dad blow his top once. A loud woman on the midnight train to Montreal was keeping everyone awake. Finally, Dad walked down the coach and put his face next to hers. 'Lady,' he said, 'will you please shut up?' I've always remembered how he said please."

Two of our eight grandchildren spoke. Ashley recalled arriving at Dartmouth. As she climbed on the bus for her freshman trip, she realized she had left her backpack at the airport. "'Holy Mackerel,' Gapa Tom said, 'I'll go get it!' He raced back to Lebanon and, just as the bus was leaving, returned with the backpack. 'Have a good trip,' he said."

Peter read a poem he had written in memory of his grandfather. "My title is 'Catch and Release.' I wasn't expecting the picture on the program." We had gone all-out with an eight-page program. On the cover Tom is holding up a yard-long Atlantic salmon, his face transformed in ecstatic joy. Not exactly catch and release.

Since pride is one of the Seven Deadlies, Tom and I must be sinners. We're so proud of those kids, and their kids.

Dick Ketchum, a friend of forty years, said, "Tom never seemed to age. That wonderful photograph of him in *The New York Times* was taken in 1991, but that's exactly the way he looked three weeks ago. It reminds me of a reply the editor Bruce Bliven made when someone asked him how it felt to be seventy-five. 'I don't feel seventy-five,' he said. 'I feel like a nineteen-year-old with a lot of things wrong with him.'"

Our rector, Andy Kline, saluted Tom "as a faithful Episcopalian, a dogged vestryman, an irrational supporter of the clergy . . . who somehow managed to keep up with Nardi, and she him, and keep their promises to one another for fifty-nine years . . .

"Listen to the tears and laughter, the love and celebration in this room today. Where has all this abundance and grace come from? Tom was God's compassionate and joyful ambassador of the Spirit to us all."

Seven priests took part in Tom's memorial service, close friends and relatives, including Red's daughter, Ann Reeder Riggs, chaplain of St. Margaret's School, and Tom's spiritual mentor Jim Crawford, rector of Old South Church. Reverend William Sloane Coffin, wrote me: "It was the best service, and I've been to many."

We read in unison the words of Psalm 90: "Our years come to an end like a sigh . . . they are soon gone and we fly away . . . So teach us to number our days that we may get a heart of wisdom."

My thoughts appeared at the end of the program:

Tom Campion had his priorities straight. When the kids carped about our aging car he said, "We may never have a Cadillac, but I mean for you to have a Cadillac of an education."

His humor was infectious—and defusing. Driving home from Maine on a blistering day, the car stuffed with kids, he turned around and said, "Remember, when I yell at you, I don't mean it."

Tom was—is—the kindest person I've ever met. How fortunate I am to have spent fifty-nine-and-a-half years with him. Wherever you are, Tom—my darling Tom—I will find you.

❦ Robert Louis Stevenson's Prayer

For our fortieth wedding anniversary in 1981, our children gave us a walking trip across Scotland. It took us five days to hike from Dundee to Oban, the narrowest waist of that wild country. Unforgettable.

In Edinburgh, Tom was captivated by the prayer engraved on a bronze statue of Robert Louis Stevenson at St. Giles Cathedral.

He learned it by heart and said it every evening before dinner.

Tom had courage and gaiety, if not the quiet mind. (Neither of us achieved that.) And down to the gates of death, he was loyal and loving.

O Lord, give us grace and strength to forbear and to persevere. Give us courage, gaiety, and the quiet mind. Spare to us our friends, soften to us our enemies. Bless us, if it may be, in all our innocent endeavors. If it may not, give us strength to encounter that which is to come, that we may be brave in peril, constant in tribulation, temperate in wrath, and in all changes of fortunes, down to the gates of death, loyal and loving one to another.

III. After Tom

Making Do and Carrying On

�֍ 45. Searching for Virginia Woolf

The Dartmouth Alumni College trip to the south of Ireland looked alluring. Tom and I always planned to go to the Ring of Kerry. Now we never would. He had been gone eight months and I missed him more every day. Would I, should I, could I, travel without him? It scared me to think about it. I'd probably lose my passport or my purse or my suitcase, maybe all three. The last time I traveled abroad alone was in 1939, when I returned from Europe on the last trip of the *SS Normandie*.

Over the years, Tom and I journeyed from Norway to Italy to Mexico to Tonga and Fiji. He took charge of the tickets and explained the currency and was always beside me with his ready laugh, quick empathy, and ironic wit. Could I go it alone? Well, I could try. I reinforced myself with my mother's adage: "A woman can do anything a man can do—but don't let them know that." I took a deep breath and sent in my check.

Then came September 11.

Along with everyone else, I was reeling with disbelief, horror, and fear. The trip to Ireland was still on, but now I was even more hesitant. *The New York Times* travel section advised: "If you're an American abroad, do not advertise your nationality. Dress like a local, avoid cowboy boots and loud conversation. Terrorists at war with the U.S. do not distinguish between military, diplomatic, or American tourists."

Nervously, I called Tommy. He had lived in Dublin for a year when he went to U.C.D. "The Irish know how to deal with terrorists—they've had lots of practice," he said. "You couldn't find a safer airline than Aer Lingus. Every year, at great expense, they ground all their planes for twenty-four hours. The Archbishop of Dublin is hoisted up in a cherry picker with a drum of Holy Water and blesses every airplane. Go for it, Mother."

Zooming toward Logan Airport in the huge Dartmouth Coach were three passengers, two students and myself. One took off his headset to tell me that the United States had started bombing Afghanistan. How awful. Maybe I should turn back? I shook my head. Tom would never do that.

I'd expected security delays at Logan airport. There were none. That didn't make me any calmer. Our plane was full, mostly Irish going home. Everyone was edgy. The Dartmouth group of thirty-two all made it, except for a North Carolina couple and the professor who was to teach us Joyce and Yeats. He decided to stay home after he heard about the bombing. That didn't make me feel any safer.

I sat next to Paddy, an Irish kid in cowboy boots who had been working at his uncle's factory in Dallas. Paddy was morose because his six-month visa had expired. "I luv Tyxas. I'm cooming back. I luv America." He gulped four cans of Guinness and passed out. His trip was shorter than mine. Tom would have laughed but I wasn't amused.

Once we landed in Ireland, my jitters subsided. When Tom and Russell and I went to Ireland in 1965 to visit Tommy, we discovered that the Irish love Americans. They all have relatives in the States. The pulverizing of the World Trade Center made Irish blood boil. Their president had declared a National Day of Mourning and closed everything, even the pubs, so the Irish people could crowd into their churches to pray for America. Why didn't we do that? Their pious distress warmed our hearts. This is a country where a woman in the elevator can say, "And did you enjoy a sweet night's sleep, dearie?"

Tourist-less Ireland was peaceful. Its emerald hills, dotted with white sheep and black and white cows, took my mind off the war. Like Glocca Morra in *Finian's Rainbow,* Ireland is magical. One should expect the unexpected.

Philip, our bus driver and instructor in things Irish, said, "The Irish don't drive on the wrong side of the road. They drive on the other side. Be careful crossing the street." He added, "We don't want anything to happen to you. Paperwork."

He never missed a chance to give the English a dig. For a bus driver, or anyone else, Philip was highly educated. He was reading Sean O'Casey: "O'Casey says the reason the sun never set on the British Empire is because God wouldn't trust an Englishman in the dark."

Our week at Acton's Hotel in Kinsale, County Cork, was blessedly uneventful. For me, the biggest hit was Blarney Castle, "home of the McCarthys"—I thought of our daughter-in-law Peggy McCarthy. Built in 1446, it sits in a green park amid huge specimen trees. People usually wait in line for hours to kiss the Blarney Stone but we sailed right in. I climbed the 130 stone steps, wishing for Tom, but this time I didn't kiss the magic rock. Without Tom to hold me, I didn't risk it.

One tourist said, "The fellow who persuaded people to come to his castle for five centuries and pay money to lie on their backs, lean out over the edge, and kiss a mossy old stone wins the prize for smooth talking."

On our free day, a Sunday, most of our group went to the Catholic Church, but Tom and I always went to the Episcopal Church, so I went alone to the Anglican St. Multose, a mistake. It is an eight-hundred-year-old church built by cruel Norman invaders on the foundation of a sixth-century Celtic church. In 1649, Oliver Cromwell, that murderous "reformer," used the church for a barracks and it still felt like a barracks.

It was the coldest church I've ever been to, and I'm not just talking climate. The fifteen worshipers who showed up at St. Multose were ancient and impervious to strangers. I sat by myself in the pew, wishing for Tom's smile to shed some warmth. One good thing happened, though. Stressing the fact that all great religions call for compassion, the minister read from the Koran: "The faithful of Allah are they who walk upon the earth modestly, and when the foolish ones address them answer: 'Peace.'"

After the service, I stood in a gray Irish mist on O'Connell Street. I felt all alone and far from home in perilous times. I recalled Tom's slogan, picked up from my family, "You're never alone if you have a good book." That's the remedy for loneliness—not any book, a good book that holds your interest.

At home I had been reading a book I discovered at the Howe Library in Hanover, an engrossing biography of Virginia Woolf by her nephew Clive Bell. Wonderful, but too big to tote. Bell tells about Woolf's first book, *Flush, A Biography*. It is the story of Elizabeth Barrett Browning's romance with Robert Browning, as told by her cocker spaniel, Flush. Very un-Woolfish. Since I dote on the Brownings, I had tried to buy a copy. Out of print of course.

Through the mist, I saw Kinsale's churchlike Temperance Hall, built in the nineteenth century to lure young sailors out of the bars. A sign outside read "Antiques and Book Fair Today." It cost one pound to enter. One pound equaled $1.19, and mine were rapidly disappearing. I hesitated. *You're never alone if you have a good book.*

I went in. The antiques were what the Irish call "nicky nacky" but the rows of old books were intriguing. The second book I pulled off the shelf was *Flush* by Virginia Woolf. I could not believe it. What a find: pen-and-ink drawings by her beloved sister, Vanessa Bell, two-inch margins, photographs of Elizabeth and Robert from the *National Portrait Gallery,* a lovely musty smell. There were even deep-red rose petals pressed between the pages. I felt giddy.

Ye gods, the price was twenty-five pounds and I hadn't bought one gift to take home. I approached the bookseller and introduced myself. He smiled broadly as we shook hands. "Gerald Feehan from Ballinlough, Cork, here."

We chatted about his books as if gossiping about old friends. He knew each one intimately. When I said I wanted to buy *Flush,* he beamed. "Good for you."

"Mr. Feehan," I said, "twenty-five pounds is a lot for a secondhand book. That's thirty dollars American."

"My dear lady, this is not a secondhand book. It's a first edition. When we go on the Euro it will cost 31.75." He paused and wiped his damp forehead. Mr. Feehan looked like a character out of Dickens: sweaty, portly, striped shirtsleeves rolled up, tousled gray hair, twinkling eyes. "Here, give me the book. I want to read you something." He handled the slim brown volume as if it were sacred, which it was. Slowly, he read with a rolling Irish inflection:

Published by Leonard and Virginia Woolf at the Hogarth Press, 52 Tavistock Square, London, 1933.

"Gerry," I said (by now we were on a first-name basis), "How do I make out the check?"

He handed me his pen and spelled his name. I wrote a check for $30 and gave him my local address. "I like your pen," I said. He looked into my eyes and gave me a warm Irish smile. Then Gerry Feehan handed me back the check.

"I want you to have this book as a gift."

I started to say, "Oh no, I couldn't accept . . ." An image of Tom flashed into my mind, instructing our children, "If somebody wants to give you a gift, whether it's a stick of gum or a bicycle, accept it graciously. Never rob anyone of the joy of giving."

"I don't know how to thank you, Gerry. I am overwhelmed."

He handed me his pen. "Here, take this, too." I shook his hand, wordlessly. "Good luck to America," he said. We hugged each other. I walked out into the mist clutching my precious Irish gifts, dazed but happy. What a wonder-full country.

The next day we left for home. On the plane, I leaned my head back against the seat and, mentally, patted myself on the back. I had done it. I had traveled abroad, even though Tom wasn't there.

But then again, maybe he was.

❦ 46. Searching for Ernest Hemingway

The older I grow, the more I feel the presence of the dead. Whenever I mope, I hear Tom saying to the kids, "Stop feeling sorry for yourself. You're better off than you think."

I felt his absence—and his presence—most strongly the second Christmas after he died, when I visited Tommy and his family in Idaho.

Jackie Kennedy said, "If you bungle raising your children, I don't think whatever else you do well matters very much." In 2001 our kids and grandkids seemed to be humming along. Tom was so proud of them all. Me, too.

Tommy and Lynn, divorced, had happily remarried. In 1998, Tommy married Ellen Feinman, also a biker and skier. Her children, Chris Feinman and Lauren Street, became part of his life. Ashley was married to a fellow Dartmouth alum, Matt Semler, and they were living in San

Francisco. Berit, Dartmouth '96, was getting her masters at UCLA Film School.

Tad, also divorced, and Peggy McCarthy were concentrating on Grady, their band-playing and sports-authority son, now twelve. Peter, Dartmouth '98, was at Boston University studying poetry with Robert Pinsky. Ned was at Union College, deep in math and music.

Toby and Anita were living in South Pasadena, pursuing chiropractic and yoga. Manolo had just graduated from the Art Center College of Design in Pasadena, where he excelled in photography. Iris was immersed in dance at the California School of the Arts.

Cissa graduated from Wellesley in 1982. She won the Barrett Fellowship for study in musical theater and spent two years at the Longy School in Cambridge. Now she was a composer and co-director of the Freelance Players, a highly successful musical theater for children in Boston. She lived in Brookline, down the street from Tad and Peggy.

Russell and Missy Jacobus had been married eleven years when they began the difficult process of adopting a baby in China. (Because of the one child law, Chinese parents usually give up a first-born daughter, hoping for a boy to support them.) In February 1995, Russell and Missy flew from Chicago to Shanghai. At the Yangzhou Children's Welfare Institute in Jiangsu Province, their eight-month-old daughter entered their hearts on Valentine's Day.

Two weeks later, the East Coast Campions gathered at Peggy and Tad's to welcome Madeleine Jacobus Campion. I wrote her a letter about that day. "Dear Maddy, Your arrival was one of the most wonderful events of our life. Tad, Peggy, Cissa, Peter, Ned, Grady, Gapa Tom, and I waited impatiently. Then Ned shouted, "Here they are!" Out of a big white car stepped your mother and your father with you in his arms. We all kissed and hugged you and everybody cried. You just looked at us with your big black eyes. Then you smiled—and we melted. We are yours forever, Maddy."

It was a long, long way to Idaho, fourteen hours from Lebanon to Ketchum. But worth it—four feet of fluffy new snow, Christmas-card perfect.

Tom and I used to play golf on the Sun Valley course, which he relished because the altitude made the ball go forever. After our games, we would visit the nearby memorial to Ernest Hemingway, surely the most hidden, most unknown memorial in America. In our college days, Hemingway was *avant garde* and so was Tom. He admired that clear-eyed honesty. "Death was Hemingway's subject," he told me. "That famous zest for life was permeated by awareness of death."

Thinking about Tom, as ever, I asked Tommy to take me back to the secluded shrine. We drove due east along a post-and-rail fence with snow hi-hats on every post. The wooden "Hemingway Memorial" sign was swinging in the wind. Tommy studied the unplowed path blanketed by four feet of snow. "Too deep," he said, "maybe later on snowshoes." I was disappointed not to pay homage, one last time, to Tom's literary hero, but there are worse problems at a ski resort than too much snow.

Christmas Eve morning Ashley telephoned. "We have a surprise for you, Cyber Grandma. Put on some ski clothes. Berit, Matt, and I are picking you up in an hour."

"Cross-country skiing? Eighty-four is too old."

They just laughed. They took me to the golf club and rented a pair of fancy Fischer cross-country skis. As Matt helped me with my boots I said, "I don't think I can do this."

"It's flat out there, Gama Nardi," he said. "You'll be fine. The grooved trails do the work for you." A lot has happened to cross-country skis since Tom bought our slowpokes in 1970. I took a tentative push. The new aerodynamic models seemed to carry Cyber Grandma as far as one of Tom's golf balls.

It was heaven. Cloudless sky, brilliant sunlight, magpies chattering in snow-laden trees. Only Tom was missing. At first I was unsteady, but the perfectly groomed cross-country trails—a wide one for skaters, a double-track for "classic skiers"—were magic. (No third trail for skiers with dogs, but this isn't Switzerland.)

"You're a classic in more ways than one," laughed Berit. I took it as a compliment.

Cautiously, I found my ski legs. Soon I was sailing along. We skied for half an hour, I puffing and blowing, they slowing way down for me. I even went downhill. That's what the little slopes felt like to me. "Where are we going?" I wheezed.

"If we tell you," Ashley said, "it won't be a surprise." We skied on. At last she pointed to the sign, almost obliterated by snow: "Hemingway Memorial." Like a lurking spirit, the memorial was invisible. We took off our skis to wade to it through the deep snow. "Remember how Gapa Tom loved coming here?" Berit said. I couldn't answer.

Two granddaughters held my hands, ahead and behind, one pulling, one pushing. "Way to go, Gama Nardi," called Matt the Encourager.

Then we saw him beside the trout stream he loved. The greenish-bronze head, atop a reddish marble shaft, gazed toward the Pioneer Mountains—white peaks jutting into a cobalt sky. Ernest Hemingway's profile is sensitive, almost delicate, far from the macho legend, the hair brushed forward, the beard trim, not bushy. It is the face of a poet, not a pugilist. Sculptor Robert Berks caught the warmth of the man who became Papa to his friends while still in his twenties.

How Tom and I treasured this protected grove. The marble bench where we used to sit was snowed under. I plopped down on a snowbank at the foot of the statue while Matt read aloud the inscription Tom knew by heart. For me it was a mystical moment.

> Best of all he loved the fall
> The leaves yellow on the cottonwoods
> Leaves floating on the trout streams
> And above the hills
>   The high blue windless skies . . .
> Now he will be a part of them forever
> Ernest Hemingway—Idaho—1939

"Why 1939?" I once asked Tom. "Hemingway died in 1961."

Ever the scholar, he repaired to the Hemingway Library to look it up. Everything in Ketchum is Hemingway: Hemingway School, Hemingway Homestead. The homestead where he shot himself in 1961 is now owned by the Nature Conservancy and is occasionally open to the public.

It turned out that those spare, exactly right words on the bronze plaque had a dramatic origin. One autumn day in 1939, when Hemingway was forty, his young friend Gene Van Guilder went duck hunting with friends. That day Ernest didn't go with his buddies. Van Guilder stood up in the boat to fire. There was a blast from a shotgun carelessly handled by one of the hunters—and Gene Van Guilder was dead.

His devastated young widow asked Hemingway to deliver a grave-side eulogy. "I'm no good in crowds," Ernest said. "I don't talk well, you know that."

But he did.

Tom found a description of the service in *High on the Wild with Hemingway*, by Lloyd Arnold. Ernest Hemingway, wearing an old tweed jacket and flannel pants, stood in the little cemetery close to the spot where he himself would be buried twenty-two years later and read from his heart.

There are no words to describe how unjust is the death of a young man . . . Gene has finished something that we all must do . . . Gene loved this country . . . with the heart of a boy who had been brought up in the West . . . He loved the hills in the spring when the snows go off and the first flowers come. He loved the warm sun of summer and the high mountain meadows, the trails through the timber and the sudden clear blue of the lakes. He loved the hills in the winter when the snow comes. Best of all he loved the fall . . .

Standing at the memorial in the Christmas Eve snow-muffled quiet, I felt the strength of Tom's presence. That bright, deep poignancy, always in my heart, deepened. I felt closer to him than I would have in any cemetery plot. Tom was firm in his belief that a departing spirit leaves only an empty shell. His shell is buried in Dartmouth Cemetery, the headstone marked simply: "Dartmouth Medical School."

I thought about my darling Tom finishing "something that we all must do." His acceptance of death was almost joyous. He loved snow and mountains and trout streams—now he is part of them forever.

In that sheltered snowy sanctuary with our grandchildren I was able, at last, to let go of Tom.

But not really—he's still with me.

A Coda

As a coda to my valentine for Tom, here is the poem our oldest grandson Peter composed for his memorial service.

Catching Tom was the fun part. Releasing him was the hardest thing I've ever done.

Catch and Release

Peter Campion

i.m. TBC (1916–2000)

Manolo and I, in sneakers and T-shirts, ran
Ahead to the brook both under the speckled light

And under his even gaze. He was a man
Whose nature it was to get the balance right

Between his kindness and sternness. Which gave
Rare reprimand real sting. But also meant

Here was this morning on the brook he could save
For grandsons: bent to his walking stick, then bent

To the water only, he held his hand
On our hands, on the orange, tugging line.

•

Swift little shadow breaking the band
Of light. Deft shadow breaking the incline

Upstream. What a strange gift it was to have
One afternoon with him two weeks ago.

Driving him home, we started up Mascoma Ave.
But he gripped his cane, and barked repeatedly, "No

This is a one-way street." Then he could see
It wasn't. What relief to sense how amused

He was at his own mistake, how the urgency
In his voice didn't sound like a man confused,

But like somebody turning from concentration.
As when his fingers slipped a barbless fly

From the rainbow's lip. Both a pilgrim at his station
And a man "gone fishing," he had in his eye

A searching sharpness. Manolo and my knees
To the silt, as he crouched down, far as his bones

Would allow, we saw it, as he watched the release,
Watched the shadow go over the speckled stones.

Index

If I listed family references, this book would be nothing but index. My family is my life.